DOROTHY PARKER

By ARTHUR F. KINNEY

University of Massachusetts, Amherst

TWAYNE PUBLISHERS
A DIVISION OF G. K. HALL & CO., BOSTON

Copyright © 1978 by G. K. Hall & Co.

Published in 1978 by Twayne Publishers,
A Division of G. K. Hall & Co.
All Rights Reserved

Printed on permanent/durable acid-free paper and bound
in the United States of America

First Printing

Library of Congress Cataloging in Publication Data

Kinney, Arthur F., 1933–
Dorothy Parker.

(Twayne's United States author series ; TUSAS 315)
Bibliography: p. 193—95
Includes index
1. Parker, Dorothy Rothschild, 1893–1967.
2. Authors, American—20th century—Biography.
PS3531.A5855Z73   818'.5'209   78-16724
ISBN 0-8057-7241-3

To the memory of

JOE LEE DAVIS:

joy in the knowing,
sorrow in the losing

Contents

About the Author

Arthur F. Kinney is Professor of English at the University of Massachusetts, Amherst. His interests range from Renaissance English literature to contemporary American literature and he has published widely in both fields. Professor Kinney is editor of *English Literary Renaissance* and field editor for studies of Renaissance authors in Twayne's English Authors Series. His recent publications include *Steinbeck and the Arthurian Theme* (edited by Tetsumaro Hayashi), *Symposium on Love* (with Kenneth W. Kuiper and Lynn Z. Bloom), *Symposium* (with Kenneth W. Kuiper and Lynn Z. Bloom), and *Bear, Man, and God* (with Francis L. Utley and Lynn Z. Bloom).

Preface

Everyone I ask has heard of Dorothy Parker. Some remember her as an urban wit of the 1920s, others as a screenwriter, while a local librarian calls her one of the first American feminists. All of them are correct. In the twenties, she was an acknowledged mistress of *bon mots*, and characters in two novels and in three plays were based on her.[1] She wrote an epigram now classic, "Men seldom make passes / At girls who wear glasses" (which, badly nearsighted, she did). She is also given credit for many clever remarks: when told at a Hallowe'en party that guests were ducking for apples, she replied, "There, but for a typographical error, is the story of my life"; and, when asked by F.P.A. to use *horticulture* in a sentence, she replied, "You can lead a horticulture but you can't make her think."[2] Later, in Hollywood, she and her husband Alan Campbell wrote part of the screenplay for the original version of *A Star Is Born* with Frederic March and Janet Gaynor and of *Sweethearts* for Nelson Eddy and Jeannette MacDonald; a decade more, and she was writing scripts for Alfred Hitchcock (*Saboteur*, 1942) and Otto Preminger (*The Fan*, 1949). She prided herself too on her intellectual independence and her successful competition—although a woman—as a wit, poet, and fiction writer among such men as Benchley and Sherwood during the brassy, flippant days of personal journalism. So "All I wanted in the world," says her current counterpart, Nora Ephron, "was to come to New York and be Dorothy Parker."[3] Dorothy Parker still seems so successful in so many ways.

But others, who knew her, knew better. For them her writing was both a disclosure of personal fears and a concealment of them. For she seems always to have been troubled: born at the wrong time and place, estranged early from her father and a spiteful stepmother, claiming or fighting poverty. During Prohibition she hung out at Tony's, at Jack and Charlie's (now "21")—and at Polly Adler's. She drank too much and suffered, from those days onward, from recurring bouts of alcoholism. She was foolishly sentimental, thoughtlessly promiscuous, frequently suicidal. Her behavior bewildered Anita Loos and disgusted Edna Ferber even as it became the basis for wisecracks by Alexander Woollcott, Robert Benchley, and others who were members of the Algonquin Hotel's "Round Table." When she loved, Dale Kramer reports, "she loved furiously; and when there were disappointments, she suffered deep pain."[4] She "so often tried to do away with herself on account of her complicated affairs of the heart," the innkeeper's daughter wrote without naming her, "that the sheer number of her attempted suicides amounted to an affectation."[5] Yet her affairs with Charles MacArthur, John McClain, and others ended abruptly when they left her for other women; two of her marriages ended in divorce; in desperation she once courted a group of New York homosexuals.

Her unhappiness resulted in an acid tongue directed at friends as well as those whose pretensions and hypocrisy had from the first led her to write satire. "This was Dottie," Sheilah Graham says of her in Hollywood, "nice to your face, cruel behind your back. I realize that she was a very unhappy woman. . . . The only way she could live with herself was to murder everybody else with her biting words."[6] This divided behavior, coaxing friendship of someone and later attacking him, finds ample testimony by Woollcott during their two decades together at New York theaters, at his elaborate houseparties on Neshobe Island in Vermont, and at the estate festivities of Bayard Swope on Long Island; and by John Mason Brown in his biography of Robert Sherwood.[7] Although she made important strides professionally—first pointing to "grace under pressure" as Hemingway's major theme while a literary critic—she remained disillusioned and alienated. Her financial success in Hollywood, where her salary during the Depression was $5,200 a week, led her to purchase a farm in Bucks County, but even here, her long-awaited pregnancy resulted in a miscarriage, and she returned to the West Coast, despising herself for "selling out" her talents to Hollywood.

Then, as the years wore on, what seemed a new Dorothy Parker matured. She became politically active. She led a labor movement for Hollywood writers, organized the Anti-Nazi League, and wrote for the Marxist *New Masses*. In what was perhaps her finest hour, she visited Madrid during the Spanish Civil War, escaping the bombs to write about the wretched suffering of the Loyalists; when she was blacklisted, she turned to the theater, to more openly autobiographical fiction, to recording, book reviewing, and teaching at California State. Throughout her life, in alternating periods of joyful elation and severe depression, she remained consistent in this: she was always loyal to the purity of the English language, strove always for compactness of phrase, authenticity and precision of tone, and clarity and simplicity of thought and feeling. Her deepest respect was paid, early and late, not to herself, her friends, or the causes she advocated so much as to her art. Yet it is her achievement in letters that is still, for too long a time now, misconstrued.

As we find it difficult to locate her essential character, so her contemporary critics disputed the value of her writing. Margaret Lawrence commented in 1936 that

> She writes and she talks in the nervous staccato of her time. Her thoughts go out with a machine-gun tempo; shot after shot in rapid rhythm. It contains no melody but a lot of noise. . . . It is a triumph of consistent follow-up shooting completely mechanized because a woman has said to herself, "I will be a modern."[8]

Her friend W. Somerset Maugham felt and wrote otherwise.

> In her stories Dorothy Parker has a sense of form which in these days, to my old-fashioned mind, is all too rare. . . . She has a tidy mind and leaves no loose ends. She has a wonderfully delicate ear for human speech and with a few words of dialogue, chosen you might think haphazardly, will give you a character complete in all its improbable plausibility. Her style is easy without being slipshod and cultivated without affectation. It is a perfect instrument for the display of her many-sided humor, her irony, her sarcasm, her tenderness, her pathos.[9]

A fellow humorist on *Life* with her, Corey Ford moans our misjudgments. "It is her cross to be best known today for her tart epigrams, rather than for her poetry or her bitter and brilliant short stories,"[10] but a close friend of her late years, Lillian Hellman, has judged that

> she wrote . . . too often in sentimental short stories about the little dressmaker or the servant as they are patronized by the people Dottie had dined with the night before. It was her way of paying back the rich and powerful, and if it is understandable in life it is too raw and unshaded for literature. The good short stories, like "Big Blonde," are her imaginative projections of what she knew or feared for herself, and have nothing to do with vengeance on the rich. Her put-them-in-their-place stories are often undigested, the conclusions there on the first page. The other stories, and much of the light verse, I think, are a valuable record of their time and place.[11]

These writers and critics, and many more, try to discern that special quality that created her "valuable record of [a] time and place" that she fixes, in bits and pieces, in our collective memories. Still we err, and too easily. Some years ago Harrison E. Salisbury attributed to her another famous epigram ("Candy is dandy / But liquor is quicker"), which is by Ogden Nash.[12] In becoming so many things to so many people, she obscured her own art. Yet that is always where her best energies went, choosing with intelligence her own literary models, modulating the taste of her times with a style crafted to a near perfection, blending her unique woman's voice with canons of classical rule. Her work, as well as she herself, needs putting in focus.

Certain clues to her life and work both can be found in two of her obsessions and in a memory from childhood. One obsession was being half-Jewish. Her father was a Rothschild, and although she dropped the name as soon as she married Edwin Pond Parker II, doubtless it is significant that she chose in Parker a successful businessman from an established Hartford family that reminded others of the father she hated. Her first book was a collaboration with the Jewish Franklin P. Adams, her first play with Elmer Rice, the subject she chose for her first book review in *The New Yorker* a novel about the intolerance shown Jews. Many of her friends at the Algonquin Round Table were Jewish (Hart, Kaufman, Ferber) as well as her Long Island host Herbert Bayard Swope and many of her associates in Hollywood (Hellman, Hecht, Herman Mankiewicz, Edwin Mayer) where, in her early days, she worked for Irving Thalberg and Sam Goldwyn. Her later marriages were to Alan Campbell, son of a Jewish mother but possessing a Gentile name. Sheilah Graham recalls that she "used to announce that she was half Jewish,"[13] and only six weeks before her death, Lillian Hellman interrupted a story in a letter to Dorothy Parker to remark, "so O.K., for the fiftieth time don't tell me you're half Jewish."[14]

In many ways, her life follows the paradigm of the second and third generation Jew from New York traced by Irving Howe: well educated in private schools, she respected education and high culture; she combined a personal self-consciousness in her writing with set pieces in the formulas of the ladies' magazines; she was attracted to the world of entertainment but distanced herself by an easygoing cynicism; she worked long and hard at her writing, although she wanted it to seem casual and spontaneous; she combined bitter (if subtle) satire of others with a running self-condemnation (both light-hearted and serious). Although her work is softer and more sentimental than, say, the stories of Bernard Malamud, there is still present some of the hardness and pity Howe finds in *The Magic Barrel*. Howe's description of the work of the New York Jewish intellectual does, in one way or another, help characterize a portion of everything she wrote.[15] Yet only once, in *The New Yorker*, did Dorothy Parker actually say what it means to be a Jew. "For the Gentile," she observed, "there is always something just a little bit comic about a Jew. That is the tragedy of Israel."[16]

Her other obsession was the art of Ernest Hemingway. She wrote admiringly of *In Our Time* and *Men Without Women*, she sailed to France to meet him and write a *New Yorker* profile on him, and she entertained him in Hollywood, helping to raise funds for his film *The Spanish Earth*. It was his example and encouragement that persuaded her to risk her life in Spain and his dedication to art that she most emulated. "A setback with a story or a poem would drive her to the depths of despair," Jane Grant tells us, "and one of her periodic efforts to commit suicide."[17] Although she was prominent in what Morton Cooper calls "a day of giants," her last recorded words, to Beatrice Ames, pursue the relentless worry that her talent did not live up to Hemingway's. "I want you to tell me the truth," she urged. "Did Ernest really like me?"[18]

And the memory from her childhood? She recalled a moment when she was five for *New Masses* when, in 1939, they asked her "What are you doing to combat fascism?" and she replied, "Not enough."

It was in a brownstone house in New York, and there was a blizzard, and my rich aunt—a horrible woman then and now—had come to visit. I remember going to the window and seeing the street with the men shoveling snow; their hands were purple on their shovels, and their feet were wrapped with burlap. And my aunt, looking over my shoulder, said, "Now isn't it nice there's this blizzard. All those men have work." And I knew then that it was not nice that men could work for their lives only in desperate weather, that there was no work for them when it was fair.[19]

Throughout her life, Dorothy Parker was quick to sympathize with those who suffered or were indentured—those she could pity because of misfortune in politics, money, race, or sex. She admired the servant class and those who, like her "Big Blonde," were defeated by conditions they could not understand or overcome. And she was as quick to attack the causes of their exploitation. From her early poetry of unrequited love to "Clothe the Naked" she attacks pretension and blindness in the middle and upper classes.

But it is equally clear, in studying her work, that she is also attracted to the status and possessions of those who are better off. She sought the stability of Edwin Parker and the Parkers of Hartford. While she understands the awful need to shovel snow to earn keep, such subsistence workers always aspire, as she herself did and partly in awe, to the condition of her aunt. She combines the child's ambition and hope with an adult's sense of outrage and cynicism at shallowness and self-deception, at the uneven and unrequited distribution of favors in this world. She did not always understand that she held mixed loyalties, although they are the foundation for the rueful attitude of much of her early poetry and fiction as well as the disappointment and disgust that characterize her essays and criticism. That memory fixes her for us, as it should, looking out on one activity, looking away from another, yet associated with both, and caught between them.

Her Jewishness gave her the felt roots of her being: a sense of being dispossessed (like the men shoveling snow), a long intellectual heritage personified by her aunt, and the desire for financial success urged by her father. Her means to all their ends were, at her best and most inspired, the means of Hemingway, through total devotion to clean, fine poetry and prose. The consequence would be a corpus of writing which, at its most creative, would be about the world's shovelers of snow designed to be read instructively by persons like her aunt. In that way Dorothy Parker could, finally and forcibly, take part in a dialogue with her aunt and point out the real significance of the blizzard; she could turn it into satire and through that into a kind of mournful, moral fable. Then her Jewishness would be vindicated—and Ernest would like her, too.

"There cannot be much doubt about it now," James Gray wrote in 1946, "Dorothy Parker is one of the few writers of our time who is destined for immortality. It is nice for us who have always cherished her gift to know that in centuries to come she will represent the sad, cocky, impudent mood of our tragic era."[20] But her cockiness is only a fraction of the achievement. She had a genuine talent for trenchant light verse but also a remarkable talent for classical epigram; she could be sentimental in her fiction and conversational in her essays, yet even here is a sardonic and a corrosive touch, for the underside of her informality is always dismay, distrust, or even anger. You cannot, I think, understand Dorothy Parker by reading only selections from the dozens of anthologies in which her work regularly appears, nor can you approach her casually; the rewards then are superficial and misleading. Only when you understand that the discipline of her writing holds in a deep hatred and despair over much that she writes of—only when you sense that the "humor" of an essay in *The Saturday Evening Post* is as bitter, as acidic, as her disdain for the intolerant guest in "Arrangement in Black and White" caught in its very title, or when you realize that "Big Blonde" is about Herbie as well as Hazel Morse—only then do you come to appreciate what are the fundamental, if complicated, forces behind her work, behind what Oliver Goldsmith called, much more genially, the "natural portrait of human folly and frailty."[21] "Great vices are the proper objects of our detestation," Fielding writes in the 1742 preface to *Joseph Andrews,* "smaller faults, of our pity; but affectation appears to me the only true source of the Ridiculous."[22] In her essential conversion of such dicta, Dorothy Parker made ridicule, in both her life and writing, the common means.

From such a perspective as I have outlined, the present study reviews Dorothy Parker's life, incorporating many facts recorded for the first time and stressing her literary work, and provides as well the first full critical assessment of her writing. In doing both, I mean to trace the sources and influences on her work as well as to assess her final achievement so as to locate what I think is her significant and unique contribution to American literature. Chapter 1 provides a biographical sketch and supplies an overview to the range of styles and genres she practiced. Chapter 2 studies chronologically most of her minor writing—her magazine essays and squibs, her light verse and early poetry, and her drama (including two later, major works, *The Coast of Illyria* and *The Ladies of the Corridor*). I have termed this "Apprenticeship" for convenience; much of this work she did not collect, and it thus often remains unavailable to the general reader. Nevertheless, these selections supply valuable background for the work discussed in Chapter 3, "Her Accomplishment," which treats her published collections of poetry and fiction and her criticism, which remains, middle and late, among her best work, and contains still some of our strongest examples of American periodical reviewing. Chapter 4, "Conclusions," attempts some brief assessment of her art as imitation and as a kind of comic melancholy.

I am indebted in this study, as any student of Dorothy Parker must be, to the pioneer biography by John Keats, *You Might As Well Live*, which has brought together some (but not all) of our scattered knowledge of her life and tested parts of the Parker legend by interviewing her friends at various stages of her life. I have likewise benefited from correspondence or discussions with Gillian Adams, Arno Bader, G. W. Bain, Leon Barron, Charles E. Beckwith, Robert E. Blackman, Louise Bogan, Charles Brackett, Jules Chametzky, Richard Ellman, Leslie Fiedler, Arnold Gingrich, Horace Gregory, Gerald Haber, Hiram Hadyn, John Harrington, Lillian Hellman, George Henderson, Michael Holahan, Barbara Holdridge, Irving Howe, Herman W. Liebert, John Lowe, Jay Martin, Robert L. Middleton, Norman Holmes Pearson, Les Perelman, Elmer Rice, Terry Roach, Howard Sackler, Allan Seager, Frederick B. Shroyer, Donald Ogden Stewart, Peter Ustinov, and Edmund Wilson. I have been supported by many libraries and staffs: in greatest measure by the New York Public Library's Main Branch, Annex, and Theatre Collection, Lincoln Center; but also by the *New York Times* library; the *Los Angeles Times* library; the Library of Congress; the National Library of Scotland, Edinburgh; British Library; Edinburgh International Festival Offices; Sterling and Beinecke Libraries, Yale; Olin Library, Cornell; the Free Library of Philadelphia; the Margaret Herrick Library of the Academy of Motion Picture Arts and Sciences; the Fine Arts Division of the Dallas Public Library; *The New Yorker* library and files; Neilson Library, Smith College; Frost Library, Amherst College; and the University of Massachusetts Library, Amherst. I also received help from the management and staff of the Algonquin Hotel, the Screen Writers Guild of America West, Paramount Studios in Hollywood, and the former staff of the Margo Jones Theatre in Dallas.

The present study is a considerable expansion of some critical remarks that first won an Avery and Jules M. Hopwood Major Award in Essay at The University of Michigan and later a Bread Loaf Scholarship in Criticism; its publication in this series was initiated and fostered by Joe Lee Davis because—for whatever reasons—he believed in the subject and in me. As professor of American Literature at Michigan for four inspiring and energetic decades, Joe Lee Davis believed in a number of minor American writers and had equally strong faith in a number of his graduate and undergraduate students, others of whom have also contributed to this series. His intelligence was matched by his devotion to those he taught, and I have come, in these intervening years, to learn how extensive was his influence and how rare his talents. He made the role of teacher the highest of callings.

ARTHUR F. KINNEY

Amherst, Massachusetts;
Cortland, New York;
Oxford, England

Acknowledgements

I am grateful to the following publishers and authors for the permissions indicated:

to Little, Brown, and Company, to quote from *An Unfinished Woman* and *Pentimento* by Lillian Hellman;

to Charles Scribner's Sons, to quote from *Short Story*, ed. Dorothy Parker and Frederick B. Shroyer; from "A Woman with a Past" by F. Scott Fitzgerald; from the collected *Letters of F. Scott Fitzgerald*, ed. Andrew Turnbull; from "Zone of Quiet" by Ring Lardner; and from *Green Hills of Africa* by Ernest Hemingway;

to Doubleday & Company, Inc., to quote from Franklin P. Adams, *In Other Words, Tobogganing on Parnassus, So There!*, and *Something Else Again* © Doubleday & Company, Inc.;

to Grove Press to quote Catullus, poems 70 and 85, in the translations by Horace Gregory;

to *The New Yorker* and to Wolcott Gibbs to quote from Gibbs' review of *Ladies of the Corridor*;

to *The New Yorker* and to the National Association for the Advancement of Colored People to quote from "Out of the Silence," "G.B.S., Practically in Person," "Profile: Ernest Hemingway," "A Certain Lady," "Lolita," "The Banquet of Crow," pseudonymous literary criticism (as "Constant Reader"), and theater criticism that first appeared in *The New Yorker*;

to the Condé Nast Publications, Inc., to quote from Frank Crowninshield, "Crowninshield in the cubs den" originally published in *Vogue*; and Robert Benchley, "The Art of Being Bohemian"; Aldous Huxley, "The Importance of the Comic Genius"; Max Eastman, "What Is the Matter with Magazine Writing?"; and Dorothy Parker, "Seven Deadly Suitors," "A Valentine for Mr. Woollcott," "Any Porch," "A Musical Comedy Thought," "The Gunman and the Debutante," "Men: A Hate Song," and essays of theater criticism originally published in *Vanity Fair*;

to Simon and Schuster, Inc., to quote from John Keats, *You Might As Well Live*;

quotations from Eric Bentley's review of *Ladies of the Corridor* reprinted from *The Dramatic Event*, by Eric Bentley, © 1954, by permission of the publisher, Horizon Press;

and "First Fig," "Second Fig," and "Thursday" from *Collected Poems*, Harper & Row, © 1922, 1950 by Edna St. Vincent Millay.

to Viking Penguin Inc. to quote from "The Bolt Behind the Blue," "The Middle or Blue Period," *The Ladies of the Corridor*, "Resume," "They Part," "War Song," "Neither Bloody Nor Bowed," "For a Sad Lady," "The New Love," "News Item," "Two-Volume Novel," "Anecdote," "Threnody," "Prophetic Soul," "Philosophy," "Pictures in the Smoke," "Words of Comfort Scratched on a Mirror," "The Last Question," "Post-Graduate," "Partial Comfort," "For a Sad Lady Who Must Write Verse," "Bohemia," "A Dream Lies Dead," "The Flaw in Paganism," "Sanctuary," "Cherry White," "Mina de l'Enclos," "Prayer for a Prayer," "Sight," "Prisoner," "Big Blonde," "From the Diary of a New York Lady," "Here We Are," "Clothe the Naked," "Soldiers of the Republic," "The Lovely Leave," "Song of the Shirt"; from Somerset Maugham's introduction to the *Portable Dorothy Parker;* and from an interview between Dorothy Parker and Marion Capron in *Writers at Work*, Vol. 1. Also for permission to quote from Alexander Woollcott's *While Rome Burns* and *Shouts and Murmurs.*

to the National Association for the Advancement of Colored People for permission to quote from letters written by Dorothy Parker to Alexander Woollcott and now held by the Houghton Library of Harvard University. I also wish to thank the Curator of Manuscripts of the Houghton Library for permitting me access to the letters.

to Holt, Rinehart, and Winston to quote A. E. Houseman's *Shropshire Lad 18* one line to quote a letter from Housman to Sydney Cockrell (January 15, 1932).

to Peter Pauper Press to quote Joseph Auslander's translation of Heine's "Es liegt der heisse Sommer."

Chronology

1893   August 22: Born in West End, New Jersey, to J. Henry Rothschild and Eliza A. (Marston) Rothschild.

?1900–   Student at Blessed Sacrament Convent, New York City; Miss
1911   Dana's School, Morristown, New Jersey.

1913   First job, on *Vogue*. Light verse published by Franklin P. Adams (F.P.A.).

1915   September: First published poem for money, "Any Porch," *Vanity Fair*.

1916–   Staff writer for *Vanity Fair*; April 1918–March 1920: replaced
1920   P. G. Wodehouse as drama reviewer.

1917   June: Married Edwin Pond Parker II.

1920   January: *High Society* with Frank Crowninshield and George S. Chappell. Fired from *Vanity Fair* for outspoken criticism; named drama reviewer for *Ainslee's* (May 1920–July 1923), contributes free-lance verse and prose to *Life*.

1921–   Contributes essays and verse to *Saturday Evening Post,*
1923   *Ladies' Home Journal, Everybody's,* and *Life*.

1922   April 30: Writes song for "No, Siree!" and acts in production; writes *Nero* with Robert Benchley for *The '49ers*. Summer: Publishes first book, *Women I'm Not Married To; Men I'm Not Married To* (with F.P.A.). December: First short story, "Such a Pretty Little Picture," in *Smart Set*.

1923   Abortion; first suicide attempt.

1924   December 1: Play, *Close Harmony* (with Elmer L. Rice) opens.

1925   Collaborates on novel, *Bobbed Hair* (*Collier's*, January 17). First film script, *Business Is Business* (with George S. Kaufman). Second suicide attempt.

1926   *Enough Rope* (poems); first European trip.

1927   October 1–March 1931: Book reviewer for *The New Yorker* as "Constant Reader." Also contributes essays and poems. Marches against execution of Sacco and Vanzetti, Boston.

1928   March 31: Divorces Parker. *Sunset Gun* (poems); column for *McCall's;* second European trip.

1929   "Big Blonde" wins O. Henry Award as year's best short story.

1930   *Laments for the Living* (stories).

1931   *Death and Taxes* (poems); contributes drama reviews to *The New Yorker* and lyrics to *Shoot the Works* by Heywood Broun. On three-month contract for MGM in Hollywood.

1933   *After Such Pleasures* (stories). 1933 or 1934: Marries Alan Campbell, also of Scottish-Jewish descent.

1934   Contributes to dialogue of *Here Is My Heart* and *One Hour Late* (both Paramount). Helps organize Screen Writers Guild.

1935   Contributes to dialogue, *Mary Burns, Fugitive*, to screenplay construction, *Hands Across the Table*, and to treatment, *Paris in Spring* (all Paramount); lyrics, *Big Broadcast of 1936* (Paramount).

1936   *Not So Deep as a Well* (collected poems); joint screenplay, *Three Married Men* and *Lady, Be Careful* (both Paramount) and *Suzy* (MGM); additional dialogue, *The Moon's Our Home* (Paramount). June: Helps found the Anti-Nazi League.

1937   Joint screenplay, *A Star Is Born*, for David Selznick; *Woman Chases Man* (United Artists). Reports on Loyalist cause from Spain for *New Masses*.

1938   Joint screenplay, *Sweethearts* (MGM); *Trade Winds* (United Artists).

1941   Joint screenplay, *Week End for Three*; additional scenes and dialogue, *The Little Foxes* (both RKO Radio).

1942   *Collected Stories*; joint original screenplay, *Saboteur* (Universal).

1944   *The Viking Portable Dorothy Parker* (poems and stories).

1947   Joint original story, *Smash Up—The Story of a Woman* (Universal-International). May 27: Divorce from Campbell.

1949   Joint screenplay, *The Fan* (20th Century-Fox); *The Coast of Illyria* (play, with Ross Evans); blacklisted in Hollywood.

1950   Remarries Alan Campbell; "Horsie" a basis for *Queen for a Day* (United Artists).

1952–   Testimony against her before HUAC; subpoena.
1953

1953   *The Ladies of the Corridor* (play, with Arnaud D'Usseau).

1955 Called before New York State joint legislative committee;
      pleads First Amendment.
1957–ocmer Book reviewer for *Esquire*.
1963
1958 Lyrics for *Candide* (musical); Marjorie Peabody Waite
      Award, American Academy of Arts and Letters.
1959 Inducted into American Academy of Arts and Letters.
1963– Distinguished Visiting Professor of English, California State
1964 College at Los Angeles.
1964 Records stories and poems for Spoken Arts, Verve; publishes
      final magazine piece in November *Esquire*.
1965 *Short Story* (anthology, co-edited with Frederick B.
      Shroyer).
1967 June 7: Discovered dead, of a heart attack, in her room at
      Hotel Volney, New York City.

CHAPTER 1

Her Life: The Events Leading Up to the Tragedy

I *The Formative Years:* Mongrel

DOROTHY Rothschild was born, two months before she was due, on August 22, 1893, in West End, New Jersey, where her family had retreated from the oppressive heat of New York City for their annual vacation. Her father, J. Henry Rothschild, was, according to Wyatt Cooper, "a fairly prosperous cloak-and-suiter"; Margaret Case Harriman recalls him as "a distinguished Talmudic scholar."[1] No relation to the prominent banking family, he was well enough off to maintain a house on West 72nd Street and a staff of servants. "Compared with all other Americans born in 1893, Dorothy Rothschild was born rich."[2] Her mother, Eliza A. (Marston) Rothschild, was a Scot, a middle-aged woman of failing health who died a short time after Dorothy's birth; the child had no memory of her, but the mixed parentage was a fact she never accepted; in late years, she professed wanting to write an autobiography if only so as to call it *Mongrel.* "That term," Cooper comments, "comes about as near as anything to expressing how Dorothy Parker saw herself: as a mongrel that wanted to be a thoroughbred."[3]

Dorothy Parker's childhood was lonely; nearest her in age was a sister nine years older. Dorothy was reared by a stepmother who was inordinately pious and whom Dorothy hated—she referred to her only as "the housekeeper"—and she was terrified of her father. Contrary to Talmudic law (by which the mother determines the Jewishness of the child), the second Mrs. Rothschild told Dorothy she was Jewish because of her father and set a course of moral indoctrination to save her soul. She sent Dorothy to a nearby school run by nuns of the Blessed Sacrament Convent; each day after

school, she asked the girl, "Did you love Jesus today?" John Keats
sums:

> It was quite a childhood: a terrifying father hammering her wrists; a
> rather lunatic stepmother hammering at her mind; a sister and a brother too
> remote in age for any communion; the servants put out of reach by social
> convention. . . . She hated being a Jew and began to think that her mother
> had deserted her by dying. She began to hate herself.[4]

She also hated her name and hoped that other children going to her
parochial school would not hold it against her; she even entertained
fantasies of being Catholic rather than Jewish.

"She was a plain, disagreeable little child with stringy hair and a
yen to write verse," she told a reporter in 1939. "The only thing she
learned at school was that if you spit on a pencil eraser, it will erase
ink."[5] Whether or not she wrote poetry, she spent much time alone,
reading. The convent taught Adelaide Ann Proctor rather than
Dickens, so she read Dickens on her own, as well as Thackeray and
all of Charles Reade. She thought her father hypocritical and her
stepmother crazy, but she put on fine manners so they would keep
their distance, and festered inside. When she reached high school,
she could continue no longer. She was "fired" from Blessed Sacrament, she said, because she insisted the Immaculate Conception
was spontaneous combustion: from an early age—even if this particular story is untrue—she learned humor could be a defense. "All
those writers who talk about their childhood! " she once commented, "Gentle God, if I wrote about mine you wouldn't sit in the
same room with me."[6]

Her parents then enrolled her in an exclusive private school, Miss
Dana's, in Morristown, New Jersey. Here amidst an affluent community she studied and boarded in an imposing Victorian house
furnished with Oriental rugs, heavy velvet curtains, overstuffed
plush sofas, and large chandeliers. Her fellow students in the small,
highly selective classes included wealthy cattle princesses, heir-
esses, Southern belles and Northern debutantes.[7] The course of
study was classical: she took up to four years of Latin and four
required years of English and Bible as well as required courses in
history, algebra, and geometry. Electives were chosen from botany,
physiology, astronomy, music, studio art, Greek, French, logic,
chemistry, physics, psychology, and banking, a traditional cur-

riculum as advanced as that of most junior colleges today. Although we do not know what she chose—later she would draw on Latin poetry and take pride in her knowledge of French—we do know that her class, like all the others, was limited to fifteen girls and, taught only by seminar, she received highly trained, personal attention. We know, too, that she was required to recite poetry; when, in the last years of her life, she made recordings of her own work for Verve and Spoken Arts, she would call on the same quiet and precise enunciations expected of the students at Miss Dana's.

Social rules at the school were strict; going to movies was grounds for suspension, smoking grounds for expulsion. Still, she wrote years later in reviewing "A Good Bad Woman" by William Anthony McGuire, "I, too, can remember those roseate days of happy girl-hood when we used to skulk off to attend like dramas, thinking that we were seeing life. Ah, youth, youth. . . ."[8] A schoolmate told John Keats, " 'I admired her as being an attractive girl; she was peppy and she was never bored. She was outstanding in school work, but I can't remember her playing games."[9]

In the evenings the girls were once more expected to listen to edifying lectures by such guests as the Reverend William E. Griffis, D. D. Since Dorothy had discovered LaRochefoucauld by that time, she must have begun to sense already the deep separation between a bright epigrammatic wit and a humorless set of clichés on Chris-tian morality, and choosing the former as the subject of her keenest interest she could, even then, strike back at her stepmother and Blessed Sacrament. Miss Dana's may also have planted seeds for her later social and political interests. The entire school met weekly to discuss current events, and the senior year focused on them: exploi-ation in the slums, reports of muckrakers, the growth of the socialist party. In this fertile atmosphere, Dorothy continued writ-ng poetry. She graduated in 1911, a member of the last class before Miss Dana died and the school went bankrupt.

II   Vanity Fair: " *'From Grave to Gay'* "

A year after she left Miss Dana's, Dorothy Rothschild's father ied, and, she told Marion Capron in an interview,

ere wasn't any money. I had to work, you see, and Mr. Crowninshield, od rest his soul, paid twelve dollars for a small verse of mine and gave me job at ten dollars a week. Well, I thought I was Edith Sitwell. I lived in a

boarding house at 103rd and Broadway, paying eight dollars a week for my
room and two meals, breakfast and dinner. Thorne Smith was there, and
another man. We used to sit around in the evening and talk. There was no
money, but Jesus we had fun.[10]

Thorne Smith was not yet famous as the author of *Topper*, and
Frank Crowninshield had come to *Vanity Fair* as editor in March
1914; the magazine, founded in 1868, was being rejuvenated by
Condé Nast, the wealthy publisher of *Vogue*. Crowninshield also
recalled that when Dorothy Rothschild was twenty,

I published a little poem of hers, the first thing she had ever written. A
cheque for five dollars encouraged her, as she told me, in the belief that she
was George Sand.
   A month later, her father died, and having to find a job, she streaked to
me for help. She had worked through the summer playing the piano,
strictly by note, for a dancing class, and even giving dancing lessons. . . .
She hadn't, she admitted, the faintest idea how to teach dancing, . . . she
wanted a literary life, and I was able to secure one for her—a job on the staff
of *Vogue*, at a cool ten dollars a week.
   But she did not last long with *Vogue*. Her first caption there, which was
designed to explain six photographs showing miscellaneous underwear, indicated that fashion would never become a religion with her. The caption
was headed, "Brevity is the Soul of Lingerie, as the Petticoat said to the
Chemise."[11]

It was wit as defense again: Dorothy Parker later said she was asked
to work with "plain women . . . at *Vogue*, not chic"; "they virginized
the models from tough babes into exquisite little loves."[12] So, in
1915, Mrs. Chase, editor of *Vogue*, transferred Miss Rothschild to
Frank Crowninshield, editor of *Vanity Fair*.
   Under Crowninshield's direction, *Vanity Fair* was turned into a
sophisticated, satirical review of literature, the arts, theater, and
society; it paid considerable attention to modern art and stylish
photography, and it kept clear of politics. The magazine that first
shaped Dorothy's style "skillfully combined a spirit of mockery with
a proper attention to its publisher's worries about what 'that old lady
in Dubuque might think,' " comments Frederick J. Hoffman. "It
was sophisticated and philistine."[13] Ring Lardner thought *Vanity
Fair* stuffy, referring to "correct Crowninshield dinner English"[14]—Crowninshield's standards reinforced those of Miss Dana's
School, rather than those of the boardinghouse.

Vogue taught Dorothy epigrammatic wit when she was forced to write clever captions; *Vanity Fair* taught her how to be "smart" rather than knowledgeable. Robert Benchley wrote in 1920 that Crowninshield

believes that the hope of a revival of Good Taste lies in those men and women who are college graduates, have some money, who know porcelains, and Verlaine, and Italian art, who love Grolier bindings, Spanish brocades, and French literature, . . . any writer who writes entertainingly [may] say practically anything he wants . . . so long as he says it in evening clothes.[15]

Crowninshield's "mind was cultivated rather than profound," Frederic Bradlee adds. "He had a deep-bedded instinct, an uncanny sense of what was and would continue to be fresh, bright, fun,"[16] and Cleveland Amory notes that the magazine "reflected America in mid-passage, as it were, between the old Four Hundred and the new Smart Set."[17]

Vanity Fair thus fostered Dorothy Rothschild's wit and taste. Before her first publication there, however, she had supported herself by playing piano for a dancing school while she wrote and donated light verse to Franklin P. Adams's newspaper columns. Her first publication for money, a poem called "Any Porch," appeared in the September 1915 *Vanity Fair*; the next month the magazine printed her first prose, "Why I Haven't Married." In the next two years, she contributed (first as Dorothy Rothschild, then as Dorothy Parker) captions for drawings by "Fish," several essays, and a number of catalogues in free verse she called "Hate Songs."

Her early recognition was heady; not only was her name frequently appearing in *Vanity Fair*, but she attended parties at the home of the publisher, Condé Nast, as Crowninshield's date. In April 1918, when Crowninshield saw her interest in drama becoming "acute," she succeeded P. G. Wodehouse as drama reviewer with a monthly column. Crowninshield remarks that "Though she was full of prejudices, her perceptions were so sure, her judgement so unerring, that she always seemed certain to hit the centre of the mark."[18]

She also helped Crowninshield with a book of his own with her bright quips; *High Society* appeared in 1920, subtitled "advice as to social campaigning, and hints on the management of dowagers, dinners, debutantes, dances, and the thousand and one diversions of persons of quality," and included "drawings by Fish, [and] the prose precepts of Dorothy Parker, George S. Chappell and Frank Crowninshield."

Short, slight, with an expensive taste for Chypre perfume, tailored suits, and large-brimmed picture hats, Dorothy Rothschild fell in love in 1917 with Edwin Pond Parker II, a lean, handsome Wall Street broker in his early twenties. He was Gentile and of distinguished ancestry: he was named for his grandfather, who had known Mark Twain and Dr. Joseph Twichell and had served as pastor of the South Church of Hartford from 1860 to 1912; and directly descended from William Parker, who had come to America with Thomas Hooker in 1636. His social credentials were impeccable; he was well-dressed and well-mannered, even though he drank heavily, sometimes a bottle a day. In May 1917, Eddie Parker enlisted in the 33rd Ambulance Company, one of 693 from Harvard, Princeton, and Yale who that spring became volunteer drivers to defend civilization.[19] In June, Eddie and Dorothy were married and, for the next nine months, she worked weekdays at *Vanity Fair* and joined Eddie weekends in Butler, New Jersey; Allentown, Pennsylvania; Charlotte, North Carolina (where he joined the Fourth Infantry Division); Camp Merritt, New Jersey; and then Brooklyn, where he shipped off to France to fight in the Allied counteroffensive of July 1918. She must have felt proudly patriotic; in June 1917 *Vanity Fair* ran sketches by Ethel Plummer entitled "Releasing a Soldier for the Front Which Is Now the Great and Paramount Duty of Every Woman in America." Dorothy Parker doted on her new husband; she wrote him daily, composing bright, witty poems to cheer him up, and in her review for the January 1919 issue of *Vanity Fair* she remarked in an aside, "I'd especially like to know how these wives of American soldiers always manage to get to France,—I've been trying to do it for the past year."[20] Parker was wounded, and the four soldiers he was carrying in his ambulance killed, by an enemy bomb, and Dorothy grew impatient for his discharge. But the war ended and he did not return. He was assigned to occupation duty in the Rhineland instead.

During Eddie's prolonged absence, in May 1919, Crowninshield hired two Harvard graduates, Robert Benchley (at $100 a week as managing editor) and Robert E. Sherwood (at $25 a week as drama editor). She lunched with them daily—she said it was in part to protect the tall, spindly Sherwood from being attacked by the im-

pish midgets then at the nearby Hippodrome vaudeville theater—
but it was Benchley who contributed more to her style.

Both Mr. Benchley and I subscribed to two undertaking magazines: *The
Casket* and *Sunnyside*. Steel yourself: *Sunnyside* had a joke column called
"From Grave to Gay." I cut a picture out of one of them, in color, of how
and where to inject embalming fluid, and had it hung over my desk until
Mr. Crowninshield asked me if I could possibly take it down. Mr. Crownin-
shield was a lovely man, but puzzled.[21]

The mordant wit of her poetry—and of the titles of all her books of
poetry and fiction—partly derives from thumbing through these
monthly journals for morticians. Benchley also supplied her with an
example of writing journalistically, covering great spaces with very
little material. He was frank enough about it; in "The Art of Being
Bohemian," in *Vanity Fair* for March 1916, he wrote,

The only trouble with this pitiless exposé of Bohemia is that I know practically nothing about the subject at all. I have only taken the most superficial
glances into New York's Bohemia and for all I know it may be one of the
most delightful and beneficial existences imaginable. It merely seemed to
me like a good thing to write about, because the editor might, while reading
it, think of a dashing illustration that could be made for it.[22]

Although this is partly the extravagance of Benchley's humor, it is
also good advice in a day when journalists were paid by the word—
advice that Dorothy followed in journalistic squibs throughout her
life.

The offices of *Vanity Fair* were at 19 West 44th Street; the nearby
hotel with the best food was the Algonquin, and Mr. Benchley, Mr.
Sherwood, and Mrs. Parker (as they called each other) ate there
often, continuing their witty conversations from work. The Pergola
Room (now the Oak Room) was then a meeting place for theater
people such as John Drew and Ethel Barrymore and for the staff of
Mencken's *Smart Set* (with offices on 45th Street). The three wits of
Vanity Fair met at the Algonquin three wits just back from the
war—Alexander Woollcott, Franklin P. Adams (F.P.A.), and Harold
Ross (who later founded *The New Yorker*)—and the six soon became
the nucleus of a regular luncheon club of literary and theater people
who spent much of their time exchanging wisecracks, "a particular
form of jest that, piercing pretense, carries a reproof."[23] The group

first gathered at a long round table between a mural of the Bay of Naples and a mirrored wall which, tellingly, reflected them back upon themselves; as they grew (and grew in reputation), the hotel manager, Frank Case, moved them into the Rose Room and gave them a round table from which the theater press agent Murdock Pemberton took their name.

Case lists as other charter members of the Round Table George and Beatrice Kaufman, Deems Taylor, Heywood Broun, Marc Connelly, Ruth Hale, Peggy Wood, Jane Grant, Margalo Gillmore, John Peter Toohey, Gertrude Atherton, Brock and Murdock Pemberton, and Edna Ferber.[24] Here, amidst inexpensive lunches of hamburger or ham and eggs, apple pie, and coffee—or free celery stuffed with roquefort, minestrone, and tea—the bon mots were exchanged. They played "I Can Give You a Sentence" using such words as *horticulture, meretricious,* and *burlesque* ("I had two soft-burlesque for breakfast"); they reviewed critically current plays and writing; they made jokes about each other and, as often, those not present. They liked puns and relished *double-entendres;* although Woollcott tried to capture the leader's role, often through his rudeness—his nickname for half-Jewish Dorothy was "Sheeny"—it was the more genial F. P. A. who became their natural director. Recording their best remarks in his newspaper column, "The Conning Tower," he helped to make Dorothy Parker famous, and as famous for her repartees as for her poetry.

The group was immortalized, too, as the Sophisticates in Gertrude Atherton's novel *Black Oxen.*[25] With such close camaraderie, there was consistent mutual admiration and much log-rolling although Edna Ferber, herself rarely admitted to the circle, has written that

Far from boosting one another they actually were merciless if they disapproved. I have never encountered a more hard-bitten crew. . . . Theirs was a tonic influence, one on the other, and all on the world of American letters. The people they could not and would not stand were the bores, hypocrites, sentimentalists and the socially pretentious. . . . Casual, incisive, they had a terrible integrity about their work and a boundless ambition.[26]

Others of the Round Table later saw the group as facile, competitive, narrow; an irresponsible game of wits that wated time and talent. Nevertheless, because the Round table became a mutually suportative society for high standards of language in an increasingly popularized theateer and jornalism, Dorothy Parker learned from this association. She seems not to have attended the group daily, and participants say she was usually shy and quiet when she did—but whatever her participation, the Algonquin lunches re inforced her interest in entertainment, celebrities, ang gossip while claiming a hatred for shallowness. It also taught her the value of a punch line, by 1921 characterizing all her light verse.

"I know of no other [group] where the percentage of success was so high," Frank Case concludes,[27] yet for Marc Connelly many years later it was Dorothy who had "the most riveting presence at the table."[28] Success did not describe "Spook" Parker, however. When he returned from Europe in 1919, he accompanied Dorothy to Algonquin lunches and to plays and after theater parties, but he was quiet, without the witty ways of his wife's new companions, and they slowly drifted apart. In his absence, Dorothy would make up stories about him—he had fallen down a manhole, he had cremated a dead person by mistake—but she must, at least at the first, have known torn loyalties. If her personal life was troubled, so was her life as a play reviewer. She enjoyed theater, but she hated most of the plays she was required to see. The excitement of her job she caught in a later column for *McCall's*—"The first-night audience is like no other assemblance of theater-goers on earth," she wrote[29]—but slowly, under the tutelage of the Round Table and with the carefree attitude of Sherwood and Benchley, Dorothy began using her wit to distance her from bad plays, just as it had distanced her from her stepmother and from Blessed Sacrament. The reviews were no less true, but sharper; instead of merely summarizing plots and performances, as she did at the start, she began to take on the sophisticated air seen elsewhere in *Vanity Fair:* she used clever, even sardonic quips to poke through the shallowness and commercialism of what she saw on stage. She compared Florenz Ziegfeld's wife Billie Burke, who overacted badly in *Caesar's Wife*, to the burlesque star Eva Tanguay, although in the review of an earlier play she had praised Miss Burke; she attacked David Belasco's *The Son-Daughter* by comparing it unfavorably to *East Is West* and to Charles Dillingham's production of *Apple Blossoms*. All three men were important advertisers in *Vanity Fair* and Crowninshield thought it necessary to reprimand her.[30] The *New York Times* reported January 13, 1920, last night, when, over a pleasantly decorated tea table at the Plaza, Mr. Crowninshield broke the news to Mrs. Parker that her days as drama critic of *Vanity Fair* were over [, s] he was assured that her work in other ways would still be valued highly by the magazine. Mrs. Parker's reception of this news was complicated by the fact that she was well aware of a recent simultaneous fire of complaint on the part of offended subjects of her criticism.

Both she and Mr. Benchley resigned because they were under the impression that it was these coinciding protests which had led to her removal as drama critic.[31]

She had had to know that the confrontation was coming. For months she had poked fun at Crowninshield's stodgy office rules, wearing a sign around her neck stating her salary, reporting to work late, or dawdling a morning away with Mr. Benchley at the Algonquin, making up a play.[32] Sherwood earlier had angered advertisers by writing an assignment on "What the Well-Dressed Man Will Wear" satirically, and he and *Vanity Fair* parted in December of 1919. But Benchley's insistence on resigning with her, out of moral indignity and professional ethics, surprised her. "Mr. Benchley had a family—two children," she later said. "It was the greatest act of friendship I'd known."[33]

Her response at the office and the Algonquin the next day was irreverent good humor. Whether her self-confidence had increased or she was suddenly relieved of an unpleasant job is unclear; but she continued to joke about it, her wit as defensive as ever. She and Benchley stayed on for their contractual sixty days, wearing red chevrons upside down, like those worn by troops mustered out of service and, the last day there, Benchley placed a sign in the lobby that read, "Contributions for Miss Billie Burke."

The bad memory of their dismissal held. In 1922 Dorothy Parker published a Valentine poem to Ziegfeld in *Life*.

> Still we're groggy from the blow
> Dealt us—by the famous Flo;
> After 1924,
> He announces, nevermore
> Will his shows our senses greet—
> At a cost of five per seat.
> Hasten, Time, your onward drive—
> Welcome, 1925![34]

And, in 1923, Benchley added an aside to his negative review of Booth Tarkington's *Rose Brier* for *Life:*

A few years ago a young dramatic critic lost her job for saying, among other disrespectful things, that Billie Burke had a tendency to fling herself coyly about like Eva Tanguay. Even in the face of this proof of divine vengeance, we apprehensively endorse the unfortunate young reviewer's judgment and assert that even after having her attention called to it three years ago, Miss Burke *still* flings herself coyly about like Eva Tanguay.

Applications for the job of dramatic reviewer on *Life* should be sent to the Managing Editor.[35]

This time, neither of them lost a job.

     III   Ainslee's; Life: *"With more technique than tact"*

When Dorothy Parker and Robert Benchley left *Vanity Fair*, they rented "a triangular cubbyhole on the third floor of the Metropolitan Opera House studios, at $30 a month," and moved in their undertakers' pamphlets and posters, two chairs, two kitchen tables, and a hatrack.[36] They were constantly together—John Keats calls theirs a father-daughter relationship,[37] doubtless to displace bad memories of J. Henry Rothschild—and when Benchley decided to buy a family house in Scarsdale, she loaned him $200 to open an account at the Lincoln Trust Company so that he could secure a down payment (although she needed the money back in a half-hour for her own expenses). Their joint quarters lasted several weeks, until Benchley got a regular job on *Life* and she, leaving Eddie and taking rooms on West 57th Street, began a job with *Ainslee's*.

There her new monthly column, "In Broadway Playhouses," permitted her to say what she wished on a stable income from May 1920 through July 1923. No longer tied to the daily routine in Crowninshield's office, she also had valuable time to freelance; by the spring of 1921, she was contributing a poem or a prose squib almost weekly to *Life*. This was good discipline; it also gave her frequent exposure, so as to build her popularity and public posture. By April 1921, her verses were introducing issues of *Life* and, in "Song of the Open Road," she employed a final twist—"I thank whatever gods look down / That I am living right here in town"— that was to become her trademark. The poem was so popular it was reprinted a month later.[38] Here she learned the forcefulness of full

rhymes and monosyllables too: "The good Saint Patrick, in his day, /
Performed a worthy act: / He up and drove the snakes away, / With
more technique than tact."[39] She used snappy lines and puns, noting Avery Hopwood's plays went "from bed to worse,"[40] but even
poetry itself was open to her criticism as she began practicing with a
poem in two voices, soon another standard form for her.

> Dark though the clouds, they are silver-lined;
>   (*This is the stuff that they like to read*)
> If Winter comes, Spring is right behind;
>   (*This is the stuff that the people need*)
>
> Smile, and the World will smile back at you;
>   Aim with a grin, and you cannot miss;
> Laugh off your woes, and you won't feel blue.
>   (*Poetry pays when it's done like this.*)[41]

She also learned to employ cliches, not just attack them; and she was
learning, too, the wit available when she made herself a butt of the
poem. The famous bohemian attitude of "Portrait of the Artist"
stems from early work in *Life* such as "Fragment."

> Why should you dare to hope that you and I
>   Could make love's fitful flash a lasting flame?
> Still, if you think it's only fair to try—
>   Well, I'm game.[42]

In addition, she published in *Life* her first literary criticism. An
outgrowth of the work on *Ainslee's*, her review of Kathleen Norris's
The Beloved Woman anticipates her later best work: "Remember
that the book is by Kathleen Norris, so everything is going to turn
out for the best, and there will never be a word that could possibly
give pain to any of her readers and make the sales fall off."[43] Other
practices in dialogue, beginning with "The Christmas Dinner" in
the December 21, 1922, issue, adumbrate her later fiction. In all
these forms, she was able to use whatever irreverence of tone suited
her fancy; for *Life* as for *Ainslee's*, there were no taboos. She worked
with the best wits on *Life*, modeled on the British magazine *Punch*,
including Benchley, Sherwood, Connelly, Kaufman, Donald Ogden
Stewart, Don Marquis, Arthur Guiterman, Christopher Morley,
and Carolyn Wells, and with them her efforts reached a climax with

the parody issues: those of 1921 and 1922, engineered by Sherwood, and that of August 18, 1925, which featured Dorothy's parody of MacFadden's *True Story* magazine with a sex confession of a model for a picture postcard; the subtitle reads, "She came to that magic Fairyland which men call BROADWAY—and was blinded by the glitter of its wickedness."[44] Between 1920 and 1922, Dorothy Parker wrote ninety-one pieces for *Life*, sixty-three poems and twenty-eight prose squibs.[45]

Her new widespread reputation was consequent to such high productivity. Even as she supplied reviews to *Ainslee's* like clockwork and supplied work regularly to *Life*, she also began writing character sketches—another exercise in preparation for her fiction—and essays for the *Saturday Evening Post, Ladies' Home Journal*, and *Everybody's*. Throughout 1922 she also supplied short pieces in prose and verse for various columns in the *Post*. Her work appeared so frequently that her name was becoming a household word, and in October 1923 she returned to *Vanity Fair*, not as an author but as an illustration: her portrait in oils by Neysa McMein, showing a demure, somewhat tense girl with delicate features, dark hair, and large, dark eyes, had just won the certificate of merit awarded by the Alumni Association of the Art Institute of Chicago.[46] It is the loveliest extant picture of her. For eating well, dressing well, now drinking well and dating a number of men often, she was writing well—and she was having the time of her life.

IV   Men I'm Not Married To; Close Harmony; "Bobbed Hair":
"This living, this living, this living"

"By the time I grew up the fight for the emancipation of women . . . was stale stuff," Lillian Hellman writes in *An Unfinished Woman*.[47] Dorothy Parker helped that liberation: she cut her hair in bangs, wore loose dresses on occasion, and competed with men professionally; "She's someone you talk to like a man," as Kaufman and Hart described a character based on her in *Merrily We Roll Along*.[48]

She kept to the journalistic and theater crowd of midtown Manhattan, rarely venturing to Greenwich Village where Edna St. Vincent Millay, Edmund Wilson, and Floyd Dell were also liberating women and morals, although Wilson once read a play he was working on to Dorothy and Benchley.[49] Instead, she partied frequently and with some abandon with her associates from the Round Table and the Broadway theater. Herman Liebert recalls visiting her in her room—a modest room with a kitchen stuck in one corner, a bathroom in another—and while he spoke to her of his writing, Benchley came in and slept on the couch; Sherwood followed, awakening him; and they wrestled.[50] This small apartment was near the studio of Neysa McMein, the locale of late night parties of the Algonquin wits. McMein was known for her homemade wine, and in her larger, shabby room they held musical evenings with Benchley on mandolin, Irving Berlin and Deems Taylor on piano, and Dorothy on triangle. Paul Robeson, then becoming an eminent bass singer, joined their parties (and gave Dorothy the germ for a later story, "Arrangement in Black and White"). Often the group would go on to the elegant Jack and Charlie's Puncheon Club[51] at 42 West 49th Street or the less elegant Tony's across the street, speakeasies where Dorothy would plead poverty and borrow taxi money to return home—or they would move on to Polly Adler's.[52] Woollcott would take Dorothy in a rented carriage down Fifth Avenue; in August 1922 they added a new place—the apartment of Harold Ross and Jane Grant at 412 West 47th Street.[53] Others sometimes joined them now: Sherwood brought Scott and Zelda Fitzgerald to meet Dorothy just after their marriage; she thought Zelda beautiful but sulky and both of them too ostentatious.[54] She also met Ring Lardner.[55]

Woollcott, meantime, had been thinking of an isolated house where such friends as Dorothy, Alice Duer Miller, and Kaufman could go to write. "Aleck had the soul of an innkeeper," Harold Ross once commented, and true to form he bought from Enos Booth in 1924 most of Neshobe Island near Bomoseen, Vermont. With the help of ten friends paying $1,000 initiation fees, he set up a kind of writing-swimming-croquet club where the Algonquin wits and their friends could go for country vacations. Howard Teichmann records that Dorothy once spent a weekend dressed only in a hat, but was finally dismissed for repeated drunkenness.[56] Little wonder Benchley thought she was getting in with the wrong crowd.[57]

She also began taking herself too seriously. Eddie, now a compulsive drinker, decided to recover in Hartford, but she declined to return there with him. So they quarreled and she left him, claiming his Protestant family detested her because her father was a Jew. " 'It was a case of incompatibility,' " Donald Ogden Stewart contended.

She was fun to dance with . . . but I think if you had been married to Dottie, you would have found out, little by little, that she really wasn't there. She was in love with you, let's say, but it was *her* emotion; she was not worrying about *your* emotion. . . . She was so full of pretense. . . . That doesn't mean she did not hate sham on a high level, but that she could recognize pretense because that was part of her makeup. She would get glimpses of herself doing things that would make her hate herself . . . .[58]

Depression set in. Her writing became more difficult and, since she was a perfectionist who always wrote slowly—"I think it out and then write it sentence by sentence. . . . I can't write five words but that I change seven"[59] —she put a towel over her typewriter so no one could know what if anything she was working on.

Gilbert Seldes blamed her depression partly on her awareness of a superior talent: " 'She had a perceptive intelligence that was really something—something the others did not have' "; she was " 'a sad person . . . as if being enormously satisfied . . . would have diminished her.'"[60] She reverted to form: she took her bewilderment, discouragement, and self-disgust out on others. Her nasty comments on what Philadelphia shirts were stuffed with, after a weekend party there as the guest of George Horace Lorimer, editor of *The Saturday Evening Post*, prevented her work from appearing in the *Post* again. On the other hand, her tearful desire to have a family and house in the country was laughed off as alcoholic sentimentality. Her poem "News Item" —sardonically titled—in F. P. A.'s column about women wearing glasses and men making passes showed contempt for men, self-pity, and, in summary, an ironic view of the universal roles of men and women: but no one took that seriously either.

They did, however, take seriously her affair with Charles MacArthur, a young reporter and budding playwright. "Her crush was as fervid as it was ill-advised," Anita Loos observes,[61] for everyone but Dorothy knew he liked all women and no special woman. Ben Hecht, who collaborated with MacArthur on *The Front Page*, recalls him as a "dashing, mysterious fellow [who] had a poet's infatuation with death. . . . There was also a wildness in Charlie, but it was well policed. . . . [H]e had to feed the daemon in him a great deal of liquor to keep it in line."[62] Soon MacArthur was also having affairs with other women. About this time Dorothy wrote "Unfortunate Coincidence":

By the time you swear you're his,
    Shivering and sighing,
And he vows his passion is
    Infinite, undying—
Lady, make a note of this:
    One of you is lying.[63]

Her despair deepened. Muriel King, who ran a clothing shop at
49 East 51st Street, remembers Dorothy as "charming, darling, and
loathsome. No, not really loathsome, disappointing. When you
thought you were friends, you didn't expect her to slap you down.
She'd come in and ask, 'What did you do yesterday?' You'd tell her.
Then she would say in a flat, bored voice, 'That is a very interesting
story.' One felt totally deflated."[64] She had as little use for herself.
Her smoking and drinking became heavy. She underwent an abortion. Remembering the undertakers' magazines, she wore perfume
with the scent of tuberoses, the scent given corpses. A short time
later, she tried to commit suicide; the hotel waiter, delivering
dinner, found her in the bathroom, her wrists slashed with Eddie's
razor. There is an eerie resemblance to the poem "Coda."

There's little in taking or giving,
    There's little in water or wine;
This living, this living, this living,
    Was never a project of mine.[65]

George Oppenheimer, later her publisher, called her " 'a masochist
whose passion for unhappiness knew no bounds.' "[66]

Now she established a pattern that would last her life, with mixed
success: she used the bad times as material for writing during the
good times. Margaret Case Harriman reports that "Everyone at the
Round Table worked hard and continuously, [in] steady and lonely
toil."[67] She met—and was perhaps inspired by—Elinor Wylie, and
Wylie's sister Nancy Hoyt records Dorothy's visits to their apartment on 9th Street just west of Fifth Avenue. "Dorothy Parker,
vivid, sympathetic and never showing the caustic side which is in
many of her poems and stories, would spend the afternoon in the
back room between the table with the typewriter and the bookshelves, a place where few penetrated."[68] The work paid off. She
conveyed her buried pain in the interior monologue of a suburban
husband trapped in a bad marriage in her first published story, one

of some power, "Such a Pretty Little Picture," in the December 1922 issue of Mencken's and Nathan's *Smart Set*. The technique resembles *Dubliners* but, for fiction then being published in America, was far ahead of its time. She also encapsulated her feelings in the poem "Interior."

> Her mind lives tidily, apart
>   From cold and noise and pain,
> And bolts the door against her heart,
>   Out wailing in the rain—[69]

She was now writing mature, autobiographical poetry she later collected in book form, to preserve.

She also began to reach out to others, to work with others. She joined the Algonquin wits in writing a parody of a European revue, *Chauve Souris*, which at the suggestion of Murdock Pemberton they called *No, Sirree!* They staged the musical on Sunday evening, April 30, 1922, in Broadway's Forty-ninth Street Theater, and invited Broadway actors and actresses to review them. Dorothy wrote a song sung by Robert Sherwood: "We've got the blues, we've got the blues, we believe we said before we've got the blues. . . . As far as we're concerned, there is no sting in death. / We've got those everlasting ingénue blues." This was part of a sketch called "He Who Gets Flapped"; Sherwood leaned languidly on the proscenium surrounded by girls. In the next sketch, "Between the Acts," Dorothy played a first-nighter in a theater lobby at intermission.[70] Woollcott thought the show potentially commercial, and rewritten and titled *The 49'ers* with a one-act "historical" drama called *Nero* by Dorothy and Benchley, it reopened in the smaller Punch and Judy Theater November 7, but closed after 15 performances to half-empty houses.[71] Also in 1922 Dorothy and F. P. A. reprinted some light free verse as a dos-a-dos book; called *Women I'm Not Married To; Men I'm Not Married To*, it had first appeared on facing pages in *The Saturday Evening Post* for June 17. The book carried their pictures on its covers.

In her *Vanity Fair* review of March 1920, Dorothy had noted that Elmer L. Rice, formerly Elmer L. Rizenstein, was the author of a mystery play that "follows the regular formula so faithfully that there is not a chance of any slip-up."[72] Now, in 1924, she wrote a formulaic domestic comedy with Rice that they first called *Soft Music* and, later, *Close Harmony; or The Lady Next Door.*[73] In the interim, Rice had written *The Adding Machine* (1923), but their joint fluff, about two frustrated people who start an adulterous affair, was tame and predictable. It has a snide child and a former burlesque star but little other chance for the acerbic Parker wit. The play tried out in Wilmington, then opened on Broadway December 1, 1924, the same night as the openings for Berlin's *Music Box Revue* and for *Lady Be Good* with Fred and Adele Astaire. It was mildly panned by critics, sparsely attended, and then, four weeks later, quietly closed. Near the end, Dorothy sent a telegram to her Algonquin friends: "CLOSE HARMONY DID A COOL, NINETY DOLLARS AT THE MATINEE. ASK THE BOYS IN THE BACK ROOM WHAT THEY WILL HAVE."[74] She had reviewed other dramatists in *Vanity Fair* and *Ainslee's* for five years and had experimented with dialogue for longer than that: the failure of *Close Harmony* must have been a great personal disappointment.[75] Yet that same year she wrote another fine story, about an abortion, "Mr. Durant," which she placed with *American Mercury*. And even while *Close Harmony* was foundering, she wrote Chapter VII of "Bobbed Hair," a collaborative novel, that appeared in *Collier's* for January 17, 1925. With an occasional biting phrase, her chapter is largely a hard-boiled gangster story, proving that in fiction, at any rate, Dorothy Parker had good command of a range of styles. Then she turned for the first time to film, and wrote a short for Paramount with Kaufman, *Business Is Business*. No matter the personal strain, her varied talents appeared inexhaustible.

V   Enough Rope; *"Constant Reader";* Sunset Gun;
     Laments for the Living; After Such Pleasures;
     Death and Taxes: *"rosemary for you and me"*

Still the highs grew higher, the lows lower. In their fictional portrayal of her, Kaufman and Hart noted the change.

The JULIA *of 1925 is fresh, buoyant, youthful, happy. There is a definite glow about her.*[76]

The JULIA *of 1927 is just beginning to show the faint traces of the woman we have seen in 1934. She has not yet acquired the flabby look of the steady drinker, but even this early in the day she is not quite sober.*[77]

Highs resulted from her newly gained popularity as a wit; her vul-
nerability combined with her speedy repartee made her acceptable
to the wealthy who liked to patronize the arts, and she, who was
always attracted to money, liked them. She also liked such famous
writers as Hemingway. Donald Ogden Stewart met him in 1924 in
Paris; when Hemingway came to New York in 1926, Stewart introduced him to Dorothy, and Benchley. Hemingway told the novelist
John Dos Passos that he found Dorothy and Benchley "obviously
attractive people,"[78] and subsequently they joined the Stewarts and
Seward Collins of *The Bookman* in sailing back to France with him.
In Paris Stewart introduced her to Gerald and Sara Murphy and,
through them, to Archibald MacLeish, Gilbert Seldes, and John
Dos Passos; they went on to the Murphys' elegant Villa Amèrica at
Antibes, where Scott and Zelda Fitzgerald joined them. Murphy,
heir to the Mark Cross leather goods business, had studied architec-
ture at Yale and wanted to be a painter. So he settled in France,
where he imported American culture and was host to American
writers, bringing jazz music to Antibes and teaching his guests
Negro spirituals.[79] He was not rich, in Fitzgerald's words, he was
"very rich," and he gave Dorothy a cottage named La Bastide
("small country house") in which to work. They all visited a small
Alpine village where she and Benchley sang Harvard songs through
the streets late one night to cheer up any students injured skiing.[80]
Later she went to the bullfights in Spain with the Seldeses and
Collins, then returned to the Riviera and Paris. But there was also a
sour note: at a party in October at the MacLeishes that she did not
attend, Hemingway toasted her—"Here's to Dorothy Parker. Life
will never become her so much as her almost leaving it"—and then
accused her of not returning his portable typewriter (which she had)
and told a dirty joke at her expense. She got her revenge: as her ship
departed, she threw overboard in his direction her own new typewriter. And then she buried the incident: her report of the trip—an
essay on Paris in the January 1927 issue of *Vanity Fair*—shows no
trace of disappointment. The Murphys visited her and Benchley in
New York in 1928 and then in the summer of 1929 they both returned, along with Stewart and Philip and Ellen Barry. "D. Parker
is on the crest," Fitzgerald wrote Hemingway exuberantly on
August 29, "tho I didn't see as much of her as I'd liked."[81] On this
trip, Dorothy showed the Murphys great generosity: she stayed in

the Swiss Alps with them through the summer, fall, and winter, at Chalet LaBruyere, Montana-Vermala, where their son Patrick, 9, was dying of consumption.

When Dorothy Parker entertained infrequently in her own rooms, across from Neysa McMein's—Thurber did a famous impersonation of Ross in her New York apartment[82]—parties were often carefree; but she attended others' parties much more often, including those at the estate of Herbert Bayard Swope at Great Neck, Long Island. Edna Ferber remembers their being "In and out, carefree as guests at an unbelievably luxurious clubhouse. . . . Tea was at six or seven, dinner at ten or eleven, supper at three or four. Good talk, laughter, games."[83] Apparently tired of tame and predictable Algonquin lunches, the Round Table moved on to more and more lavish, more and more frenetic parties on Long Island. The Lardners lived next door to the Swopes' mansion, where Dorothy once watched others play croquet on the neighboring lawn by flashlight: " 'Jesus Christ,' " she remarked, " 'the heirs of the ages!' "[84] For Dorothy was not always welcome. Bennett Cerf records that she "could scarcely be considered the ideal week-end guest. Her hostess at one such gathering was described as 'outspoken.' 'Outspoken by whom?' rasped Miss Parker. That evening she wired a friend in New York, 'For heaven's sake, rush me a loaf of bread, enclosing saw and file,' " and Gaines records that Lardner stopped inviting her because it was impossible for him to work when she was there.[85] It was, Lillian Hellman says, vengeance on the rich. Such revenge inspired mature stories, too, like "Song of the Shirt, 1941" and "I Live on Your Visits."

Dorothy's self-punishment—her alternating lows—was the other form of despair. Although she underwent psychiatric treatment with Dr. Alvan Barach—later Woollcott would, too—in 1925 she attempted suicide again with an overdose of sleeping pills. Following her recovery, she began another affair, with another wealthy man but now a discriminating patron of the arts as well—Seward Collins, editor of *The Bookman* and heir to a national chain of tobacco stores. He accompanied her to Europe in 1926 but they quarreled frequently, and she sent him home midtrip, spending the remainder of her journey with the honeymooning Stewarts. Another affair followed in 1927 with John Garrett, a businessman who reminded her friends of Eddie Parker. This too did not last; she may have revealed the reason in "Ballade at Thirty-Five":

> Ever a prey to coincidence,
> Always I knew the consequence;
> Always saw what the end would be.
> We're as Nature has made us—hence
> I loved them until they loved me.[86]

In 1927, G.T. Hartmann painted a new portrait of her in *Arts and Decoration* that shows a sour woman, but by then the old Algonquin group, her only "family," was breaking up. And in the spring of 1928, she went to Hartford to testify privately to Eddie Parker's cruelty. She won a divorce on March 31.[87]

Dorothy Parker's poetry now took on a wary tone, but not her relationships. One night at Tony's she met John McClain, a recent college football star, now a clerk on Wall Street. He was in his early twenties, she was thirty-eight. Their affair was sordid.

Mr. McClain, to use his own words, considered himself to be a hell of a swordsman, a he-whore, and he told his roommates that he intended to roll up a score with well-known women in Society, on the stage, and in the literary world. . . . It was not long, however, before Mr. McClain began to complain that she would not leave him alone. . . and he was tired of such nonsense.[88]

She tried suicide a third time with a fistful of barbituates after warning her friends, then sought a loan to get released from the hospital. She became sentimental and self-pitying, choosing young actors as escorts and concentrating on homosexuals, saying she needed good fairies to take care of her. But, Beatrice Ames said, "She respected her talent even more. . . . She had an absolute, solid gratitude for her talent. She said to me, 'I'm betraying it, I'm drinking, I'm not working. I have the most horrendous guilt,' "[89] and Vincent Sheean recalls: "If the doorbell rang in her apartment, she would say, 'What fresh hell can this be?'—and it wasn't funny; she meant it. . . . I think she drank because of her perception. She wanted to dull her perceptions. Her vision of life was almost more than she could bear."[90]

This guilt and agony, bolstered by a quick wit and sardonic humor, awarded her the rueful attitude she conveyed in her poems. She kept publishing them—in *Life*, *Vanity Fair*, *The New Yorker*, and F. P. A.'s column in *The World*—and in 1926, during her first trip to Europe, Horace Liveright published *Enough Rope*. This

collection of her poems went through eleven printings, an unprecedented bestseller, and her fame spread further; she was, says
Keats, the prisoner of her notoriety. But no one took seriously as
experiential a poem as "Resumé":

> Razors pain you;
> Rivers are damp;
> Acids stain you;
> And drugs cause cramp.
> Guns aren't lawful;
> Nooses give;
> Gas smells awful;
> You might as well live.[91]

Instead, critics like Genevieve Taggard, reviewing *Enough Rope* for
the *Herald-Tribune*, noted: "Dorothy Parker runs her little show as
if it were a circus,"[92] and Marie Luhrs wrote in *Poetry* that "in its
lightness, its cynicism, its pose, she has done the right thing." They
had in mind poems like "They Part":

> There's rosemary for you and me;
>   But is it usual, dear,
> To hire a man, and fill a van
>   By way of *souvenir?*[93]

Such a reputation was due largely to F. P. A., recording her bon
mots in his column, "The Conning Tower," and publishing imitations and parodies of her work; he also included her in entries for his
"Diary of Our Own Samuel Pepys."[94] Critics acclaimed her even as
the public made her popular. Edmund Wilson wrote in *New Republic*:

I believe that, if we admire, as it is fashionable to do, the light verse of Prior
and Gay, we should admire Miss Parker also. She writes well: her wit is the
wit of her time and place; but it is often as cleanly economic at the same
time that it is as flatly brutal as the wit of the age of Pope; and, within its
scope, it is a criticism of life.[95]

In *The Bookman* for March 1928, John Farrar wrote that she "has
become the giantess of American letters, . . . ready to eat up any
poor Jack who shows his head bearing signs of enthusiasm, sentimentality, or quaintness."[96]

She was aided immeasurably by *The New Yorker*. Founded by Harold Ross and Jane Grant with the financial support of Raoul Fleischmann, the baking magnate, the new weekly announced in its first issue (February 21, 1925) that Dorothy was, along with Connelly, Kaufman, Woollcott, Alice Duer Miller, Ralph Barton, and Rea Irwin, one of the "Advisory Editors," a ruse she agreed to so that Ross could obtain sufficient backing. Ross hoped to capture the suavity and sophistication of New York and to combine it with the irony and mot juste of the Round Table. He wrote in a prospectus:

The New Yorker will be a reflection in word and picture of metropolitan life. . . . Its general tenor will be one of gaiety, wit and satire, . . . It will be what is commonly called sophisticated, in that it will assume a reasonable degree of enlightenment on the part of its readers. It will hate bunk . . . . *The New Yorker* will be the magazine which is not edited for the old lady in Dubuque.[97]

"The old lady in Dubuque" was a direct challenge to Crowninshield's *Vanity Fair*, but *The New Yorker* nearly failed at first. Ross insisted on both clarity and casualness, and Dorothy Parker found this recipe instructive, although she only contributed two poems, an essay on a typical clubwoman, and a drama review under a pseudonym during the first year. From an original print run of 15,000 copies in February 1925, circulation fell to a precarious 2,700 by August.[98] The Algonquin group did not take Ross seriously. But he finally persuaded Fleischmann to loan him more money and, in time, the magazine caught on, while *Vanity Fair*'s circulation decreased.

Probably out of friendship to Ross and Grant, for the money, and for the freedom they gave her, rather than for vengeance on Crowninshield, Dorothy agreed to review books for *The New Yorker* each week beginning in October 1927 and continuing, off and on after 1929, through 1931. Her column was first called "Recent Books" but, starting in November 1927, "Reading and Writing," and she signed it "Constant Reader." The acerbity she had found at *Vanity Fair* and improved at *Ainslee's* provided *The New Yorker* now with some of its best known lines. She praised Hemingway and Lardner, but reported of Margot Asquith's autobiography, "The affair between Margot Asquith and Margot Asquith will live as one of the prettiest love stories in all literature"; of William Lyon Phelps' *Hap-*

piness, "It is second only to a rubber duck as the ideal bathtub companion"; and of Milne's whimsey, "Tonstant weader fwowed up."[99] As usual, she was awkward in praising, but perceptive, intelligent, and biting in dispraise, trying to slip her puns past a wary, irritated Ross.[100] She added a personal note to many columns, giving "Constant Reader" the identity of a poor, hard-working, but put-upon woman who cheerfully obliged publisher and readers. Her column was interrupted by an appendectomy—"a mere scratch" ("Back to the Book-Shelf," August 25, 1928, p. 60)—and her trip to the Murphys, which led to a description of Switzerland in the column for January 24, 1931 ("Home Is the Sailor," p. 62).

But she did not concentrate exclusively on her work as "Constant Reader." In 1928, following the affair with Collins and the divorce from Eddie but before she met McClain, she gathered her poems from the magazines and newspapers and published a second volume. *Sunset Gun* also garnered high commendations. As far away as London, Leon Whipple noted in *The Survey* that "She takes refuge, as moderns will, in irony and satire, but for the first time since Suckling or Heine we have self-satire, not social satire. . . . The verse creates a valid mood of pathos or wistful reminiscence."[101] Also in the winter and spring of 1928, she wrote a column on the New York scene for *McCall's* and, in the summer and early fall, essays on Shaw and on the movies for *The New Yorker*, remarking in this last, "I share the general high hopes for the increasing perfection of the talkies" ("G.B.S., Practically in Person," July 7, 1928, p. 28). What made her proudest, however, was her profile of Hemingway, "The Artist's Reward," in the issue for November 30, 1929, where she called him "far and away the first American artist" (p. 28) and praised him for avoiding New York. "He has the most valuable asset an artist can possess—the fear of what he knows is bad for him" (p. 29).

In 1929, she helped Marc Connelly, a friend from Algonquin days, type out the final script for *The Green Pastures*, but she also began drinking more heavily, missing magazine deadlines. She collected her stories for her friend George Oppenheimer, moving from Boni and Liveright to Viking, and *Laments for the Living* appeared in 1930, after Oppenheimer locked her away with a bottle to work through the proofs.[102] These stories range from bright dialogues of youth ("The Sexes") and recollections on the morning after ("You Were Perfectly Fine") to serious stories about the death of an old man ("The Wonderful Old Gentleman") and bitter attacks on intolerance ("Arrangement in Black and White") and adultery ("Mr. Durant," "Big Blonde"). Of them, T. S. Matthews wrote: "We recognize her own style: style which is apparently compact of merely reported speech, but which has a bite, nevertheless, as individual and unmistakable as Ring Lardner's or Hemingway's."[103] In 1931 Dorothy Parker collected her last poems for Viking in *Death and Taxes*, also to fine reviews (except in *Poetry*); in *Saturday Review* for June 13, Henry Seidel Canby thought her work "verse of a Horatian lightness, with an exquisite certainty of technique, which, like the lustre on a Persian bowl, is proof that civilization is itself a philosophy."[104] But she was too often still considered the wit, not the poet. She complained retrospectively to Marion Capron:

I was following in the exquisite footsteps of Miss Millay, unhappily in my own horrible sneakers. My verses are no damn good. Let's face it, honey, my verse is terribly dated—as anything once fashionable is dreadful now. I gave it up, knowing it wasn't getting any better, but nobody seemed to notice my magnificent gesture.[105]

Her second volume of stories, *After Such Pleasures*, appeared from Viking in 1933. The book juxtaposes some well-known monologues ("The Waltz;" "From the Diary of a New York Lady") that surveyed the pretensions and shallowness of society with more sympathetic portraits of a plain middle-aged woman ("Horsie") and a fading actress coarsened by her decline ("Glory in the Daytime"). "It's fun to see the lamented English language rise from the Parisian boneyard and race out front with the right jockey in the saddle," Ogden Nash commented in the *Saturday Review*,[106] and Mark Van Doren noted in the *English Journal* that "Drunk or sober, angry or affectionate, stupid or inspired, these people of Mrs. Parker's speak with an accent we immediately recognize and relish."[107] In addition, in 1931, Dorothy filled in as drama critic for two months at *The New Yorker* while Benchley went to Hollywood, and contributed lyrics to Heywood Broun's revue *Shoot the Works*, which also featured a skit based on her story "You Were Perfectly Fine." No matter how joyful or despairing she became, she retained contact with the Algonquin friends who had encouraged her from the beginning.

Two other events occurred in this second major period of production, 1925–1933. She became a political and social activist for the first time, and she won her major literary award. The case against Nicola Sacco and Bartolomeo Vanzetti for robbery and murder in South Braintree, Massachusetts, on April 15, 1920, went through eight years of litigation while many protested, at home and abroad, that their ignorance of American ways and their avowed anarchism prevented a fair trial and condemned the innocent. Benchley was implicated when a close friend told him that Judge Webster Thayer had vowed he " 'would show them and get those guys hanged.' "[108] On August 11, 1927, the day of their execution, Benchley and Edna St. Vincent Millay went to Boston to plead a stay from Governor Fuller, and Millay read, in a rally on Salem Street, her poem "Justice Denied in Massachusetts." Sympathetic groups from New York marched with placards up Tremont Street to the State House grounds where they walked slowly back and forth outside a meeting of the Governor's Council. When a crowd gathered, two patrol wagons came up and police grabbed "as many marchers as they could";[109] of the forty-four protesters, thirty-nine were arrested, including John Dos Passos, Benchley, and Dorothy Parker. She was fined five dollars, and she later told papers "she had been treated roughly" by police. Her presence helped to sensationalize the event, but two scholars have since claimed that "the demonstrations were [not] dominated by unrealistic Bohemianism. . . . [O]nly a few writers were active; those who did participate were intelligent, practical, and thoroughly aware of their civil rights."[110] Those who noticed an increasing sympathy in her fiction over the cold ruefulness in her poems could not have been surprised.

The best example of this sympathy came in Dorothy's most daring story. In 1929 she told of her own alcoholic depressions, ill-fated love affairs, and attempted suicides in the story of Hazel Morse. Like Dorothy, Hazel Morse was terrified of her loneliness and despair but thought by her friends to be a party girl, always good for laughs.[111] The mode was new for Dorothy Parker and would seriously challenge her popular reputation as a wit, but she wrote "Big Blonde" with astonishing power and technique: she reduced long years of a woman's life into short panels and compressed an entire autobiography into a short story. From more than 2,000 entries, "Big Blonde" was awarded the eleventh annual first prize of $500 in the O. Henry Memorial Prizes for the best short story appearing in an American magazine for that year. As far away as Cannes,

Fitzgerald was elated. A master of the form of short story himself, he urged Max Perkins at Scribner's to sign Dorothy on at once. "Just now she's at a high point as a producer and as to reputation," he wrote. "I wouldn't lose any time about this if it interests you."[112] Dorothy, also in France then, must have been pleased—if she ever knew.

> VI *Hollywood;* Not So Deep as a Well; New Masses;
> Here Lies: *"the poet speaks not just for himself"*

Writing on "Movies—The Eighth Art" in the March 1920 issue of *Vanity Fair*, John Emerson and Anita Loos predicted that "the scenario writer must be the central figure."[113] Few writers then paid any heed, for talkies were not yet developed and New York theater was in a period of unprecedented growth.[114] Rising costs, greater risks, and keener competition from the talkies, however, caused many writers whom Dorothy knew to drift to the West Coast in the late 1920s, along with actors, directors, and musicians, for the lure of big salaries and a new art form was too great to ignore. Dorothy herself signed a three month contract with MGM in 1931.

But she did not stay—having spent all her life in the family house or in apartments and hotels in midtown Manhattan, she could not leave the city for long. Its pace, feel, and attitudes were too fundamentally her own. So she returned, lived off the sales of *Death and Taxes* and *After Such Pleasures*, and, drinking steadily now, wrote when and where she could. Not much appeared. Ogden Nash dedicated *Hard Lines* to her (among others) in 1931, and she wrote parodies of his irregular, rhyming verse.[115] In 1932 she accepted Thurber's offer to introduce his book of drawings, *The Seal in the Bedroom and Other Predicaments;* in 1932 and 1933 she wrote six stories for *Harper's Bazaar* and two each in 1933 and 1934 for *The New Yorker;* and in 1934 she published a profile of Woollcott in *Vanity Fair* and an account of a dog show for *Cosmopolitan.* She collected her three volumes of poetry, with a few omitted, as *Not So Deep as a Well* (1936). But now reviews were mixed, as Dorothy Emerson pointed out in the March 13 issue of *Scholastic* magazine.

When *Enough Rope* appeared, some reviewers hailed her as an immortal poet, and others ranked her with the best of our serious poets. Now the praise has undeniably diminished. Many in estimating her *Not So Deep as a Well* declare that the flippant brokenheartedness, the playing with bitterness and folly, seem somewhat outworn. The difference cannot be explained by any change in her work.

The change is in the times. Her poems were timely in the predepression era, when it was fashionable to be irresponsible and bitter. . . . [N]ow it's "smart to be thrifty." . . . Though Dorothy Parker's poems are not fine enough to give lasting rather than passing interest, they are expertly written, unusually diverting and amusing, and it is safe to predict that you and I will continue reading them and quoting them for years to come.[116]

Such reviews were kind but, for someone who had surrendered her poetry as so many wisecracks, they were hardly encouraging. Nor was she content with her stories.

Her friends nonetheless stuck by her. Oppenheimer, with the aid of George and Beatrice Kaufman, complimented her as the bright but eccentric Mary Hilliard in a 1933 comedy, *Here Today*, but it closed in five weeks.[117] Early the next year, Edward F. Gardner tried adapting the stories of *After Such Pleasures* for the stage with his wife Shirley Booth in some of the leading roles; it lasted only twenty-three performances. Both counteracted the brutal portrait of her, with her puffy eyes, self-pity, and girlish crushes, drawn by Charles Brackett in *Entirely Surrounded*. There were still moments of fun, too: the Algonquin crowd, now the Moriarty crowd, celebrated the end of Prohibition (December 5, 1933) at Jim Moriarty's new establishment, the Marlborough House at 15 East 61st Street; in February 1934 she joined Woollcott and Benchley in supporting a waiters' strike at the Waldorf-Astoria Hotel;[118] and she stopped going around with various young gay escorts from the theater and took up living with one of them, Alan Campbell, whom she met at the Howard Dietzes'. And in 1934, while Kaufman and Hart were ridiculing her as Julia Glenn and the Algonquin crowd itself as actresses at Le Coq D'Or restaurant in the Broadway hit *Merrily We Roll Along*, she and Alan Campbell went West.

They traveled to Denver in a 1929 flivver, along with two Bedlington terriers, arriving in early June for Alan's acting job in summer stock at the Elitch Gardens theater. At some point—Dorothy said it was partly because of the morality of Denver—they were married, but she gave variant stories on when and where.[119] At the time, Dorothy was forty; Alan was twenty-nine, the son of a Scottish tobacco man from Richmond, a long-time landed cavalier, and a Jewish mother, daughter of a kosher butcher. Dorothy never knew his father and from the start disliked his mother, but Alan, who in New York had cooked and cleaned for Dorothy and helped to temper her drinking, seemed to many—despite a difference in age—to be a good husband for her. Even in Denver where, she complained to Woollcott in a letter, Alan spent most of his time away from her in rehearsal or performance, she was relaxed and happy; "We have met three or four nice people, which is big for a continent. I thought I was going to hate it, and I love it. I love being a juvenile's bride and living in a bungalow and pinching dead leaves off the rose bushes. I will be God damned."[120]

After his job in Denver, they drove on to Hollywood, where they lived briefly in Oppenheimer's house before joining other screenwriters in the Garden of Allah. The Garden of Allah, a Spanish mansion bought in 1918 by the Russian actress Alla Nazimova on a lot between Hollywood and Beverly Hills, had been made into an ugly, uncomfortable bungalow hotel as an investment, "a world within the world of Hollywood."[121] Here the Campbells partied each afternoon with Benchley, McClain, John O'Hara, Eddie Mayer, Muriel King, Frances and Albert Hackett (all writers), and the comic actor Charlie Butterworth. Dorothy "wore the weirdest clothes," Sheilah Graham recalls, "tennis shoes and black stockings with a blouse and skirt."[122] Dorothy and Benchley put up money for founding Romanoff's, soon another hangout, and then she and Alan bought an imposing house of their own, with a white colonnade and servants, in Beverly Hills.

The Campbells had signed up with Paramount to begin work on an original story for Carole Lombard and Lee Tracy on September 5, 1934, and they did contribute to dialogue for *Here Is My Heart* and *One Hour Late* but they were never credited with any work. Instead, Dorothy recalled bitterly in 1939, she wrote the words for one song for *The Big Broadcast of 1936*, "played golf all day and sent her chauffeur around to the studio every week to pick up her salary check."[123] The weekly pay was $5,200—equivalent to $8,200 today—and Dorothy, true to form, spent it as quickly as it came in: $86 on one hat and $628 on handmade lingerie at 1935 prices.[124] True to form also, she despised the same wealth she adored and hated wasting her talents on Hollywood. Her letter to Woollcott some time later from 520 North Canon Drive in Beverly Hills confirms her anger and despair over manufactured writing, beneath the defensive smartness:

54   DOROTHY PARKER

Alan and I are working on a little opera which was originally named "Twenty-two Hours by Air," but it has been kicking around the studio for a long time, during which aerial transportation has made such progress that it is now called "Eleven Hours by Air." By the time we are done, the title is to be, I believe, "Stay Where You Are." Before this, we were summoned to labor on a story of which we were told only, "Now, we don't know yet whether the male lead will be played by Tallia Carminati or Bing Crosby. So just sort of write it with both of them in mind." Before that, we were assigned the task of taking the sex out of "Sailor Beware" [sic] They read our script, and went back to the original version. The catch for the movies, it seemed, was that hinge of the plot where the sailor bets he will make the girl. They said that was dirty. But would they accept our change, that triumph of ingenuity where the sailor just bets he will make another sailor? Oh, no. Sometimes I think they don't know *what* they want.

Her friendship with Helen Hayes and her admiration for James Cagney and Crosby mitigated the cynicism of her writing—"Aside from the work, which I hate like holy water, I love it here"—yet she continued to be restless when not writing something that gave her commitment and pride.[125]

Woollcott considered her and her friends "slaves, indentured servants, or dupes" and "He not only pitied them but told them so to their faces or through the mails." Her friend Ben Hecht, who had also left New York to write films, thought they were contributing to "trash," and Dorothy and Benchley often talked about their jobs with anger.[126] She was courted by McClain and O'Hara, and in 1935 she met the close friend of her later years, Lillian Hellman,[127] but these friendships did not suffice. She and Alan quarreled frequently, and their drinking grew worse, her language more vulgar, her attempted suicides more frequent.[128] Having enough, she escaped.

By 1936 she was back in New York, reading the reviews of *Not So Deep as a Well*, which was then going through five printings—a popular success, if not always a critical one—and gathering up her royalties, which for 1935–1937 amounted to more than $32,000. Part of this she used to buy a "pitifully inexpensive" drawing of Scott Fitzgerald by his wife.[129] But she found her city " 'shabby and tired. Somehow you feel betrayed.' "[130] So she and Alan found another escape—the *New York Times* announced on August 24 that the Campbells had bought one hundred and eleven acres near Doylestown, Pennsylvania, in a Bucks County then largely unsettled, and were restoring a colonial fieldstone farmhouse there. "It has fourteen rooms and three fireplaces and overlooks the Delaware River with the Netcong Mountains of New Jersey in the distance. It had been in the possession of the Fox family from 1775 until the new owners bought it from Franklin G. Fox of Easton. . . . They plan to occupy it Sept. 1."[131]

The house, Dorothy later told Gilmore Millen, was once used as a station on the underground railroad and would be ideal for her dogs, now numbering nine. Another filmwriter in Hollywood had suggested the possibility, and now, in rural Pennsylvania, they were gutting and remodeling the interior, doing the living room in nine shades of red, putting mirrors in the dining room to bring more landscape in, lining rooms with bookshelves, and constructing a butler's pantry and servants' quarters. They brought in their own electricity for $3,000, later put in a swimming pool for $2,600, spending in all $98,000 to improve their $4,500 purchase. At last, she had the country house of which she dreamed.

But come September they were not in Fox House; on September 24 they were back home in Beverly Hills working for David O. Selznick on *It Happened in Hollywood*. They had needed money; in time Dorothy's name (but not Alan's) would be on a directory of esteemed writers in the new Thalberg Building,[132] but they continued, nearly always, to work as a team—Alan seriously, Dorothy diffidently—both on films where they were given credit and those where they were not. Dorothy sent Woollcott a parody of the Hollywood milieu, but the work situation itself was not altogether funny.[133] Then, Donald Ogden Stewart recalls,

The competition was very great—you couldn't make mistakes because there were other writers waiting to step in and fix your script up the way you were fixing somebody else's. . . . In those days the first thing you had to learn as a writer if you wanted to get screen credit was to hold off until you knew when they were going to have to start shooting. Then your agent would suggest you might be able to help. The producers had the theory that the more writers they had to work on the scripts the better they would be. It was the third or fourth writer who always got the screen credit. If you could possibly screw up another writer's script, it wasn't beyond you to do that so that your script would come through at the end . . . it became a game to be the last one before they started shooting so that you would not be eased out of the screen credit.[134]

Dorothy herself said in a lecture later printed in *Seven Arts,*

I tell you, nobody can do anything alone. You are given a script that eight
people have written from a novel four people have written. You then, they
say, write dialogue. What a curious word. Well you know you can't dialogue
without changing scenes. While you are doing it, eight people back of you
are writing beyond you. Nobody is allowed to do anything alone. I think
that's most of the trouble with the movies.[135]

Charles Brackett writes that she received equal credit for work
largely accomplished by Alan,[136] but it was Dorothy who was hired
to add women's dialogue or bright repartee. She added witty lines,
as William Wellman added slapstick, for Selznick's *Nothing Sacred*
(1937), a Ben Hecht script that "provided a fine cynical view of
small-town narrow-mindedness and big-city exploitation,"[137] but
she got no screen credit. Nor did she and Alan receive credit for
their work on *Passport for Life* for Garson Kanin or *Dynamite* for
Cecil B. DeMille.[138] Adela Rogers St. Johns has commented that

Like a lot of famous writers they had been brought to Hollywood for more
money than they had ever before seen, and then discovered they couldn't
write a shooting script. . . . So some poor underpaid fellow would have to
sweat it out to get a script. This would cause Dorothy and many like her to
weep and wring their hands and say how much they hated Hollywood.[139]

If Dorothy never liked her work in Hollywood, Alan enjoyed
working on scripts and apparently was very good at it. In 1936, the
Campbells received screen credits for three films. *The Moon's Our
Home,* adapted by Isabel Dawn and Bouce DeGaw from a novel by
Faith Baldwin with additional dialogue by the Campbells, was a
Walter Wanger film for Paramount starring Margaret Sullavan,
Henry Fonda, and Charles Butterworth; the reviewer for the *New
York Times* noted that "an occasional spout of dialogue. . . justifies
the hiring of Dorothy Parker for the re-write job."[140] Dorothy and
Alan were given joint credit for the screenplay, with Horace Jackson
and Lenore Coffee, for *Suzy,* an MGM film based on a novel by
Herbert Gorman that starred Jean Harlow, Franchot Tone, and
Cary Grant. The third film was *Lady, Be Careful,* adapted by the
Campbells and Harry Ruskin from the play *Sailor Beware* by
Kenyon Nicholson and Charles Robinson for Paramount. The film

starred Lew Ayres and the *New York Times* commented on it as caustically as Dorothy did by implication in her letter to Woollcott.

> That superbly efficient wet-wash technique of the Hollywood laundries, which consists half the time in removing not only the dirt but the shirt as well, has been applied in the case of "Lady, Be Careful" by some of the most highly paid spot removers on the Paramount staff. Dorothy Parker, a gifted washerwoman, . . . Alan Campbell, and a literary consultant named Harry Ruskin have done such a thorough job of scrubbing that if the playwrights hadn't luckily sold their idea to Hollywood long ago they couldn't recover a penny by suing the screen authors for plagiarism. . . . [There remains] scarcely a saving ounce of the Parker vitriol to justify the change.[141]

Dorothy may have thought little about this or any film at any time of the writing in Hollywood, may have given her attention to her own stories, on which she kept working, or on the farm. She had another interest, too. In July 1932 *The Golden Book Magazine* had quoted Dorothy as saying, "The only full life for a woman is marriage and babies."[142] She was probably then being witty and smart; but she was serious on December 15, 1936, when she told the *Los Angeles Times* that she was pregnant and that they expected a child in June. She and Alan returned to Bucks County—always now a place of stabilizing retreat—and set up facing typewriters, working on scripts there. In her spare time, she began knitting baby clothes. But she was forty-three, and in her third month she miscarried.

So other films followed. In 1937 they worked on their most famous picture, *A Star Is Born* with Frederic March and Janet Gaynor. Selznick got the idea from the 1932 film *What Price Hollywood?* with Constance Bennett and Lowell Sherman (RKO); it was developed by William Wellman and Robert Carson and rewritten by Dorothy and Alan. In his customary way, Selznick then asked Rowland Brown, and Budd Schulberg and Ring Lardner, Jr., to do other rewritings secretly, but Wellman heard of this and much of the Wellman-Carson script was restored. The film won several Academy Awards, including one for best original story, which went to Wellman and Carson. Alan's and Dorothy's screenplay was likewise nominated, but it did not win.[143] The *New York Times* said of *A Star Is Born* that it was "the most accurate mirror ever held before the glittering, tinseled, trivial, generous, cruel, and ecstatic

world that is Hollywood. . . . [T]here are vibrance and understanding in their writing, a feeling for detail and sympathy for the people
they are touching. . . . Its script is bright, inventive, and forceful."[144] Also that year, Dorothy and Alan joined Joe Bigelow of
Variety on *Woman Chases Man*, an antic farce for Goldwyn starring
Miriam Hopkins and Joel McCrea and studded with Dorothy's trenchant wit: a "crud" defined as "an old man who puts his shoes on
backwards and crawls around on newspapers" and a "flab" (Hopkins)
as "a young snip who climbs ladders upside down blindfolded."[145]
In 1938 they wrote a sentimental script for *Sweethearts* with Nelson
Eddy and Jeannette MacDonald,[146] and in 1939 a screen play from
Tay Garnett's story for *Trade Winds* produced by William Wanger
and starring Frederic March and Joan Bennett. Frank S. Nugent
remarked in the *New York Times* that the film was "glibbly written,"
where "Mr. March has a good line to toss for every toss of the
Bennett shoulder."[147]

Meantime, at the farm and in Hollywood, Dorothy was able to
complete only three stories. *The New Yorker* published "But the
One on the Right" in 1937 and *Scribner's* took "Clothe the Naked"
in 1938. This last departs radically from Frank Fenton's portrait of
Dorothy in *Vanity Fair* for 1935—

Dorothy Parker
AS SHE looked at him critically she knew that she was
going to love him forever—all that night—[148]

but Edmund Wilson might have had her in mind also when he
wrote in the *New Republic* for July 21, 1937,

Have we not all had dear friends who have gone West with a smile on their
lips and who have never returned again? . . . . It never occurs to us that
they may have been the authors of the dreadful stuff which we hear the
smooth-faced phantoms croak between kisses and pistol-shots. . . . Yes, as
Alva Johnston tells us, Mr. Goldwyn always wants the best writers. And
there they are cooped up in their little cells, like school children doing
exercises for teacher . . . . The great aim is to be a favorite of teacher's.
There they are blowing in their money on goofy Los Angeles houses and on
gigantic cocktail parties where they talk about their salaries and their op-
tions and always speak of their superiors with respect. There they submit to
be spied on by their employers and to have their letters opened and read.

Dorothy agreed with Stewart that films could be "a powerful weapon in the defense of our democratic heritage."[158] Dalton Trumbo and others, meantime, tried to write antifascist sentiment into their film scripts, and some writers began broadcasting on local radio stations belonging to Jack Warner. Dorothy attended the Western Writers Congress held at the Scottish Rite Auditorium in San Francisco in mid-November 1936; called to protest the social and cultural decay implicit in fascism, members of the congress signed a call to "the writers of the West, where the liberty-loving tradition of the pioneer is still fresh."[159]

"I cannot tell you on what day what did what to me," Dorothy told *New Masses.*

There I was, then, wild with the knowledge of injustice and brutality and misrepresentation. . . . At that time I saw many rich people, and—in this I am not unique—they did much in my life to send me back to the masses, to make me proud of being a worker, too. One must say for the rich that they are our best propagandists. One sees them, clumsy and without gayety and bumbling and dependent, and $300,000,000 doesn't seem much, as against mind and solidarity and spirit. I saw these silly, dull, stuffy people, and they sent me shunting. It is not noble, that hatred sends you from one side to the other; but I say again, it is not unique.[160]

During trips to New York, she remained active, in 1936 joining a committee of authors working for Roosevelt's reelection, in 1937 supporting a dinner for the Anti-Nazi League at the Biltmore.[161]

In 1936, André Malraux, who flew a plane for the Spanish Loyalists, made his first trip to Hollywood to raise money for their cause. The Falangists had deposed the puppet Spanish king in 1931, and since then their aristocratic government, a coalition of large landowners, the church, and the military, had sought to keep down the workers. Dorothy's friend Ring Lardner, Jr., wrote his mother in defense of the Spanish People's Front: "That is what Marx meant in his analysis of the course of a decaying capitalism. . . . That is what Fascism is—the last refuge of a minority intent on maintaining a system which has collapsed and which can no longer provide enough work and enough bread for the people."[162] Malraux spoke at Lillian Hellman's home and delivered a major address at the Philharmonic Auditorium. Dorothy invested $500 along with Hellman and others in *The Spanish Earth*, a pro-Loyalist documentary that Hemingway Joris Ivens.

On August 17, 1937, Dorothy and Alan, with Hellman and Hammett, sailed to France on the *Normandie*, ostensibly on vacation. In Paris, Dorothy introduced her friends to the Murphys and rejoined the wealthy with what Lillian Hellman terms "her excessive good manners."[164] She also saw Thurber, who later wrote of her to E.B. White, "It is the easiest thing in the world nowadays to become so socially conscious, so Spanish war stricken, that all sense of balance and values goes out of a person."[165] Leland Stowe shamed her into going to Spain, and her report on the difficult trip, published by *New Masses*, is deeply troubled, displaying admiration and anger. She tells how fertile and productive the fields are in Valencia, but contrasts them with Madrid.

Six years ago almost half the population of this country was illiterate. The first thing that the republican government did was to recognize this hunger, the starvation of the people for education. Now there are schools even in the tiniest, poorest villages; more schools in a year than ever were in all the years of the reigning kings. And still more are being established every day. I have seen a city bombed by night, and the next morning the people rose and went on with the completion of their schools. . . . I do not know where you can see a finer thing.[166]

Returning to America, Dorothy did as she had with "Big Blonde"— she recorded her meeting with some American soldiers in Spain, almost without change, into the story "Soldiers of the Republic," which she published in *The New Yorker*. It was slice-of-life, bare of detail and strong, and it so impressed Woollcott that he reprinted it privately for friends, declaring at first that it was better than Tolstoy or Stephen Crane, and, later, that "Certainly it comes nearer to telling the reader exactly what she is like than anything else she ever wrote."[167]

In 1938 Hemingway and Ivens brought the final cut of their film to California for a private screening at the home of Frederic March. With others, Dorothy contributed $1,000 that night, providing a sum large enough to buy an ambulance for the Loyalists, and then she invited the guests on to her place for nightcaps. On January 7, 1939, Dorothy commanded attention in the national press and magazines by speaking at the home of Leon Henderson, New Deal economist, in Washington, D.C.

"A humorist in this world is whistling by the loneliest graveyard and whistling the saddest song," she said. "There is nothing funny in the world any more.

"If you had seen what I saw in Spain you'd be serious, too. And you'd be trying to help those poor people."

When she finished speaking she was crying.[168]

So were some guests, including social and political leaders and the Spanish ambassador, DeLos Rios. That spring, following a mass protest of 2,000 in Madison Square Garden against Nazi outrages, Dorothy told *New Masses* that the days when poets of light verse wrote about disliking parsley or ladies' clothes were over. "It is no longer the time for personal matters—thank God! Now the poet speaks not just for himself but for all of us—and so his voice is heard, and so his song goes on."[169]

Then, on September 1, 1939, Russia allied herself with Germany and invaded Poland. The political movements in Hollywood broke or halted and the Anti-Nazi League changed its name to the Hollywood League for Democratic Action, concentrating not on "concerted action" against Hitler but neutrality, denouncing "the war to lead America to War." The romance with communism had turned attention from the economic practices in Hollywood and given writers self-respect. Now, left out on a limb, they retreated to past convention. Scott Fitzgerald wrote Gerald Murphy,

The heroes are the great corruptionists or the supremely indifferent—by whom I mean the spoiled writers, Hecht, Nunnally Johnson, Dotty, Dash Hammett, etc. That Dotty has embraced the church and reads her office faithfully every day does not affect her indifference. So is one type of Commy Malraux didn't list among his categories in *Man's Hope*—but nothing would disappoint her so vehemently as success.[170]

Dorothy turned to what she had as reliable resources. She gathered up her fiction, added "Soldiers of the Republic" and "Clothe the Naked," wrote a new story about an aging woman's affairs with young men ("The Custard Heart"), and published her collected stories under still another funereal title—*Here Lies.* And she had to be content with the same compliments she won with *Not So Deep as a Well.* In between there had been a new Dorothy Parker that caused her much lifeblood and pain, but no one now noticed. So she pulled herself in, and went on.

VII   The Portable Dorothy Parker; The Coast of Illyria; The
      Ladies of the Corridor; Esquire: *"I've got troubles"*

Alan was right: neither of them was given a script to write in 1939
and 1940. Woollcott joined them in Hollywood in 1940, and then, in
1941, there was work again. In 1939 Dorothy and Alan had gone to
Baltimore for the opening of Lillian Hellman's play *The Little Foxes;*
now, in the course of the film production with Bette Davis, Hellman
had to return to New York, and Dorothy helped by writing additional scenes.[171] Both Dorothy and Alan adapted *Week End for
Three* for Tay Garnett from a story by Budd Schulberg, but Thomas
M. Pryor, in the *New York Times,* reported that "the fine acerbic
hand of Miss Parker is only fleetingly detectable in a couple of
situations."[172] Dorothy's "Horsie" also supplied one of three original stories for *Queen for a Day,* and in 1942 she wrote, with Peter
Viertel and Joan Harrison, the original screen play for Hitchcock's
Saboteur.

With America's entrance into World War II, Alan, a graduate of
Virginia Military Institute, enlisted, at age forty, in the Army Air
Force and Dorothy accompanied him to the enlistment center at
Philadelphia. She was proud of the sight—"All the while we were
there," she wrote Woollcott, "that line kept lengthening, and men
were still coming in when we left. That goes on every day, all day.
Jesus, Alec, I guess we're all right." Her comments came in her
longest letter—five legal-sized pages crammed with single-spaced
typewriting frequently interrupted by an unusual preponderance of
typing errors. Her faith was renewed, sparked again as in the
Loyalists' cause, and one incident at the center belongs equally well
to "Soldiers of the Republic." She continues, in the letter to
Woollcott,

The greater part of the room is for the men who are going to camp that
day. They all have their bags, and the only time I busted was at the sight of a
tall, thin young Negro—"lanky" I [believe] is the word always
employed—carrying a six-inch square of muslin in which were his personal
effects. It looked so exactly like a bean-bag . . . And then I realized I was
rotten to be tear-sprinkled. He wasn't sad. He felt fine. . . . I was ashamed
of myself. And yet, dear Alec, I defy you to have looked at that bean-bag,
and kept an arid eye. That, of course, has nothing to do with war. Except,
also of course, that a man who had no more than that was going to fight for
it. . . .

She could have been back in childhood again, at her rich aunt's house, the black enlistee similar to the men shovelling snow. As if her life collapsed into one metaphoric scene, her aunt was also represented—the other side of her whole body of fiction.

While we were standing there [at the railroad station], there came up to me a fat, ill-favored, dark little woman, who said to me, "Parn me, but aren't you Doorthy [*sic*] Parker? Well, I've no doubt you've heard of me, I'm Mrs. Sig Greesbaum [deliberate error?], Edith Greenbaum, you'd probably know me better as; I'm the head of our local chapter of the Better Living Club, and we'd like to have you come talk to us; of course I'm still a little angry at you for writing that thing about men not making advances at girls who wear glasses, because I've worn glasses for years, and Sig, that's my husband, but I still call him my sweetheart, he says it doesn't matter a bit, well, he wears glasses himself, and I want you to talk to our club, of course we can't pay you any money, but it will do you a lot of good, we've had all sorts of wonderful people, Ethel Grimsby Loe that writes all the greeting cards, and the editor of the Doylestown Intelligenser, and Mrs. Mercer, that told us all about Italy when she used to live there after the last war, and the photographs she showed us of her cypresses and all, and it would really be a wonderful thing for you to meet us, and now when can I put you down to come talk to us?"

The awful distance between Dorothy and her neighbors even in rural Pennsylvania increases.

I said I was terribly sorry, but if she didn't mind, I was busy at the moment. So she looked around at the rows of men—she hadn't seen them before, apparently; all they did was take up half the station—and she giggled heartily and said, "Oh, what are those? More poor suckers caught in the draft? "

And an almighty wrath came on me, and I said, "Those are American patriots who have volunteered to fight for your liberty, you Sheeny bitch!" And I walked away, already horrified—as I am now—at what I had said. Not, dear, the gist, which I will stick to and should, but the use of the word "Sheeny," which I give you my word I have not heard for forty years [this directly to Woollcott!] and I have never used before. The horror lies in the ease with which it came to me—And worse horror lies in the knowledge that if she had been black, I would have said, "You nigger bitch"—Dear God. The things I have fought against all my life. And that's what I did.

Well, so anyway, then they came down to the train, and then I left before the train pulled out, because flesh and blood is or are flesh and blood.

So again she was proud—this time of a mature man who refused to be an officer, who enlisted as a private; and again she was alone, vulnerable. For the only time in all her correspondence—the smart alongside the private and personal—she tells Woollcott of her family, of her attempt to reach out to her siblings, to reach back to the Rothschilds.

On the way back from Philadelphia, I telephoned my brother and sister—whom I had neglected to inform I was back in the East. I got my sister, and said Alan had enlisted and had gone. She said, "Oh, isn't that terrible? Well, it's been terrible here, too, all Summer. I never saw such a Summer. Why, they didn't even have dances Saturday nights at the club."

So then I tried my brother, who is not bad, but I got my sister-in-law. I told her about Alan. She said, "Oh, really? Well, of course, he's had a college education. That's what's holding Bertram back—he never had a college education." (She has a son named Bertram, approximately thirty-five) "He'd just love to be an aviator, but of course he hasn't got a college education." I skipped over Bertram's advanced age for the aviation corps, and explained that the college-educated Alan had enlisted as a private. "Oh, really? " she said. "Oh, listen, Dot, we're going to take a new apartment, the first of October. It's got two rooms that the sun simply POURS in—and you know how I love sun! " I don't, Alec.

Honestly, if you were suddenly to point a finger at me and say, "Dorothy Parker, what is your sister-in-law's opinion of sun? " I should be dumfounded.

Jesus Christ. People whose country is at war. People who live in a world on fire, in a time when there have never before been such dangers, such threats, such murders. . . .[sic]

Well.[173]

Here, in an exposed and troubled time, she knew the days of witty epigrams on girls who wear glasses, like the companionship of the smart set, had vanished. Her talent, like her reputation, was of another time; her serious, halting feelings now had no successfully equivalent form.

So Dorothy accompanied Alan to Miami Beach for his ground school training.[174] As she did with Eddie, Dorothy went with Alan wherever she could—even to Smith College where she agreed timidly to visit a class—but soon he was shipped overseas to England. She tried to enlist then as a WAC but, at fifty, she was too old; she attempted to go abroad as a war correspondent, only to learn that her association with the Anti-Nazi League had branded her a "premature anti-Fascist" and a possible subversive: the government would not grant her a passport. So she moved restlessly from Hollywood to New York, from the farm to Lillian Hellman's on Martha's Vineyard; for three weeks she visited Somerset Maugham—who still carried her books bound in leather in his traveling library—in South Carolina. And she tried to bury herself in her work: a scathing portrait of a self-contented war supporter, "Song of the Shirt, 1941," was published in *The New Yorker*; a painful autobiographical story about a serviceman's foreshortened leave with his wife appeared in the same magazine in 1943. In 1942 Modern Library published her *Collected Stories*—a reprint of *Here Lies* with a Foreword by F. P. A.; she dedicated the book to Lillian Hellman. An issue of *House and Garden* that year printed her essay on Fox House, "Destructive Decoration," but the tone is forced: "So our drawing-room is in pink, rose, scarlet, magenta, vermilion, crimson, maroon, russet, and raspberry. The colors are not tagged and I doubt if you would know that they were all present. But you would, or at least I pray you would, know that you were in a pretty room, a gay room."[175] In the summer of 1942 she wrote the introduction to a limited edition of Hellman's *Watch on the Rhine* put out by the Joint Anti-Fascist Refugee Committee to raise funds.

> The woman who wrote this play and the men who made these drawings give this, their book, to those who earliest fought Fascism. Most of those warriors died; on the stiff plains of Spain, behind the jagged wire of French prison camps, in small echoing rooms of German towns. Few of their names are told, and their numbers are not measured. They wear no clean and carven stones in death. But for them there is an eternal light that will burn with a flame far higher than any beside a tomb.[176]

In turn, Woollcott included Dorothy's work in anthologies for servicemen *(As You Were)* and the general public *(Innocent Merriment)*.

Clearly, Dorothy was at loose ends. In 1943 she introduced Thurber's *Men, Women, and Dogs* and, despairing of a way to serve, wrote a second forced essay for the May *Mademoiselle* arguing that women ought to take over men's jobs to free them for the front.[177] In 1944 Hellman dedicated *The Searching Wind* to her—a play about fascist Italy in 1922, Nazi Germany in 1923, and the physical amputations and spiritual appeasements of war—and Dorothy began to renew her political efforts. She took the platform at the

July 1943 Emergency Conference to Save the Jews of Europe at the Hotel Commodore in New York, declaring that four million Jews were in daily jeopardy in Europe and urging support to permit them free passage into Turkey. On September 27, 1944, she and Clifton Fadiman appealed to the Women's Division of the New York War Fund, urging funds for the USO and the UN. The women raised over $82,000, surpassing their goal by a third, and Dorothy returned to thank them in November.[178] At the Hotel Astor in November she made an appeal for children's books, appearing as a member of the National Council of American-Soviet Friendship and presenting an exhibit of books to the wife of the Russian consul. Recalling her estrangement from Eddie, she wrote an essay for the July 1944 *Vogue* warning wives of returning servicemen to prepare themselves to welcome men partly unknown to them. *Reader's Digest*, finding this naive and unpatriotic, reprinted the essay in September with replies from clergymen and others. So her wit was gone, the film assignments few, military service closed to her, and her public speeches—difficult for a timid woman—for fund-raising only, while her personal essays were publicly rebuked.

Perhaps to earn her more money, Viking published *The Viking Portable Dorothy Parker* in 1944, giving Somerset Maugham $250 for an introduction in which he praised her "faultless ear," her "beautifully polished" poetry and her "art of enduring significance."[179] The book had a large number of printings, but it received mixed reviews once more. Her old friend John O'Hara praised her work in the *New York Times*, but J. Donald Adams' negative judgment there was more typical.

Dorothy Parker, both in her prose and her poetry, might almost be used as a symbol (so far as American literature goes) for that kind of exceedingly clever and polished writing which derives from an attitude. Even at its best, and its best is very good indeed, an aura of artificiality envelops it. It is a kind of writing that has no very deep roots in human life; the blooms it produces are showy, they abound in color and sparkle like the morning dew with wit, but they have no fragrance, and some . . . fade at an astonishing pace.[180]

These critics apparently overlooked the dedication—"To Lieutenant Alan Campbell"—and a new poem she wrote for him, "War Song":

Soldier, in a curious land
  All across a swaying sea,
Take her smile and lift her hand—
  Have no guilt of me.
Soldier, when were soldiers true?
  If she's kind and sweet and gay,
Use the wish I send to you—
  Lie not lone till day!
Only, for the nights that were,
  Soldier, and the dawns that came,
When in sleep you turn to her
  Call her by my name.[181]

It was sad, and wonderfully generous in spirit and intention.

1945 started out like previous years: Dorothy became acting chairman of the Spanish Refugee Appeal and began a drive for clothes. Viking published the *Portable F. Scott Fitzgerald,* for which she chose the contents—but, unable to do the introduction on time, asked John O'Hara to do it for her.[182] And then the war ended and, in grim echo, Alan did not come home, but stayed with occupation forces in London. Bewildered, hurt, angry, she blamed another homosexual affair and for two years wrote nothing, but drank heavily. In 1947, Alan sued her for divorce in Las Vegas, saying separation made them strangers, but he later allowed her to divorce him on May 27. She sold Fox House—for $40,000.

In 1947, Dorothy returned to Hollywood and Walter Wanger to write *Smash-Up—The Story of a Woman* with Frank Cavett. The film starred Susan Hayward as an alcoholic in a performance that added significantly to her reputation, but the critics found the script unconvincing and arbitrary, a kind of soap opera. In 1949 Dorothy adapted Oscar Wilde's *Lady Windemere's Fan* for an Otto Preminger film with Jeanne Craine, Madelaine Carroll, and George Sanders. Her collaborator was a handsome but much younger man, Ross Evans; they began a new affair. Dorothy and Evans published a story—which sounds much like Parker alone—in the December 1948 *Cosmopolitan;* "The Game" tells of two newlyweds destructively attacked by a spiteful older woman; it is one of her most bitter stories. They wrote a play, *The Coast of Illyria,* based on the life of Charles and Mary Lamb, which opened in April 1949 at the Margo

Jones Theatre in Dallas. But the unrelieved characterizations of the
Lambs, and of Coleridge, Hazlitt, and DeQuincey who visit them,
prevented its going on to Broadway. It ran three weeks in Dallas,
and closed permanently despite plans for European productions.[183]
With these failures and no bids from Hollywood, Dorothy and
Evans flew to Mexico for a vacation, where Evans left her for a
woman with a dress shop in Acapulco, and Dorothy returned to
New York.

This was not a good time for her. Broken by the affair with Evans,
she was blacklisted in June 1949 by the California State Senate
Committee on Un-American activities in its fifth biennial report.[184]
Dalton Trumbo attacked the blacklists in a book that he gave
Dorothy and that she liked.[185] A brief respite followed for her when
she and Alan were remarried on August 17, 1950, and then, in
September 1951, screenwriter Martin Berkeley recited before the
House Un-American Activities Committee a list of Hollywood
communists—and again Dorothy, and Alan too, were cited, and the
Joint Anti-Fascist Refugee Committee named as a communist-front
organization.[186] That Dorothy was involved in supplying overseas
libraries and information centers led to a McCarthy subpoena in
June 1953. And in late February 1955, the New York State joint
legislative committee found misuse of the JAFRC funds and called
up Dorothy Parker, who as national chairman had signed most of the
checks. She denied knowing the financial records, but admitted
signing checks that " 'were used to help people who were help-
less.' "[187] When asked outright if she were a communist, Dorothy
pleaded the First Amendment.

Through the strain of governmental witchhunts, Alan was unable
to get work in Hollywood but would not leave; Dorothy wanted to
return "home" to New York. They quarreled, drank more, and
agreed to a separation a little more than two years after their remar-
riage. Dorothy settled in the Hotel Volney, off Madison Avenue in
the east seventies, and soon was collaborating for the theater again,
this time with a former colleague on *New Masses*, Arnaud D'Usseau.
He was the author of *Deep Are the Roots* and *Tomorrow the World*,
a distinguished playwright, unlike Evans, and together they produced Dorothy's last drama, *The Ladies of the Corridor*. She
brought to this unflinching portrayal of lonely people living in a
hotel all that she knew of the Volney and added scraps of Alan,
Alan's mother, and herself in her portraits of a dipsomaniac-suicide,

a mother who controls her son (accused of homosexuality), and an older woman who falls in love with a young man. The play opened on October 21, 1953, at the Longacre Theatre, staged by Harold Clurman and starring Betty Field, Edna Best, and Walter Matthau. *The Ladies of the Corridor* was named the best play of the year by George Jean Nathan and it was, Dorothy said, "the only thing I have ever done in which I had great pride."[188] But she was asked to change the play's ending, making it false, she thought, and the play closed after forty-five performances. The best review came from John McClain; other critics, misunderstanding the play, were harsh.[189] And "failure in the theatre is more public, more brilliant, more unreal than in any other field," Hellman has said.[190]

But Dorothy was writing again. In 1954, *A Star Is Born* was remade with Gloria Swanson and William Holden, and Alan and Dorothy were again given credits. In 1955 Dorothy submitted two of her best stories to *The New Yorker*, "I Live on Your Visits" and "Lolita," that were quite possibly spinoffs of her last play. In 1957 *The New Yorker* published another fine story, "The Banquet of Crow," about an estranged couple and the woman's fantasy of possible reconciliation.

Dorothy's reconciliation was real, however; she and Alan reunited in 1956 and moved into a house at 8983 Norma Place, West Hollywood. But it was, with momentary bright spots, downhill from there. They worked on *The Good Soup* for Charles Brackett and Marilyn Monroe, but it was never released; and then there were no more assignments. So they lived on alcohol and unemployment checks. Dorothy was asked to join Richard Wilbur and John Latouche in writing lyrics for Leonard Bernstein's musical version of Voltaire's *Candide*, with the book by Lillian Hellman, and she finally managed one song, "Gavotte," sung in the play by Sofronia:

> I've got troubles, as I said.
> Though our name, I say again, is
> Quite the proudest name in Venice,
> Our afflictions are so many,
> And we haven't got a penny.

She wrote one other song, for Candide in the Eldorado scene, that was not used. The musical, a brilliant success recently, did not have a good first run; the original production lasted only seventy-three performances.

Yet amidst the squalor of the small bungalow Alan and Dorothy bought—they had long since sold the house in Beverly Hills—she was sought out again. Harold Hayes of *Esquire* asked her to do monthly book reviews resembling those of "Constant Reader." The first appeared in December 1957, others irregularly; writing was painfully difficult for her now: "It is a high-forceps delivery every time we manage to get [one] out of her," Arnold Gingrich, publisher of *Esquire*, remarked.[191] She did receive a standing ovation from the National Institute and American Academy of Arts and Letters on April 30, 1958, when she received a citation and the Marjorie Peabody Waite Award for her fiction and poetry; they inducted her as a member on May 21, 1959. In November 1958 she joined Robert Gorham Davis to conduct a symposium at the Writers Club of Columbia University's School of General Studies. She appeared on David Susskind's Chicago television show, "Open End," where she reported that new fiction sent her by *Esquire* was "appalling."[192] In May 1962, WNEW-TV dramatized three of her stories ("The Lovely Leave," "A Telephone Call," "Dusk Before Fireworks") with Margaret Leighton and Patrick O'Neal, although Dorothy complained to the press that she was not paid for it.[193]

She also returned to campus. Her friend Frederick B. Shroyer, who in 1965 would co-edit with her an anthology of short stories, suggested that she succeed Christopher Isherwood as the Distinguished Visiting Professor of English at California State College, Los Angeles, to teach courses in Twentieth Century American Literature and Major British Writers. Dorothy got lost in the maze of corridors, told the *Los Angeles Times* she found eighteen thousand students and one hundred fifty parking lots, and was interviewed by the student press.[194] "Her classes were largely of an informal and personally reminiscent nature," Professor Charles Beckwith, then chairman of the department, recalls,[195] but she was a huge success. Caedmon Records, who first interviewed Dorothy in 1956, recorded her work with Shirley Booth in 1962,[196] and she read her own works for Spoken Arts and Verve records. In the fall of 1963, Dorothy moved back to New York for the last time; "A silver cord," she once wrote, "ties me right to my city."[197] Another young man, Wyatt Cooper, interviewed her for *Esquire* and began taping her autobiography. She was interviewed on WBAI by Richard Lamparski. She wrote book reviews through 1963, covering two hundred eight books, then stopped; in November 1964 she published her last work for the magazines, captions for John Koch's paintings of New York City for *Esquire:* "As only New Yorkers know, if you can get through the twilight, you'll live through the night."[198] She was, by now, alone and lonely; she still drank a great deal, ate little, and lost a great deal of weight. Often she would be drunk for days. And, saddest of all, the girl who wore glasses was now going blind.

VIII   *The Events Leading Up to the Tragedy:*
         "just a lot of people telling jokes"

Brendan Gill thinks Dorothy Parker's increased suffering was due to her early exaggerated reputation; her associations with lesser talents such as Woollcott and Kaufman, and the sharp shift in literary and national sensibility during and after the Depression: in short, Dorothy Parker outlived her time.[199] Of this last, Dorothy thought so too. On January 28, 1943, she had attended Woollcott's funeral, "quipless."[200] On November 21, 1945, Benchley died unexpectedly of a cerebral hemorrhage, and Dorothy, then staying in his cottage at the Garden of Allah, presided over the West Coast wake at Romanoff's. Dashiel Hammett's funeral was January 10, 1961; by then, Fitzgerald too was dead—she was one of the few who attended his funeral where she recalled his line about Gatsby, " 'Poor son of a bitch' "[201]—and Hemingway had shot himself. And on June 15, 1963, Alan, fifty-eight, took too many sleeping pills (as Eddie Parker had), and Dorothy found him dead in their bed. This loss was greatest. As Wyatt Cooper noted in *Esquire*,

They were very much alike, much more alike than most people realized. Not only their humor—Alan wrote the funniest letters I've ever read—but their likes, their dislikes, their prejudices, their fears, and their critical judgments were almost interchangeable. They had the kind of unspoken communication of those who know all there is to know about each other.[202]

"Her captains and kings had long departed," Shroyer writes. "I saw her at the Volney before she died . . . and she said, in effect, that all those she loved were dead, and that she, herself, had been dead for a long time."[203] Her own view was more sardonic. "People ought to be one of two things, "she wrote. "Young or old. No; what's the good of fooling? People ought to be one of two things, young or dead."[204]

So she grew sad, disappointed, bitter at the end. In 1940, she had told Donald Ogden Stewart that her early years had been wasted: she had chosen unimportant topics, her love poetry had been formulaic, and her experimentation with French verse forms merely smart fooling around. "We were little black ewes that had gone astray; we were a sort of ladies' auxiliary of the legion of the damned. And, boy, were we proud of our shame! . . . I think the trouble with us was that we stayed young too long."[205] When she was seventy, she told Associated Press reporter Saul Pett that there were no good humorists left, that she never said half the quips attributed to her, and that Millay did great harm by suggesting that poetry was easy. The Round Table, too, had been overpraised: "This was no Mermaid. These were no giants." Even her California students were "ignorant prigs. . . . They don't read."[206] A year before she died, her drunkenness led to an accident that hospitalized her.[207] Three months preceding her death, she was guest of honor at a fashionable dinner party given by Gloria Vanderbilt Cooper; she arrived dressed in a golden sheath dress her hostess had bought her for the occasion. In the week before she died, she called her friend Beatrice Ames to ask if Hemingway really liked her.[208] She was helping to plan "The First Dorothy Parker Quartette" (Variety, June 14, 1967) when, on June 7, police found her dead, of a heart attack, in her room at the Volney. She was alone except for a dog—her inevitable dog; this time, a poodle named C'est Tout. The New York Times' obituary appeared on page 1 and then, inside, covered a full page.

About one hundred fifty literary and theater friends gathered at Frank Campbell's chapel at Madison and 81st Street for her funeral: she was dressed in Mrs. Cooper's golden gift dress. Zero Mostel— who had been called before the McCarthy hearings with her— spoke, noting that there would be no formal ceremony if she had had her way. Lillian Hellman also addressed the mourners.

She was part of nothing and nobody except herself; it was this independence of mind and spirit that was her true distinction, and it stayed with her until the end, young and sparkling. . . . She never spoke of old glories, never repeated old defeats, never rested on times long gone. She was always brave in deprivation, in the chivying she took during the McCarthy days, in the isolation of the last, bad sick years. The remarkable quality of her wit was that it stayed in no place, and was of no time.[209]

She left $20,000—the bulk of her estate—to Martin Luther King, Jr., a man whom she admired but had never met.

"You see," Woollcott wrote in 1934, "she is so odd a blend of Little Nell and Lady Macbeth":[210] as usual, he saw deeply and found the paradox within her. Her bitterness finally was not over a public who misunderstood her but her own self-betrayal. Nathaniel Benchley has written of his father words applicable to her.

> He had a theory that everyone tends to become the type of person he hates most, and when he gave up writing he gave up the one thing in which he had honest pride. He had never been able to write all he wanted, he felt that he had burned himself out on the mass production of trivia when he should have been doing something better.[211]

But for our best emblem of Dorothy, Woollcott is again the authority.

> There was, at one time, much talk of a novel to be called, I think, *The Events Leading Up to the Tragedy*, and indeed her publisher, having made a visit of investigation to the villa where she was staying at Antibes, reported happily that she had a great stack of manuscript already finished. He did say she was shy about letting him see it. This was because that stack of alleged manuscript consisted largely of undestroyed carbons of old articles of hers, padded out with letters.[212]

A perfectionist, she could not bear to disappoint others; yet she found it painful to see work that would betray the standards she most respected. Her tragedy was that she could not write more and more easily; our misfortune is that we have yet to take true measure of what she did accomplish.

CHAPTER 2

Her Apprenticeship: Essays, Light Verse, Drama

I Preliminaries: "expert advice"

"TO look upon life with the eye of understanding is to see men the prey to passions and delusions,—the very comment on which can be nothing else but satire."[1] This remark in a popular 1922 book on Horace, one of Dorothy Parker's favorite poets, summarizes the perspective common to all of her writing: essays, verse, drama, fiction, criticism. The premise, a loose summing of Horace's first satire, recalled for her those classical roots she had learned at Miss Dana's, roots that she could translate into the demands of those popular, sophisticated magazines where most of her early work appeared. But, as she knew, this form of humor had its own demarcations. Aldous Huxley, among others, made this clear in an essay she also knew: "satire, the comedy of manners, and wit are not creative, like pure comedy. Satire and the comedy of manners depend on the actual life they portray and mock at, with greater or less ferocity; while wit is an affair of verbal ingenuity."[2] Dorothy's contribution to the humor of her period was a combination of classical practices with her own very personal tone, a tone of the carefree but victimized "little woman," which gave to her work its special profile, its recognizable hallmarks.

Dorothy Parker's work is thoroughly grounded in a world of taste and manners—in a world where values, integrity, and discipline are not only admirable but necessary. This perspective may stem directly from her life at Miss Dana's where classes discussing the promises of socialism and the shortcomings of capitalism, the need for ethics and the irrelevance of institutionalized religion to the sufferings and weaknesses of mankind were held in a highly disci-

76

plined class day set amidst the Oriental rugs and glass chandeliers of the well to do. There is no evidence that there, or anywhere else later, Dorothy ever sensed an incongruity between discussions of the downtrodden and the environments in which they were held. The discrepancy, rather, was between mankind's privations and mankind happy and fulfilled. As if her writing arose from such discussions, her work observes social facts and customs, sees them representatively rather than in particularities, and then invites the happy or scornful laughter of critcism. She invites people (as a generality or type) to change, just as she urges the imperatives of change in social and political life. Amusement comes from performances and conditions. Her satire is thus an act of preservation (and of hope). Her friend Gilbert Seldes wrote in 1924 that "Satire is like parody in admitting the integrity of the subject; it is a pruning knife for the good of the tree."[3] That idea, too, is classical in origin.

Dorothy Parker's writing, therefore, sanctions not morality so much as compassion and proper behavior—"proper" meaning both "functional" and "refined." Usually her works insinuate her criticism, providing their own sense of decorum, while she herself practices a restraint, balance, and attempted urbanity that lends her work not so much tact and subtlety as an air of control even in the use of conversational diction. What she strives for is an elegant casualness. The discrepancy between the seriousness of her aim and the playful tone of her presentation provides not only a kind of cool satire but a forceful, because constricted, irony. Indeed, her work is so cool in its fundamental bitterness that she has from the first appealed to a very wide audience—both those wishing simple amusement and those who recognize her sardonic wit.

To locate Dorothy Parker's unique flavor, it is simplest to keep in mind her short poems where, despite the compactness of the form, all her attitudes and techniques are in play. Here as elsewhere she concentrates on a specific situation or moment, the foreground sharply focused in time and space. Her images and her diction (formal or informal) are synecdochical: she has a fine gift for appropriate selectivity of detail. Often, but not always, she extends her canvas by burlesque, pun, or paradox; often too the wit is reflexive, and irony becomes irony of the self (and even of the poem, of poetry). By restricting her scope, her concentration on the paraphernalia of life never clutters her line as it never clutters her point of view.

What *is* complicated, however, are the levels on which even her simplest poems and stories function. At first reading, they are commentaries about what is open to ridicule, about the ridiculous. They expose correctable human failings; her chief means are repetition ("I Live on Your Visits"), dullness *(Close Harmony)*, and hyperbole ("One Perfect Rose"). By such means we not only see but see through the pretense or shallowness she describes in her stories and dramatizes in poems and plays. Pushed harder, her works discuss failings not only of a poem's persona or a story's protagonist but equally of us, of her readers. When we are amused by her work (and only amused) we are trapped, because we are never meant to agree with her characters. Sympathy, for her, does not mean consent. Our involvement, potentially if not actually, is what supplies irony to her work, gives it the double edge, the sardonic twist. Pushed hardest, the third level at which her works operate reveals her as author and her insistent desire to expose, which, because it becomes universal, reveals the mordant quality of her own mind. Here the tone is neither angry nor despairing; there is, rather, a rueful acceptance, an edged stoicism. It is this quality that has led some critics to find a certain "smartness" or "urbanity" in her work. Such descriptions may be accurate as far as they go, but the hardness they are describing is not so much an easy formula for writing as it is a consequence of her perspective. All of these characteristics are relatively available to the careful reader of "Neither Bloody Nor Bowed."

> They say of me, and so they should,
> It's doubtful if I come to good.
> I see acquaintances and friends
> Accumulating dividends,
> And making enviable names
> In science, art, and parlor games.
> But I, despite expert advice,
> Keep doing things I think are nice,
> And though to good I never come—
> Inseparable my nose and thumb![4]

It is easy, in reading such a poem, to suppose we are to agree with the attitude of sophisticated flippancy. A quick reading, for enjoyment, will be content with this. But it is not the poem. Friends who "accumulate dividends" are business people who quantify things— not only wrong in Dorothy Parker's lexicon but surely also in our own. So the source of wisdom in the poem is tainted. There are other clues: we could hardly admire someone whose reputation depends on "parlor games," but to align this with science and art suggests the shallowness—not the wise flippancy—of the persona. The word "nice" is so limp, moreover, that the poem itself is not, finally, fully accomplished. Such are the clues we must look for in a corpus as carefully crafted as Dorothy Parker's. As for the last two lines, they are a cheap theatrics, a gesture irrelevant to such larger issues as the quantification of life or the false values attributed to ability at parlor games.

When Dorothy Parker wishes, her language has a kind of classical purity and vigor, a fine power of expression stemming from simplicity, lucidity, and economy; for her, disciplined language is also a matter of taste. Like Horace, she writes satires that are seen as a form opposed not to tragedy (that would be comedy) but to epic. She deals with the commonplace, the everyday, even the trivial if it reveals something useful. In "For a Sad Lady" no word is out of tune, everything is carefully placed.

> And let her loves, when she is dead,
>   Write this above her bones:
> "No more she lives to give us bread
>   Who asked her only stones."[5]

Here the risk is not to be taken too lightly but to be considered too sentimental. Yet look carefully. The commonplace language of the first two lines melds into—but is not discrepant from—the biblical diction of the last two lines. The irony is clear if we see the conflicting uses of "her" in lines 1 and 4; even the internal rhyme of "loves" and "above" (lines 1, 2) suggest how the obvious ignores the meaningful. Since the poem's chief irony is that the woman could give things no one wished, she is a "lady"—it gives new significance to a clichéd word of the 1920s—but the "unfortunate" belongs not to *her* but to *them*, her "loves." Her willingness to be ignored, Dorothy Parker is saying, suggests the depth of her love—always ready to nourish as bread does—even as it points to the shallowness of "love" by the "loves." Their shallowness is caught in the act of providing a grave marker, but a grave marker that misunderstands and so, not properly honoring the lady, gravely critiques those providing the memorial.

Like Horace, Dorothy Parker weighs every word; she employs both its conventional context and the context in which she places it; she notes the attitude of the persona, the reader, and the poet. Hers is an art which *unwinds* its meanings. Like Horace, her work only appears extemporaneous; it is really skillfully *fashioned*. And like Horace, who wanted to become Rome's leading satirist by applying his personal stamp, she finds her own tone, reveals her own sensibility. Repeatedly her attitude is that of a woman who is lazy or carefree but is nevertheless put upon, exploited, unfortunate in life and love. When Dorothy Parker is careless, her work goes flat, words function unequally, and her attitude can collapse into sentimentality. The poems, plays, and stories become thin, or, worse, maudlin and bathetic. Her achievement is not consistent. But at her best—in the art of the epigram or the brief word portrait—she is without peer in her time.

II Essays: "That's, as someone has phrased it, that"

Dorothy Parker's early work—in essay, light verse, and drama—is not as skillful as the best of her poetry, fiction, and criticism, but it was useful apprentice work for her, and examining it helps us to see the components of her craft and how she worked to master them. Most of her earliest work was on assignment for such magazines as *Vanity Fair* or *McCall's* or free-lance for magazines similar in standards and content. They printed, even then, journalism of a high sort, which Max Eastman discussed in a pointed essay in *Vanity Fair* for June 1916, shortly after Dorothy began working there. "Magazine writing," he wrote, "is professional. It is work and not play. And for that reason it is never profoundly serious, or intensely frivolous enough to captivate the soul. It lacks abandon. It is simply well done. Amazingly well done."[6] Such writing was slick; moreover, the writer's goal—to fill up space—contributed a kind of thinness.

It is amazing what the mere necessity of earning a living can do to an English prose style. If you were offered $5.00 a paragraph, would you divide your paragraphs in the broad, logical manner of Macaulay? Well, for five cents a word, you will not write words with the weighty brevity of Emerson or Epictetus. You will write like an indictment clerk.[7]

Popular magazines required Dorothy to choose everyday ideas and to carry brief thoughts a great distance. It is surely arguable that such practices led, later, to such well-known monologues as "The Waltz" and "From the Diary of a New York Lady," but it is not arguable that they resulted in such overspun pieces as her portrait of Beatrice Herford, a popular monologuist, in an essay called "A One-Woman Show" (*Everybody's*, March 1921), where Dorothy transforms eight facts into two long pages of appreciative commentary (pp. 34–35).[8] Another example of extreme padding is the opening page of the May 1919 issue of *Vanity Fair*, "So This is New York!," which depends on a shaggy dog story (p. 21). She also leisurely recounted the formulaic stories of "The Christmas Magazines" (*VF*, December 1916, p. 83), her criticism of film ("If I Were a Movie Manager," *VF*, June 1918, pp. 84, 88), and the unwanted do-gooder ("Good Souls," *VF*, June 1919, pp. 47, 94).

Turning to typed persons, she found a particularly popular subject in her first essay on the overly refined ("Are You a Glossy?," *VF*, April 1918, pp. 57, 90) and so followed it with an inferior sequel ("How to Know the Glossies," *VF*, May 1918, pp. 59, 89) in which "glossies" are made not only more foolish but also more vulgar. Her best experience, in retrospect, came in writing captions on courtship, divorce, and stereotyped men for sketches by the British artist "Fish."[9] Unlike the essays, here Dorothy learned selectivity and economy, as well as the clever phrase that combines quips with clichés, a distinctive feature of her mature style.

And then there was Peggy. Really, he couldn't have found a more perfect home body than Peggy—civil to her parents, pleasant to have around a bridge table, fond of children and potted plants. Nothing could have been sweeter—until she took him out motoring with her. He is here portrayed at the moment of registering a silent vow that if he ever gets home all in one piece, he will never gaze upon Peggy again. ("On the Trail of a Wife." *VF*, December 1919, p. 61)

In these slight pieces, the objects of the satire are customs or manners, and the mode is personal, whether as commentary, narrative, or literary parody. Although the works seem chatty and predictable, Dorothy had already begun to write critically by using a viewpoint that, while it seemed informed, was often naive, sharing the false values of what was apparently under attack.

In time her sketches were elongated and grouped, while she continued to practice selectivity and compression. Broad classifications—such as the "Seven Deadly Suitors" which she claimed kept her single[10]—allowed her to stretch these paragraphs into the length required of fuller articles. "Maximilian, Table D'Hote Socialist" illustrates her new technique.

He was an artist and had long nervous hands and a trick of impatiently tossing his hair out of his eyes. He capitalized the A in art. Together we plumbed the depths of Greenwich Village, seldom coming above Fourteenth Street for air. We dined in those how-*can*-they-do-it-for-fifty-cents table d'hotes, where Maximilian and his little group of serious thinkers were wont to gather about dank bottles of sinister claret and flourish marked copies of "The Masses." I learned to make sweeping gestures with my bent-back thumb, to smile tolerantly at the mention of John Sargent; to use all the technical terms when I discussed Neo-Malthusianism. Maximilian made love in an impersonal sort of way. He called me "Comrade" and flung a casual arm across my shoulders whenever he happened to think of it. (*VF*, October 1916, p. 12)

With such sketches she learned to dramatize rather than narrate, to let her readers accumulate and interpret her details; her writing was, instinctively, practicing the "iceberg theory" that Hemingway subsequently advocated. Although she occasionally leaned on verbal quips and her portraits soon became formulaic, her vocabulary limited, she had moved past explicit commentary. She now insinuated her judgments as well as her values. Other anthologies, characterizing women's circles, dinner parties, guests at summer resorts and residents of apartment houses appeared in *Ladies' Home Journal* and the *Saturday Evening Post*, and one—on "Men I'm Not Married To"—was reprinted as part of a book in 1922.[11] "Is Your Little Girl Safe?," (*VF*, September 1918, pp. 46, 48), a parody of a silent film script, juxtaposed brief narrations to flash on the screen with directions on how to film each scene; here the satire is in the discrepancy between the two summaries as well as between the parody and the reader's responses. Later, Dorothy would use this technique to fine advantage in her poetic dialogues and in monologues ("The Waltz") that imply a second voice; what is surprising, and to her credit, is that within the commercially oriented craft of popular journalism, she had already successfully located the fundamental means of her satire.

Relatively early, then, she was writing essays that were longer but not nearly so thin as those of other writers. "The Education of Gloria" (*LHJ*, October 1920, pp. 37, 124) pretends to sketch one person while actually indicting upper class exclusivity.

> She was congenitally equipped with a restfully uninquiring mind, an amiable submissiveness of spirit, a readily formative point of view. . . . It is Mrs. Tomlinson's social position, as her friends so well know, which supplies the major part of her repertory of conversational topics. It ranks next to her good breeding as a subject for continuous discourse and self-congratulation. . . . Yet, it was stressed, it was her duty always to be charitable. (p. 37)

If we place this story alongside a mature one, "Song of the Shirt, 1941," we can see how Dorothy Parker's talents matured.

Other essays, on spiritualism, homebodies, summer resort life, and suburban life also turn to fictional characters, or types, as a basic means of satire.[12] "Professional Youth," one of her best early works, profiles a young writer as an economical way to burlesque an entire generation (*SEP*, April 28, 1923); this is presented as a story-within-a-story, implying a whole series of receding mirrors for her subjects—and her readers as well. Her concurrent series of short poems in *Life*, "Figures in American Folk Lore," makes a neat parallel.

Five years later, returning to magazine essays, she added another dimension to her work with a naive perspective that became its own means for parodying middle class values. This was first apparent in her *Vanity Fair* report on a Paris trip where she parodies the magazine's desired "sophistication" by making gossip equivalent to historical data from a guidebook.

> Ah, *doucement*, driver, *doucement* here, for we are passing the spot where F. Scott Fitzgerald, one wild black night, bought the 15 by 18 rug from the astounded Armenian street-vendor, and, a few minutes later, lost it—a feat before which the notorious losing of the bass drum pales to the commonplace. A little farther on, although historians debate the exact spot, Donald Ogden Stewart, at five minutes before midnight on July 1, 1925, flung himself into a taxicab and cried hoarsely to the driver, "To the *Bastille*, and drive like the very devil! I've got to get there before it falls!". ("The Paris That Keeps Out of the Papers," January 1927, p. 71)

From January to May 1928 she wrote monthly columns for *McCall's*, succeeding Gene Stratton-Porter, in which she satirized herself as a New Yorker, supplied an epitome of "The New York Type," discussed opening night at the theater, the arrival of spring in the City, and parodied her own excessive love for dogs.[13] Conversely, she used the personal element seriously in her literary portraits and in her political accounts of the Spanish Civil War.

Of these two groups, the portraits are less well wrought. They retreat to a thin patina, polishing a few facts as Eastman had warned might happen. "G.B.S., Practically in Person" *(NY*, July 7, 1928), reviews a film of Shaw.

As Shaw appears on the screen (and the audience, the typical movie audience, applauds wildly at the sight of him, which enthusiasm certainly made a better and more thoughtful girl of me), somewhere in the trees of the pictured background, a thrush can be heard singing. Later, when his act is nearly done, you hear the squawk of a peacock. I don't, myself, go in much for symbols; but many do, and they say they get a lot out of it. (p. 28)

The *New Yorker* profile of Hemingway (November 30, 1929) is embarrassing when she discusses her inability to rise to the occasion, to say anything new; it is also marred by her total adoration.

He lives, for a bit of every year, in Paris—which is how the expatriation stories started. He and his wife do this because they like it, and because their rent is not high. (He doesn't make much money—not half as much as you do.) They form no part of the dancing-and-light-drugs life of the French capital. Their apartment has no telephone; . . . He writes there, mostly in bed, and he reads books that have a great many things going on in them— novels by the elder Dumas, and books and books and books about the Crusades. ("Profiles: The Artist's Reward," p. 29)

She is considerably better at "A Valentine for Mr. Woollcott" *(VF*, February 1934). There is a coyness to some of it, but there is also, on occasion, a succinct, incisive summary of the man.

He has, I should think, between seven and eight hundred intimate friends, with all of whom he converses only in terms of atrocious insult. It is not, it is true, a mark of his affection if he insults you once or twice; but if he addresses you outrageously all the time, then you know you're in. . . . He is at the same time the busiest man I know and the most leisured. He even has time for the dear lost arts—letter-writing and conversation. . . . Alexander

Woollcott's enthusiasm is his trademark; you know that never has he written a piece strained through boredom. (pp. 27, 57)

Here, in small compass, she manages to isolate all those features drawn at some length in our succeeding biographies; she even saw correctly, in his extraordinary fondness for Hamilton College, that eventually he would wish to be buried there (p. 27). Although her intelligence, taste, and commitment to art all merge in these portraits, they are still subject to an artificial pose and rely on coy phraseology ("That's, as someone has phrased it, that").

Technique evaporates before substance in the direct, somber political pieces she wrote in defense of the Spanish Loyalists and in explanation of her own late political awakening; these rise to superb reportage. She stands with the best; Hemingway had written "On the American" in *New Masses* for February 14, 1939, "Just as the earth can never die, neither will those who have ever been free return to slavery. The peasants who work the earth where our dead lie know what these dead died for. There was time during the war for them to learn these things, and there is forever for them to remember them in."[14] Hemingway wrote this editorial after filming *The Spanish Earth*; Dorothy Parker's remarks follow a single searing visit to Spain and are more sharply photographic:

the streets are crowded, and the shops are open, and the people go about their daily living. It isn't tense and it isn't hysterical. What they have is not morale, which is something created and bolstered and directed. It is the sure, steady spirit of those who know what the fight is about and who know that they must win.

In spite of all the evacuation, there are still nearly a million people here. Some of them—you may be like that yourself—won't leave their homes and their possessions, all the things they have gathered together through the years. They are not at all dramatic about it. It is simply that anything else than the life they have made for themselves is inconceivable to them. Yesterday I saw a woman who lives in the poorest quarter of Madrid. It has been bombed twice by the fascists; her house is one of the few left standing. She has seven children. It has often been suggested to her that she and the children leave Madrid for a safer place. She dismisses such ideas easily and firmly. Every six weeks, she says, her husband has forty-eight hours' leave from the front. Naturally, he wants to come home to see her and the children. She, and each one of the seven, are calm and strong and smiling. It is a typical Madrid family. ("Incredible, Fantastic, . . . and True," *New Masses*, November 23, 1937, pp. 15–16)

Again she is using exemplum rather than generalization and clean
bare prose. She also knows how to use her own persona.

While I was in Valencia the fascists raided it four times. If you are going to
be in an air raid at all, it is better for you if it happens at night. Then it is
unreal, it is almost beautiful, it is like a ballet with the scurrying figures and
the great white shafts of the searchlights. But when a raid comes in the
daytime, then you see the faces of the people, and it isn't unreal any longer.
You see the terrible resignation on the faces of old women, and you see little
children wild with terror. (Ibid., p. 16)

Synecdoche, apostrophe, juxtaposition: all her means are
employed with great force and belie a new, grim sensibility. She
still maintains control; the sentences are painstakingly formed, the
anecdotes expertly placed. John Bright wrote to *New Masses* from
Hollywood,

Congratulations to you and Dorothy Parker for the most moving piece yet
on the Spanish war. Not only moving and beautiful. But true and diggingly
deep. Perhaps the essence of the entire struggle in Spain is in her observa-
tion that "I don't think there will be any lost generation after this war" . . .
because "they are fighting for more than their lives. They are fighting for
the chance to live them."[15]

This essay, "Incredible, Fantastic . . . and True," is her best. A later
one, "Not Enough," is less disciplined, more erratic.

I cannot talk about it in these days. All I know is that there I saw the finest
people I ever saw, that there I knew the only possible thing for mankind is
solidarity. As I write, their defense in Catalonia against the invasion of the
fascists has failed. But do you think people like that can fail for long, do you
think that they, banded together in their simple demand for decency, can
long go down? They threw off that monarchy, after those centuries; can men
of ten years' tyranny defeat them now?
    I beg your pardon. I get excited. (*New Masses*, March 14, 1939, pp. 3–4)

In her later essays, Dorothy Parker learned, as in time she learned
with her fiction, poetry, and drama, that drawing on deep autobiographical resources results in less artificial but more substantial—
and more powerful—art.[16]

III   *Light Verse: "counting up, exultingly"*

When the wry, regular, and apparently easy poems of Dorothy Parker were selected for her first book in 1926, she had been writing and publishing short verses for more than eleven years. The poetic performances in *Enough Rope* are uneven in quality, but nearly all of them are superior to her earliest trials. Louis Kronenberger has commented on why this is so:

[T]here is more good serious poetry in English than good light verse. If poets are born, light verse writers are not. No trances guide their pens: the freshness and gaiety we ask of them must be achieved through practice and drudgery . . . . Unless the versification is accompanied by substance and mood, the result is in the long run unhappily hollow . . . . Something beyond a corner of our minds must be affected—whether by sheer nonsense, which gets its effect beyond the mind, or by wit, which floods the mind with an enlarging light, or by warmth or spontaneity or the laughter of the body of a pleasantly sensuous appeal. Obviously the best light verse is also poetry.[17]

Given her range of choices, Dorothy Parker was determined from the start to write satire from her woman's point of view—to exaggerate reality through stereotype, repetition, cataloguing, or hyperbole—rather than to write nonsense verse. She also wanted her verse to be simple, as colloquial as possible, for that way she could extend her satire to those who spoke as her lines speak—but she found, even composing longhand (later, with criticism, she would compose on the typewriter), that she continually crossed out words that were not simple enough. She was encouraged in her search for substance coupled with a simple style by F. P. A., when he was on *The Mail* and she was still at *Vogue*. Her first published poem, "Any Porch," is still awkward.

> "I'm reading that new thing of Locke's—
>   So whimsical, isn't he? Yes—"
> "My dear, have you seen those new smocks?
>   They're nightgowns—no more, and no less."
> "I don't call Mrs. Brown *bad*,
>   She's *un*-moral, dear, not *im*moral—"
> "Well, really, it makes me so mad
>   To think what I paid for that coral! "

"My husband says, often, 'Elsie,
    You feel things too deeply, you do—"
"Yes, forty a month, if you please,
    Oh, servants impose on *me*, too." (VF, September 1915, p. 32)

The poem continues for six more stanzas, but topics are haphazard;
as there is no patterned scansion, there is no accretive or accumula-
tive power to the fragments of conversation, pointed as they are.

It did not take Dorothy long to learn that the iamb was her most
forceful foot and that strictly iambic meter had a kind of dog trot
rhythm that would reinforce the commonness of the ideas and of the
people she would write about. Clichés, too, worked better when
falling into taut quatrains and full rhymes. We do not know how
many unpublished starts she made after "Any Porch," but her second publication, "A Musical Comedy Thought," shows improve-
ment.

My heart is fairly melting at the thought of Julian Eltinge;
    His vice versa, Vesta Tilley, too.
Our language is so dexterous, let us call them ambi-sexterous,—
    Why hasn't this occurred before to you? (VF, June 1916, p. 126)

The poem relies too heavily on a Nash-like neologism, but her third
published poem has married simple diction, iambic meter, and full
rhyme without any crutches. "The Gunman and the Debutante"
begins,

A wild and wicked gunman—one who held a gang in thrall—
    A menace to the lives of me and you,
    Was counting up, exultingly, the day's successful haul—
As gunmen are extremely apt to do.
A string of pearls, a watch or two, a roll of bills, a ring,
    Some pocketbooks—about a dozen, say—
An emerald tiara—oh, a very pretty thing!
    Yes, really, quite a gratifying day. (VF, October 1916, p. 120)

The trisyllabic *tiara* is a particular challenge, but even this early,
Dorothy Rothschild attempted to work into regular metrics the long
and unusual word, as would the mature Dorothy Parker.

Somewhat surprisingly—and disappointingly, from our later
perspective—Dorothy Rothschild now began parodying vers libre,

then especially fashionable. Beginning with the February 1917 *Vanity Fair*, she wrote a series of "hate songs" in which her compact descriptions of typed personalities resemble the captions she had written for *Vogue*. The satire is glib, the targets wide, the rhythms of stanzas (which vary in length) slack. "Men: A Hate Song," the first, is subtitled "I hate men. They irritate me" and opens with the "Serious Thinkers."

> There are the Serious Thinkers,—
> There ought to be a law against them.
> They see life, as through shell-rimmed glasses, darkly.
> They are always drawing their weary hands
> Across their wan brows.
> They talk about Humanity
> As if they had just invented it;
> They have to keep helping it along.
> They revel in strikes
> And they are eternally getting up petitions.
> They are doing a wonderful thing for the Great Unwashed,—
> They are living right down among them.
> They can hardly wait
> For "The Masses" to appear on the newsstands,
> And they read all those Russian novels,—
> The sex best sellers. (p. 65)

The strength of such poetry lies in a distanced tone and clever observations. It is also a poetry that must always hit the bull's-eye, and so quickly grows tiresome. But such poems made her very popular then, and she went on to write more for *Vanity Fair* and a good many for *Life*, on relatives (with a stanza on husbands from a liberated woman's perspective); on actresses, actors, bohemians, slackers, and office colleagues; on bores, the drama, parties, movies, books, the younger set, summer resorts, wives, and college boys; and F. P. A. and others parodied or imitated the form.[18]

Dorothy Parker's free verse can be likened to prose lists and conversational fragments she wrote for *Life*, but with another parody, called "Oh, Look—I Can Do It, too" in *Vanity Fair* for December 1918 (p. 48), she began turning her attention to French forms, the ballade and rondeau, made popular by Eugene Field, Austin Dobson, and F. P. A. Still she remained satiricial; still she strove to look casual. "Ballade of Big Plans" takes its chorus from

Julia Cane: "She loved him. He knew it. And love was a game that two could play at." The last stanza and envoy read,

> Recollections can only bore us;
> Now it's over, and now it's through
> Our day is dead as a dinosaurus.
> Other the paths that you pursue.
> What is she doing to spend her day at?
> Fun demands, at a minimum, two—
> And love is a game that two can play at.
>
> Prince, I'm packing away the rue:
> I'll show them something to shout "Hooray" at.
> I've got somebody else in view.
> And love is a game that two can play at.[19]

She also attempted an "Excursion Into Assonance" (*The World*, August 17, 1928, 11:1), and the sonnet form for more serious poetry. In this last she often echoes Edna St. Vincent Millay and Elinor Wylie,[20] but she employs this form least often and, when she does, is often tonily flabby and sentimental, her poetry losing much of its normal power and effectiveness.

At the same time she was finding her best verse form, Dorothy Parker grew in her mastery of the witty line. Yet, generally speaking, the wit matured later than her control of form. As late as 1921, "The Passionate Freudian to His Love" relies on puns.

> So come dwell a while on that distant isle
>   In the brilliant tropic weather;
> Where a Freud in need is a Freud indeed,
>   We'll be always Jung together. (*Life*, April 28, 1921, p. 596)

By 1922 she discovered the residual wit available in poetry by which the last line, supplying a contrary attitude, provides the poem with a backward-looking tension. She begins such contrasts in the early "Idyl".

> While, all forgotten, the world rolls along,
>   Think of us two, in a world of our own
> Now that you've thought of it seriously—
>   Isn't it grand that it never can be? (*Life*, July 7, 1921, p. 3)

Soon this became predictable, so she tried other overriding structures, such as "moral tales" where the punch line in the final maxim both opposes the preceding lines with its more distanced tone and moves the particular into a congruent generalization.

> Gracie, with her golden curls,
> Took her mother's string of pearls.
> Figuring—as who would not?—
> It would pawn for quite a lot.
> Picture, then, her indignation
> When she found it imitation!
> Though her grief she tries to smother,
> Grace can't feel the same towards Mother!
> All pretence and sham detest,
> Work for nothing but the best. (*Life*, May 4, 1922, p. 7)

Here the poem can also satirize the greed and affectation of those who would pretend to wealth. Another exercise in affecting overall structure is her "Somewhat Delayed Spring Song."

> Crocuses are springing,
> Birds are lightly winging,
> Corydon is singing,
>   To his rustic lute;
> Sullen winter passes,
> Shepherds meet their lasses,
> Tender-tinted grasses
>   Shoot.
> All the world's a-thrilling,
> Meadow larks are shrilling,
> Little brooks are trilling,
>   You, alone, are mute;
> Why do you delay it?
> Love's a game—let's play it,
> Go ahead and say it—
>   Shoot! (*SEP*, September 30, 1922, p. 105)

Last to be developed in her light verse was what has become the recognizable Dorothy Parker persona, that of the woman who is both exploited and thick-skinned, who is put upon but can equally well put down others. "Song" suggests this with cynical wisdom.

> Clarabelle has golden hair,
>   Mabel's eyes are blue,
> Nancy's form is passing fair,
>   Mary's heart is true.
> Chloë's heart has proved to be
>   Something else again;
> Not so much on looks is she,
>   But she gets the men. (*SEP*, November 18, 1922, p. 93)

"Folk Song" has the same idea, but reverses the roles.

> Rafe's a fine young gentleman;
>   Tom's with virtue blest.
> Jack, he broke my heart and ran,—
>   I love him the best. (*Life*, October 16, 1924, p. 7)

Another early "Song" contrasts peaceful countryside and the more desirable city life (*SEP*, July 29, 1922, p. 46). Because her wit came to rely on the transformation from one stance to another in the closing lines, she was keenly aware of diction, sound, and rhythm. After recounting a series of lovely natural flowers, "Woodland Song" ends: "But my favorite blossoms, I'm here to aver, / Are American Beauties at five dollars per" (*Life*, June 22, 1922, p. 1). "Invictus," built by clichés, has still more subtlety.

> Black though my record as darkest jet,
>   Give me, I beg, my devil's due;
> Only remember, I've never yet
>   Said, "How's the world been treating you?"
>   (*Life*, January 27, 1921, p. 161.

So tight is her control by 1923 that she can be compared, and fruitfully, to Heinrich Heine.[21] "The Temptress," which appeared the year of *Enough Rope*, is every bit as good as the poems she collected, but ends with a sentiment she might not want in the book.

> Ah, could I tempt assorted gents
> As sure as I can Providence,
> A different story I'd rehearse,
> And damned if I'd be writing verse! (*Life*, November 18, 1926, p. 15)

Little wonder that by then her "little woman" persona was being widely imitated.[22] She had found, by trial and error, the subject and stance that distinguish the best of her poetry.

IV   Drama: "we were pretty once"

"The essence of drama is not words but action. Plays are written to be enacted," Elmer Rice, co-author with Dorothy Parker of *Close Harmony; or, The Lady Next Door* (1924), has said.[23] This distinction draws our attention to the best part of *Close Harmony*, as Robert Benchley noted in summing the play for *Life*.

A poor little guy who is "happily married," except for the fact that he is miserable, meets a neighbor's wife who isn't even "happily married." They find that they have something in common. She plays the piano and he plays the mandolin—when his wife will let him. They get together one afternoon and he picks out "The Blue Danube" to her accompaniment and, inflamed by the nominal success of this, they sing "The Sunshine of Your Smile" together. The delicate writing of this scene, combined with the practically perfect work of James Spottswood and Wanda Lyon, makes it just about as heartbreaking a thing as we have ever seen on the stage.[24]

Heywood Broun agreed in the *Sunday World:* "The scene at the piano and round about is the most authentic and interesting combination of actuality and theatrical effectiveness which I have seen this year."[25] The difficulty, however, is that the play seems to be written *only* for this scene.

The situation bears strong resemblance to Dorothy's first story, "Such a Pretty Little Picture," which also examines a man trapped in an unhappy marriage, outwardly conforming but inwardly rebeling. *Close Harmony* reveals such frustration by showing certain surface similarities between Ed Graham, a suburbanite with a nagging wife and a critical daughter ironically named "Sister," and Belle Sheridan, Sister's piano teacher and a former burlesque star whose husband, now out of work, spends his time in the City with other women. Their Saturday afternoon commiseration for each other leads to mutual affection and plans for an elopement. But Sister, at a children's birthday party with her mother, is hit in the stomach, and Ed is confronted with family responsibilities he cannot bring himself to leave. Belle understands, although she plans to leave her husband, anyway. "I hate to leave you here, Ed. But it's all right, I guess. Look—I'm the way I am—and you're your way—and Bert's his—I guess we're all better off where we belong. You see, don't you?"[26] He does, but the magic of their hours together, which gave her the strength to leave Bert, gives Ed renewed strength within his home. He sends his visiting sister-in-law back to New Bedford, tells his daughter to stop complaining, and instructs his wife to prepare eggs for dinner, since he burned the roast while distracted with Belle. Then Ed takes down his mandolin. But he does not play it. *"After about eight bars he gradually leaves off playing, takes the pipe from his mouth and looks out into space as* THE [final] CUR-TAIN FALLS" (p. 91).

In this predictable domestic comedy, Dorothy Parker makes triviality her chief weapon in exposing the mediocrity of the middle class. Even her attempts at witty repartee (pp. 39, 41, 43, 44, 60–61) are clichéd. Worst of all, Ed, with whom we are to sympathize, is, for all of the change he undergoes in the play, no less mediocre, his dialogue no less stereotyped. If he has any insights worth recording, they are caught only in pantomime as the curtain falls—and thus are insufficiently rendered. Although Woollcott praised the play as Chekhovian in its attempt to make art out of the commonplace, *Close Harmony* lacks the psychological development of Chekhov's plays, even if it employs in the mandolin a Chekhovian symbol. Louis Bromfield now seems more accurate: "If one goes often enough to the theatre in New York there comes a moment when one more play of middle class life is simply too much," he wrote in *The Bookman* for February 1925. "There have been too many of them."[27] *Close Harmony* opened in Wilmington, Delaware, to fairly warm reception on November 21, 1924, and in New York on De-cember 1, where it ran twenty-four performances before closing quietly late in the month in which it began. " 'It was dull,' " Dorothy later said. " 'You have my apologies.' "[28]

Dorothy Parker's second play, *The Coast of Illyria*, written with Ross Evans (1949), is far more ambitious. This unrelieved portrayal of the tortured lives of Charles and Mary Lamb takes its title, sar-donically, from *Twelfth Night*, which the Lambs are then tran-scribing for children: "There were a brother and sister. . . . who were shipwrecked off the coast of Illyria." In the third act, Charles glosses the title (Original playscript, Act 3, p. 6 [p. 3–6]): they are shipwrecked eternally, because Mary's threatened insanity drives him to drink and his alcoholism brings on her madness.

The play opens happily enough. Charles is courting Fanny Kelly, a successful actress at Drury Lane; they plan to announce their marriage when Mary, whose last fit of madness has hospitalized her, returns home. Fanny no sooner leaves than Coleridge arrives—the self-destructive Coleridge complaining about Wordsworth's disapproval of him and his own hellish pains of mind and body. His anxiety and despair, his near-madness of speech and need for laudanum which he carries with him, embody the tragedies of Mary *and* Charles: he is both an emblem of the play's impossible tragedies and a forewarning of what the remaining acts will unfold. Although Charles and Coleridge are offset in the first act by the lovely dignity of Mary, who appears cured, and the sweetness of the Lambs' permanent houseguest George Dyer—who gave away all his money, Charles tells us, because his head is uniformly wrong while his heart is uniformly right—there is an underlying concern that Mary's mental stability is only temporary. Again Dorothy Parker knows how to *enact* scenes: Charles must destroy the Hogarth picture of Bedlam on one of Mary's treasured glasses before she returns and so he smashes it in the fireplace; Coleridge places his vial of laudanum on the mantel to show he intends to abstain forever; the Lambs' writing desk, always before us on the stage, stands neatly arranged but unused.

The deep and bitter tragedy of loves too promising to be lost and too sensitive to withstand living, captured superbly in the characterization of Coleridge in Act I, embodies the world of the play in Act II—where it expands almost unbearably. As Fanny's gaiety opened the first act, so the promise of a Thursday night at the Lambs' with good food, sparkling conversation, and games of whist opens the second. But Hazlitt comes to complain of his wife—he has just seen her in whorish dress riding in a carriage with another man and they nearly ran him down, spattering him with mud. Coleridge arrives, back on drugs and bringing in tow a blond boy of nineteen, Thomas DeQuincey, who is learned in books and shares Coleridge's love for opium. To add to his troubles, Charles has bought a set of "The Rake's Progress" in oils for Mary, only to learn that the gallery delivered the Bedlam scene that might bring on her a permanent madness. Mrs. Kelly is horrorstruck by the guests and leaves when Coleridge reads aloud from Charles' "Confessions of a Drunkard," for she will not allow her daughter to marry a man widely known as an alcoholic and brother of a girl who murdered their mother with a kitchen knife.

If the first act signifies paradise lost and the second act pandemonium, the third act is hell itself. A week has passed and Charles has been drinking day and night, for he has had no word from Fanny. When his employer Mr. Wilberforce arrives from the East India Company to announce that Charles has not been fired but given a pension for life so that he may devote all his time to writing, and when Fanny arrives to tell him that her mother kept his letters of entreaty from her and so only now has she learned of his continued love for her, things seem about to right themselves. Mary, however, cannot live without Charles; Fanny cannot live with them both. Charles wishes to be a married man and a father—to have a fuller life than that of a brother—but he cannot resign the responsibility of his sister, cannot commit her to Bedlam, which Hogarth has put before him (and us) in all its horror. As the play ends, Fanny leaves Charles, and Mary, threatened by their marriage, sinks into another period of insanity. .Charles stands alone, asking for something to hate, and hating the burden of being everything to his sweet sister who cannot let him go lest she lose her mind in the giving.

The Coast of Illyria is a rich play, partly historical, with an extraordinary range of characterization and an authentic dramatization of loneliness, terror, and despair. It realizes, in an especially vivid way, the classic notion of tragedy as a necessary choice between impossible alternatives. The anguish that produces art of great loveliness—at one finely staged moment, Coleridge recites "Kubla Khan"—suggests the ineradicable cost of what is precious in life; the multiple portraits of self-hatred embody the haunted love that likewise produces some of our best literature. The dialogue, moreover, is crisp and cogent, insinuating the shabby life of nineteenth century London with a natural ease. The play ran in Dallas from April 4–23, 1949, but another production in Edinburg was cancelled.[29] Keats says that Dorothy was content that it folded in Dallas although it was voted the best play of the season at the Margo Jones Theatre,[30] but if the play can be faulted, it must lie in the total starkness of plot and presentation. Dorothy's mordant quality here chokes off any humor, any real joy, and the play is as painful to read or see as it must have been painful to live.

The Ladies of the Corridor, written with Arnaud D'Usseau in 1953, carries forward some similar themes. This drama, Eric Bentley wrote, is a story about the derelict women who live in hotels. A young one, who has a husband that uses a whip and keeps the company of call girls, takes to drink, disgusts herself by sleeping with the desk clerk, and commits suicide. An old one, concealing behind her old lace the arsenic of maternal tyranny, forces her son into spending his life with her by threatening to expose the fact that he had given up his last job under suspicion of homosexuality. A middle-aged one has a pathetic love affair with a younger man. As a kind of chorus commenting on the three principals, there is, on the one side, a successful career woman and, on the other, a couple of hags whose life is death.[31]

Thus the chief difference from *The Coast of Illyria* is that the characters here are drawn from Dorothy Parker's own life, the setting a midtown Manhattan hotel where she was then living.[32] In his largely negative review, Bentley agreed that "The ladies our authors had in mind are important because they exist. And if there is a scandal in their existence—or their situation—it should by all means be loudly announced,"[33] while Brooks Atkinson, one of the play's severest critics, commented "that unattached ladies of venerable years are pathetic and lonely creatures," but added that "nearly everybody knows that without having to go to the theatre."[34]

For Dorothy, the play's theme is the "appalling human waste," and the Hotel Marlowe a microcosm of the larger American society.

"We're trying to show a part of American life—and a very large part of it," she said. "There is an enormous population of women alone. . . . It's not so much age as manlessness—and they should be better trained, adjusted, to live a life without a man.

"I think in many cases they're contented women; they wouldn't change places with anyone, and if you possibly told any of them they were miserably unhappy, they'd think you were insane. But some of them don't know they're dead—that curious death in life with which they are content. . . . It sounds too pompous, I know, . . . but I don't think tragedy is too big a word because the waste is unnecessary." (*NYT*, October 18, 1953, 3:4–5)

There is more wit in *Ladies of the Corridor* than in *Coast of Illyria*, but it is mordant humor, self-directed. Humor and dread were always closely related in Dorothy Parker's mind—it is one of the chief strengths of all her work—and here it functions brilliantly, the rueful and cruel jokes displaying among the aging women a last shared personal and psychic stay against the terror of emptiness. If it

seems a meager response, it is a tactic grown from deep self-awareness, now hoary with age.

The Ladies of the Corridor also takes its title from literature, from
T.S. Eliot's "Sweeney Erect," and from the beginning, the play
stretches by such allusions to incorporate larger dimensions than a
midtown hotel. The drama incorporates two of Dorothy's stories—"I
Live on Your Visits" and "Lolita"—as well as her own experiences
with Eddie, McClain, Alan, and Alan's mother. The play is presented as a mosaic in which a chorus of two women showing disparate consequences of living in hell (a hotel of "no exit" that is
through repeated allusion made metaphorically the Inferno) comment on the lives of others damned to join them there. Act I
supplies case studies—through arbitrary days in their lives—of
three dead souls; the intermission allows us to see that they are all
the same person and all fragments of the chorus in the lobby, that
any day is like any other, so that we have been tendered not slices of
life but capsule biographies; Act II shows the consequences of the
characters themselves realizing their fate as we have come to understand it. How they face their own new awareness of the death in life
that is "their living, their living, their living" is the point of the play.

The setting, Hotel Marlowe in the East Sixties, is for this study of
death-as-emptiness the crossroads of the world.

> *The Marlowe is an old hotel with an atmosphere that suggests another
> and more opulent era. It is not shabby, it is efficiently managed, but there
> has been no attempt to modernize its decorations, which are considered part
> of its charm. It has but few transient guests and no commercial trade.
> Occasionally a married couple is found living there, and sometimes a
> bachelor, but most of the suites and single rooms are occupied by ladies
> alone. Mostly they are widows (there are seven and a half million widows in
> the United States); some less fortunate are divorced; and there's an in-
> frequent nondescript who is only separated.[35]*

In the lobby sit as a Greek chorus two derelicts, Mrs. Gordon and
Mrs. Lauterbach, whose running comments provide bankrupt social
judgments and deathlike interpretations, *thanatos* embodied and so
verified. Mrs. Gordon's tag—"Well, what's new on the Rialto?" (p.
5)—is at once at attempt to be witty and a metaphor to suggest that if
all the world's a stage, here the stage is meant to be all the world.
She is the most theatrical, the most artificial (she frequently changes
her nailpolish, [p. 7]), for her life is altogether vicarious: she lives the

lives of hotel residents in daytime and the lives of movie actors at night. Her kleptomania—she steals a blue ashtray from Mrs. Lauterbach and some of Mildred Tynan's cards after Mildred commits suicide—suggests her fundamentally parasitic nature. Mrs. Lauterbach's more pathetic loneliness—she wants to see her son at Thanksgiving, but he hasn't invited her and she is afraid that if she writes him it will seem like "pushing" (p. 6)—is ignored by Mrs. Gordon, blind to compassion. Because of the coldness of the one, the warmth of the other, their relationship is peculiarly unrewarding, infertile.

The hotel guests, however, seem to hold out more promise. Mrs. Nichols has found an accommodation to life with her son Charles: she manages their affairs through investments and joins her son in stamp collecting (another allusion to the Marlowe as microcosm, [pp. 38–39]). Charles Nichols, whose chief occupation is "Gray Lady," a nurse companion to his mother, spends each day at the zoo. His mother forces the significance of this on him.

All [the animals] in their nice clean cages, nice and warm? . . . . Poor caged things. And yet they say that when one of them escapes he's frightened out of his wits. He doesn't know what to do. Why is that, Charles? . . . . Too much soft living, I expect. And too much care—yes, and affection. I've always heard the keepers are extremely fond of them. (p. 42)

Such obvious analogy with her son, an accused homosexual who has retreated to her parasitic care of him, does not damage the fabric of the play so much as point to her monstrosity and viciousness.

Just as Mrs. Nichols first appears a gentle and well-bred woman, Mildred Tynan seems at first a typed dipsomaniac. Drink, she tells the maid Irma, "makes you a different person. You're not yourself for a little while, and that's velvet. . . . A couple of drinks, and I've got some nerve. Otherwise I'm frightened all the time" (p. 45). But she has a desperate kind of wit—"I'm giving up solitaire. I can't win even when I cheat" (p. 45). "Maybe I could give music lessons to backward children. . . . I finally got so I could play the "Minute Waltz" in a minute and a half" (p. 49)—that shows how frightened she remains, even after drinking. For the drinking is a consequence not of fear in the present but of searing memories from the past with her husband.

Once I got started—God, how he hurried me along. So when we went to the country club, Mrs. John Tynan would fall down on the dance floor and her husband would carry her out. And everybody would say, "Oh, that poor man, and look how sweet he is to her! Poor, dear man." Holy John Tynan, the Blessed Martyr of Santa Barbara. Yes, and the call girls, two and three at a time, and the whip in the closet. (p. 113)

As then, hers is still a life of lies, and her hope in finding a new job at Irma's suggestion, like the hope in the bottle and in the driven affair with the bellhop Harry, is futile. She knows pretense is her life— and that her life is pretense. Her suicide is superbly plotted (she has only a superficial resemblance to Hazel Morse, the "Big Blonde"), but her final line is embarrassing.

The chief character is Lulu Ames who upon the death of her husband in Akron moves to this crossroads to begin a new life near a son and daughter-in-law who do not want her. Her friend Connie tells her how to cope.

LULU: Is there a man, Connie?
CONNIE: No; oh, no. After Ben died there was a long stretch when I sat and looked at the wall. Then, a long time after that, there was a man—a lovely man. I was young again.
LULU (gently): What happened, Connie?
CONNIE: He found somebody who was young for the first time. So then there was a succession of transients. If that shocks you, Lulu, it shouldn't. The one-night stands don't do any good; I found that out. There's got to be fondness, and there's got to be hope. Lulu, please—this new life must be all you want it to be. Only don't let yourself get lonely. Loneliness makes ladies our age do the goddamnedest things. (pp. 28–29)

Lulu finds a young man whose solitude after the breakup of his marriage mirrors her own. For a while, their relationship is tender and successful; but Lulu does not want to attend young peoples' parties with Paul and, their affair threatened, she grows nervous about possibly losing him. She too uses humor as a defense while back of the wit is terror. "Look, Lulu," Paul tells her, "two people, no matter what their feeling, mustn't feed entirely on each other. If they do, all that's left of them is a little heap of bones" (p. 86); the comment is true for them, for Mrs. Nichols, for the women in the lobby. But like them, Lulu cannot help herself and the relationship collapses "Because the sweetness has gone out of it—the loveliness"

(p. 108). The paradigmatic relationship anticipates Mildred's death in the next scene, for her actual suicide is only a more visible form of the spiritual suicide shared by all the others. Earlier, Lulu had traced their common despair to larger social patterns. "We were told you grew up, you got married, and there you were. And so we did, and so there we were. But our husbands, they were busy. We weren't part of their lives; and as we got older we weren't part of anybody's lives, and yet we never learned how to be alone" (p. 97). The terms in which each woman confronts her despair—or state of sin, of damnation—become interchangeable with the other women of the Marlowe—they are all Francesca to a Paolo (p. 86), their paths circular and futile, as in Dante's picture of hell.

The Ladies of the Corridor is thus symphonic in structure, Mildred's death at the end only echoing an earlier death in the same room where Viola Hasbrook covered all her mirrors before her life ended: with mirrors or without, the repetitive patterns of life lead only to the awareness or fact of death. In such a beautifully orchestrated play, with deeply and individually etched portraits all fusing at the close, only the ending rings false. Lulu Ames should, by the dynamics of the play, become another Mrs. Lauterbach, and that is what Dorothy Parker knew and wrote. But the producer wanted it changed, and so Lulu replaces Paul with needlepoint: that, perhaps, is what misdirected such critics as Bentley.[36] Except for this and for occasionally cheap jokes rather than brittle ones (pp. 35, 55, 56, 60, 115), the play is an unrelenting study of internal pain and terror. What seems exaggerated in the opening scene becomes, in the course of the play, metaphorically and then literally possible: a *danse macabre* exposing the loneliness and despair of old age. In our time of senior citizens' colonies and nursing home scandals, this drama still pierces deeply.

But with these last two plays, we move beyond Dorothy Parker's apprenticeship; here we have begun to appraise her chief accomplishments.

CHAPTER 3

Her Accomplishment: Poetry, Fiction, Criticism

I *Premises: "Call her by my name"*

A rewarding way to study Dorothy Parker's mature work is to see how she embodies in it more and more of her own life. We have just seen how a work as impersonal as *Close Harmony* can descend to the artless and the trivial and how, conversely, a play as personal and autobiographical as *The Ladies of the Corridor* can gain richness, substance, and authority. Dorothy Parker had learned in writing her plays, as she did in the evolution of her essays and light verse, the inherent value in imaginative application of experience, starting with a personal perspective as a handy persona and moving, more and more, toward a personal aesthetic. Her accomplished poetry, fiction, and criticism illustrate the success of this development.

II *Poetry: "To follow a thread of song"*

Dorothy Parker's maturity is clearly visible when we compare a late poem like "War Song" (see p. 69) with an early poem from *Enough Rope* (1926), "The New Love."

> If it shine or if it rain,
>   Little will I care or know.
> Days, like drops upon a pane,
>   Slip, and join, and go.
>
> At my door's another lad;
>   Here's his flower in my hair.
> If he see me pale and sad,
>   Will he see me fair?

> I sit looking at the floor,
>   Little will I think or say
> If he seek another door;
>   Even if he stay.[1]

"The New Love" is essentially negative, its wit grounded in a rueful attitude, self-deprecation, and world-worn cynicism; the poem has a kind of half-cheerful heartlessness that echoes early Millay. "War Song," on the other hand, is more positive. The later poem is also more realistic and willing to settle for less, not self-deprecating but not boasting either; instead, the persona has reconciled herself to the way of the world. "War Song" is essentially generous in spirit and, if it has any echoes, they are of the mature A. E. Housman.

Yet these distinctions are subordinate to the similarities: the simplicity of diction, clarity of stance, easiness of rhyme, and settledness of form and presentation; each has its own lapidary effect. Such common qualities—which distinguish all her best poems—are neoclassical and together they define all the mature work, whether they result from her Latin training at Miss Dana's or reach her by way of her contemporaries. Roman poetry lies just behind the epigrammatic poems of Dorothy Parker.

a. *Confluences: "I have lived with shades"*

"Every good copy of verses is inspired by the elder poetry," John Jay Chapman wrote in *Vanity Fair* for July 1919.[2] Not one but two classical traditions merged during the period that Dorothy Parker advanced from her light verse, largely inconsequential, to her mature and substantial poetry; although no one has yet paid sufficient attention, these two strains caused a remarkable revival in interest in Roman poetry in the earlier part of the twentieth century. One tradition, the more learned and serious, stemming from Catullus, arose with Housman and reached Dorothy Parker largely through the work of Millay and Elinor Wylie. The other, beginning with Eugene Field's imitations of Horace, reached Dorothy Parker through later imitations by F. P. A. Her best poems marry both traditions.

A recent scholar has identified Catullus as the first Roman poet who shaped short lyrics by his own independent, wisecracking personality, reflecting personal sentiments rather than serving the larger community.[3] Earlier, when Dorothy Parker was writing

Enough Rope, a popular book on Catullus held that he was "the pioneer. . . in the epigram and the lampoon," that "His language is sometimes that of the nursery, sometimes that of the drawing-room, sometimes that of the street corners; [in each] he wastes no words."[4] Catullus wrote forty songs of hate, ranging from two to forty lines, his work often revealing "his open contempt for shams. . . . It was Catullus who taught Europe, and America, how to sing tender songs of love, to phrase bitter words of hate; who 'pointed the way to a more exact prosody and a richer versification'; who showed us how to flash on the mental retina whole pictures in a single word."[5] Harrington quotes Walter Pater, " 'Catullus' expression of emotion has the Greek qualities of definiteness, adequacy, point, and necessary limitation.' "[6] Although the poetry was immediate in reference and impact, the moments chosen were eternal ones; Catullus compounded sharp wit, ingenuity, and elegance of expression from songs of beauty to hard poems of savage invective. His poems could be solemn or reckless in attitude, fostering an "urban consciousness,"[7] the clean precision of his lines and the economy of phrase resulting from quip and cliché with a relative absence of simile and metaphor. In all these primary characteristics, "He set the pace for epigram throughout the centuries"[8]—and he wrote verse astonishingly similar to that of Dorothy Parker. As an example, here is number 70 in a contemporary translation by Horace Gregory.

> My mother says that she would rather wear the wedding-veil for me
> than anyone: even if Jupiter himself came storming after her;
> that's what she says, but when a woman talks to a hungry,
> ravenous lover, her words should be written upon the wind
> and engraved in rapid waters.

Compare Dorothy's "Prophetic Soul" (*Enough Rope*, p. 56) with Catullus' number 85:

> I hate and love.
>   And if you ask me why,
> I have no answer, but I discern,
> can feel, my senses rooted in eternal torture.[9]

Confessional yet highly disciplined, conversational yet poetically rendered, the work of both poets displays a controlled imagination. Distanced reflection and careful analysis merge. And both poets are structurally similar, opening with a summary sentiment, continuing by amplification and parallelism, and concluding with a bright summary or, more often, a turn or counterturn frequently involving a change in attitude, sometimes involving a pun. Catullus and Dorothy Parker share a forced (and threatened) personal integrity before failed love affairs and a disintegrating society. Catullus' misfortune with Lesbia, Dorothy's with many men, allow them to juxtapose a grim reality with a struggle to preserve the image of an ideal lover; for both, cynicism results.[10]

Catullus was revived in the work of A. E. Housman, a classicist known for reciting the Roman poet before his classes, even during battles at Vincy and Verdun, and who published an eleven-page discussion on obscenities in Catullus and other Latin poets.[11] "The unanimous verdict of the Housman admirers," writes Cyril Connolly,

is that he is essentially a classical poet. Master of the Latin language, he has introduced in English poetry the economy, the precision, the severity of that terse and lucid tongue. His verses are highly finished, deeply pagan; they stand outside the ordinary current of modern poetry, the inheritors, not of the romantic age, but of the poignancy and stateliness, the epigraphic quality of the poems of Catullus, Horace, and Virgil, or the flowers of the Greek Anthology.[12]

Just how closely he resembles Dorothy Parker can be seen in *A Shropshire Lad*, number 18:

> Oh, when I was in love with you,
> Then I was clean and brave,
> And miles around the wonder grew
> How well did I behave.
>
> And now the fancy passes by,
> And nothing will remain,
> And miles around they'll say that I
> Am quite myself again.

As for American poets, Housman felt Millay "the best [one] living," from whom he "got more enjoyment [than] Frost or Robinson."[13]

Edna St. Vincent Millay studied Latin poetry as a child and as an adult carried with her a "tiny, shabby brown leather" copy of

Catullus' poetry; in the Village, she talked about Catullus with Edmund Wilson over peach brandy. She was equally fond of Housman, once chasing him a half-mile through Cambridge "just to get a glimpse of his face, a nice face"; she was also close to Harrison Dowd who set part of *A Shropshire Lad* to music.[14] Both poets find a place in her poetry, in her recklessness and reserve, in her devotion to learning, in her creativity and rebellion.[15] Like Dorothy, Millay deals with unrequited love and with sexual affairs that are "just as real and true as any other," bringing to them "a pertness, a saucy impudence—even a certain heartlessness" that reminds us of Dorothy's poetry.[16] For our purposes, *A Few Figs from Thistles* (1922) is most apposite. The opening poems are indistinguishable from Dorothy's.

> First Fig
> My candle burns at both ends;
>   It will not last the night;
> But ah, my foes, and oh, my friends—
>   It gives a lovely light!
>
> Second Fig
> Safe upon the solid rock the ugly houses stand:
> Come and see my shining palace built upon the sand![17]

So is "Thursday":

> And if I loved you Wednesday,
> Well, what is that to you?
> I do not love you Thursday—
> So much is true.
> And why you come complaining
> Is more than I can see.
> I loved you Wednesday,—yes—but what
> Is that to me?[18]

And, as with Dorothy Parker, death as well as love becomes an omnipresent theme in Millay's poetry.[19] Among other contemporaries, the "small, clean technique," the miniaturist art of Elinor Wylie, has also been compared to her friend Dorothy Parker's.[20]

Dorothy learned much of her art of poetry from Catullus and the Catullan tradition in England and America, but it was the Horatian tradition that taught her the inevitability of man's failings, and that led to her rueful and cocky tones. There is some likelihood that the *Odes of Horace* that she knew at Miss Dana's School was that translated by W. E. Gladstone (1894) which emphasized the *compression* of his verse. Warren H. Cudworth's text (1917) appeared just as she was seeking out her own form; in his preface, Cudworth stresses the tight *form* of Horatian poetry.[21] But Dorothy Parker was far from alone in this interest; Louis Untermeyer's popular little book *Including Horace* pointed out ways in which he was seen as contemporary.

Horace in his own mood [is] light, slyly mocking, petulant, often downright flippant. In spite of his immortal literary harem, his Lydias, his Chloës, his Pyrrhas, his Lelages, there is never in all of Horace's erotic rhymes the note of genuine passion. . . . The note is always that of sophistication. . . . Over and over again he tells us to enjoy the present and distrust tomorrow.[22]

Structurally, Horace's *Satires,* like Dorothy's, often begin with a hyperbole, develop by antithetical ideas, or end with a surprise, a twist. Horace wrote his fashionable poetry for his own inner circle, the friends of Maecenas resembling for him what the Algonquin wits did for Dorothy Parker; but as Grant Showerman wrote in 1922, Horace detached himself from the crowd so that he could see and comment on the folly of his fellow men. He is tamer and less involved than Catullus, although Horace too could use his own person as the subject or perspective for his poetry.[23]

The modern tradition of imitating Horace began with Eugene Field who was taught classics by his father and whose managing editor on the Chicago *Daily News,* F. W. Reilly, persuaded him to try his hand. Field's methodology was a conscious one. "[Horace's] was a joyous spirit and certainly he would express himself rhythmically and with mirthful lightness if he were now on earth. So I try to interpret Horace in a way to bring his pagan poetry up to date. At least I give him the best I have in the shop."[24] Field's imitations appeared in his newspaper column *Sharps and Flats;* in the winter of 1890 he was convinced by a friend, Francis Wilson, that he should publish a whole book of such poetry. *Echoes from the Sabine Farm* appeared in 1896. Field's work was brief, colloquial, and critical— but never savage or trenchant like Dorothy Parker's. He appeals frequently to Roman allusions in his originals, as in "To Chloë (II)":

> Chloë, you shun me like a hind
>   That, seeking vainly for her mother,
> Hears danger in each breath of wind,
>   And wildly darts this way and t'other; . . .
> But Chloë, you're no infant thing
>   That should esteem a man an ogre;
> Let go your mother's apron-string,
>   And pin your faith upon a toga![25]

Field perhaps gave his most serious attention to these imitations. He defended them at length in 1891, but he died before completing his ambition to write Horace's biography. His work was widely hailed and itself imitated.[26]

F. P. A., who worked on Chicago newspapers during Field's last years, brought the idea of imitating Horace to New York City with him, and his own imitations became a popular feature in his "Conning Tower" column in the New York *World*; Dorothy herself tried her hand at them there. "The patron of the smart," as Gilbert Seldes called F. P. A.,[27] made it possible (in the words of Don Marquis) "to admit our learning and still be honorable men."[28] F. P. A.'s imitation of the same ode to Chloë (Book I, ode xxiii) reads,

> Nay, Chloë, dear, forget your fear,
>   Nor like a frightened fawn outrun me;
> No savage I to horrify—
>   You shouldn't shun me.
> Come Chloë, queen, you're seventeen;
>   There's many a precedent to back us.
> Why shouldn't you be Mrs. Q.
>   Horatius Flaccus?[29]

His imitation of Book I, Ode v also uses a popular expression.

> What lady-like youth in his wild aberrations
>   Is putting cologne on his brow?
> For whom are the puffs and the blond transformations?
>   I wonder who's kissing you now.[30]

Long sections of each of F. P. A.'s early books, published during the time he was encouraging Dorothy Parker, are given over to such imitations of Horace—and of Propertius, Catullus, and Martial.[31]

F. P. A. learned from imitating Horace the precision, simplicity, and compactness that distinguish his light verse as they distinguish Dorothy's poetry: he served her as an important model. He also turned to puns, as in "The Atmospheric Complex."

> Give me the balmy breezes!
>   Give me the raging storm!
> Give me the gale that freezes!
>   Give me the zephyrs warm!
> Give me the searing tropic!
>   Wind on my cheek and hair!
> And, while we're on the topic,
>   Give me the air[32]

Like Dorothy Parker, F. P. A. was fascinated by the theme of unrequited love and challenged by the difficult word, as in "The Return of the Soldier."

> Lady, when I left you
>   Ere I sailed the sea.
> Bitterly I bereft you
>   Told me you would be. . . .
> Arguing *ex parte*,
>   Maybe you can tell
> Why I find your heart
> A. W. O. L.[33]

The legacy of Horace, summed Showerman in 1922, was "to be straightforward and rapid and omit the unessential; to be truthful to life; . . . to be appropriate in meter and diction."[34] Horace spawned such imitators because they, as he, were discontented with their lot (Book I, satire i).

Still "the model and type of the epigram . . . which have not been surpassed in any literature" is Martial, and Dorothy Parker may have known the Martial text by J. H. Westcott (1897). The chief characteristics of the Martial epigram are wit and point, as in "News Item" or "Two-Volume Novel" by Dorothy.

> Men seldom make passes
> At girls who wear glasses. (*Enough Rope*, p. 85)

> The sun's gone dim, and
>   The moon's turned black;
> For I loved him, and
>   He didn't love back. (*Sunset Gun*, p. 70)

Paul Nixon notes in *A Roman Wit* (1911) that Martial was an urban wit; his poetry offers as its reward an "intellectual appreciation, not an emotional reaction,"[35] and it is Westcott's text that tells us most about how Dorothy Parker's generation perceived the classical epigrammatist.

> The fact that Martial's character was not a strong one, that he felt no consciousness of a moral mission, that he was neither greatly better nor worse than people about him, that he reflects so thoroughly the spirit of his age, makes him more interesting to us and more instructive in his way than many a sterner author. . . . His satire stings more than it wounds. And at his best he reveals a tenderness and pathos which prove a genuinely affectionate heart, or a refined delicacy which is hard to reconcile with coarseness of feeling. . . . Martial's versification is admirable, being clear, tasteful, and careful, without being pedantic or over precise.[36]

Nixon's 1911 translations illustrate these techniques.

> Philo swears he was never known
>   To dine alone:
>   He was not.
> Dine at all, when it comes about
>   He's not asked out,
>   He does n't.[37]

> Your clients' applause for your poems,
>   Pomponious,
> Would prove not your metres but menus
>   Euphonious.[38]

"The point, whether dependent on a pun, or an ambiguous phrase, on a new meaning given to a word, or an antithesis," writes Walter C. A. Ker in 1930, "is sharply brought out. And the words fall into their places with a fitness that suggests the solution of a puzzle: the reader feels that no other words could have been employed. He is never turgid or pompous: all he touches with a light hand."[39] The understanding the Algonquin wits had of Martial, as of Catullus and

Horace, points the way to the resources and the hallmarks of Dorothy Parker's major poetry.

b.   Enough Rope: *"The sweeter the apple, the blacker the core"*

J. F. [John Farrar] wrote in *The Bookman* for March 1927 that "Dorothy Parker in *Enough Rope* . . . collects some of her fragile verses, and the effect is devastating. Singly, they are lovely. As a volume, they are terrifying; but only as they reflect what seems to be a fiery, discontented personality"[40]; the *New York Times* dismissed the poetry of her first book as "flapper verse."[41] The most considered praise came from Edmund Wilson, a student of Catullus in Greenwich Village, who wrote in *New Republic* for January 19, 1927,

Mrs. Dorothy Parker began her poetic career as a writer of humorous verse of the school of Franklin P. Adams. . . . Her present book is, however, quite different. During the last two or three years, Dorothy Parker—though still in the pages of Life and the New Yorker—has emerged as a distinguished and interesting poet. . . . Perhaps few poems in this book are completely successful: they tend, on the one hand . . . to become a little cheapened in the direction of ordinary humorous verse and, on the other, to become too deeply saturated with the jargon of ordinary feminine poetry, . . . But her best work is extraordinarily vivid: it has a peculiar intensity and frankness which, when they appear in poetry, seem to justify any style or method, no matter how strange to literary convention.[42]

In *Poetry* for April 1927, Marie Luhrs added: "Here is poetry that is 'smart' in the fashion designer's sense of the word. . . . Mrs. Parker has her own particular field of frank American humor. She is slangy, vulgar, candid, and withal subtle, delicate and sparkling. The soul of wit distinguishes most of her pieces. . . . For all their pertness and bravado they mirror, in most cases, quite genuine and profound experiences."[43]

Enough Rope (1926) appeared from Boni and Liveright for two dollars, in a gray dustjacket with yellow lettering—"A woman supplies enough rope to hang a hundred Egos"[44]—and a dangling rope for illustration; it went through eight printings, a phenomenal bestseller. For the uninitiated, the plaintive, self-pitying tone of the spurned woman must have seemed obvious and trite ("The Small Hours," p. 12) or brightly, if superficially, sophisticated ("Wail," p. 22). While the book's title suggests her conscious adoption of the role of satirist, one bemused by the human situation and sufficiently superior to poke fun at it, the poetry of Part I, treating such commonplace themes as unrequited love, loneliness, death, and hypocrisy, makes the book appear commonplace. Attempts to be otherwise, as with "The Immortals" (p. 44), strain self-consciously but are actually poor parodies of "serious" love poems.

But this is to take the worst poetry in the book as our norm. If we examine the best of it, we see already that terseness and strength whereby classical form supplies foundation and limitation to both situation and sentiment. Compare "Anecdote":

> So silent I when Love was by
> He yawned, and turned away;
> But Sorrow clings to my apron-strings,
> I have so much to say. (p. 25)

Here is the precision and distillation characteristic of Martial at *his* succinct best. This is a very much more disciplined poem than "Threnody," which opens the volume.

> 1 Lilacs blossom just as sweet
> Now my heart is shattered.
> If I bowled it down the street,
> Who's to say it mattered?
> 5 If there's one that rode away
> What would I be missing?
> Lips that taste of tears, they say,
> Are the best for kissing.
>
> Eyes that watch the morning star
> 10 Seem a little brighter;
> Arms held out to darkness are
> Usually whiter.
> Shall I bar the strolling guest;
> Bind my brow with willow,
> 15 When, they say, the empty breast
> Is the softer pillow?
>
> That a heart falls tinkling down,
> Never think it ceases.
> Every likely lad in town
> 20 Gathers up the pieces.

> If there's one gone whistling by
> Would I let it grieve me?
> Let him wonder if I lie;
> Let him half believe me. (p. 11)

The explosive conceit of the heart as bowling ball is at once cocky and exaggerated, although it frees the quatrains, opening them up for the drama of an undefeated spirit. Dorothy Parker knows already how form can constrict when density is sought and can just as easily loosen the spirit within the form when she wishes to dramatize a willful and even reckless vitality.

However different the immediate tones of "Anecdote" and "Threnody," close reading reveals the same careful plotting of diction and sound; they are exacting as voiced feelings. Simple language, taut or loose, coiled or sprung, is economic, direct, even astringent. "They say"(l. 7) is not a linefiller, but an indication of the persona's naive reliance on sophistication that is assumed, not real; the victory she scores, then, in the last lines, assuring her alliance with the code of "them," only points out to us her equal shallowness for we cannot take such clichés seriously. Dissociated as we are from the persona's sentiment (ll. 1–2), her sudden loss of the one fine metaphor (wrenchingly changed in l. 17) shows us the ironic distance between poet and persona. The liberating metaphor (l. 3) is also misplaced and grotesque, a product of the personal. So too the authentic colloquialisms that insistently revert to clichés. In this equivocation that guarantees satire, Dorothy Parker provides a wit as controlled as the Roman poets', yet in an idiom very much her own.

Enough Rope is dedicated to Elinor Wylie, whose personal copy was inscribed, "With love, gratitude, and everything." This gift to a serious poet—not one of the light versifiers who contributed doggerel to *Life* and "The Conning Tower"—anticipates some serious changes Dorothy Parker made when collecting these poems from earlier publication in the magazines.[45] Some of the poems here are still early and unsuccessful ("A Portrait" [p. 45], "Chant for Dark Hours" [p. 50], "Verses for a Certain Dog" [p. 57]), but others, like those she revised, already show her mastering her craft. The themes that run through the volume are those with which she was by now identified: unrequited love, loneliness, and death. Yet note her control in such poems as "For a Sad Lady":

> And let her loves, when she is dead,
> Write this above her bones:
> "No more she lives to give us bread
> Who asked her only stones." ("For a Sad Lady," p. 34)

If her imitations of Horace lack the wide-wheeling energy of F. P. A. ("Renunciation," p. 62), when she brings her own voice to the classical form, she is unsurpassed ("Unfortunate Coincidence," p. 51). That she manages in far briefer compass shows that she is primarily a miniaturist.

To appreciate the peculiarly successful poetic of *Enough Rope*, we must see how Dorothy Parker starts with the briefest possible situation, catches it at a split moment, and dramatizes it through a voice unaware of the clichés on which it rests.

> Because your eyes are slant and slow,
>   Because your hair is sweet to touch,
> My heart is high again; but oh,
>   I doubt if this will get me much. ("Prophetic Soul," p. 66)

The interior monologue advances amusement through its innocent self-condemnation. Consider the technique of "Philosophy."

> If I should labor through daylight and dark,
>   Consecrate, valorous, serious, true,
> Then on the world I may blazon my mark;
>   And what if I don't, and what if I do? (p. 79)

Every word is measured here; the polysyllables of line 2 add variety and counterrhythm to lines 1,3, and 4, but they are defeated by the honesty, the rueful forthrightness of the monosyllables that completely enclose them. The poem, collapsing on a line that, removed from this freshening context, is one of the tritest lines of everyday conversation, shows us how we are, for the moment, suspended between a commonplace language and sentiment and a uniquely forceful—a memorable, mnemonic—poem.

Dorothy Parker's poetry appears thin partly because it is dramatic, not ruminative. But by puns, clichés, and unhappy word choices, her poems invite us to reflect on the sharp difference between poet and persona. It is this implied contrast—one we as readers *sense*—that provides point and force. The unwinding process of thought is in us, as with "Interview" (p. 106).

> The ladies men admire, I've heard,
> Would shudder at a wicked word.
> Their candle gives a single light;
> They'd rather stay at home at night.
> They do not keep awake till three,
> Nor read erotic poetry.
> They never sanction the impure,
> Nor recognize an overture.
> They shrink from powers and from paints . . .
> So far, I've had no complaints.

Here the punch line is no surprise; the controlling idea lies in the exaggerated sentiment of line 1, the parody of Millay in line 3, the excessive catalogue of lines 4–9. The last line is merely a resolution of what is said and what we expected. Even more embedded is the satire of "Pictures in the Smoke."

> Oh, gallant was the first love, and glittering and fine;
>   The second love was water, in a clear white cup;
> The third love was his, and the fourth was mine;
>   And after that, I always get them all mixed up. (p. 101)

The inability of the persona here to rescue even her first lover from romantic jargon—to award him reality—is a certain indication of the hollowness of her own self, of her own attitude towards love. The poem is clearly self-condemning.

This is not to deny a sprightly laughter; Dorothy Parker's poems are also *fun*. In assessing both the absurdity of human behavior generally and the foolishness of her personae in particular, she is much like the Horace of the *Satires* and of F. P. A.'s imitations.[46] But *Enough Rope* remains an uneven collection throughout. Some poems are highly imitative of Housman (pp. 6, 26), Millay (pp. 11, 24, 29, 30), Eliot (p.32) and, even, medieval balladry (pp. 14, 49) and Herrick (p.89), although here too she supplies her own final signature (as in "Portrait of the Artist"). Her best work echoes Martial (pp. 25, 78, 83) with the forcefulness of childlike diction, masculine rhymes, and a strong reliance on nouns and active verbs. Her strange mixture of romantic and classic checks any wrong impulse or self-posturing aside from that of her persona, and supplies what Maugham calls her "many-sided humor, her irony, her sarcasm, her tenderness, her pathos"[47]—a stiff upper lip alongside haunting disappointment and implied recalculation ("One Perfect Rose"). As Genevieve Taggard has it,

This quaint, slightly cock-eyed world where men and women go around
making chest developing gestures in the direction of each other, colliding
like drunken electrons, apologizing ("So sorry!"), never looked more piti-
fully ridiculous through the lens of any poet's microscope than it does
through Dorothy Parker's. It is hard to tell how she gets her hard-bitten
comedy unless by the device of always correcting the way the specimen
looks by the evidence of how it feels—or vice versa. Mrs Parker has such a
corrective habit in her work . . .[that next to Millay, it is] whisky straight,
not champagne.[48]

Shrewd and fastidious, in modulated language and tight form, trenchant humor opposing clichéd love conventions surprises, engages,
and amuses us, as in "Words of Comfrot to be Scratched on a Mirror
in Part II:

> Helen of Troy had a wandering glance;
> Sappho's restriction was only the sky;
> Ninon was ever the chatter of France;
> But oh, what a good girl am I! (p. 83)

In the best of this book, Dorothy Parker is already the most accomplished classical epigrammatist of her time.

c.   Sunset Gun: *"Authors and actors and artists and such"*

The unprecedented success of *Enough Rope* made critics and
reviewers in popular journals more cautious in reviewing Dorothy
Parker's second volume of poetry, published two years later, 1928.
Nearly all of them sought characteristics to praise, as if the *consen-
sus gentium* took on inviolable authority; so the reservation of the
critic for the *New York Times* is worth remembering.

In these verses [of *Enough Rope*] perfected with simplicity of words and
fine craftsmanship—there is more than facility—there is an outspoken
manner that explodes pretense sharply and turns its sorrow into mordant
wit.
   Sunset Gun has the same exuberant vitality. And again there is the
tinctured mixture of the sad and the gay, suggesting that it is better to laugh
than cry. And if one may be pardoned such ungallantry—the girl grows
older—a mature note of intensity is apparent in her lyric note. She does not
now have to depend on the last line reverse twist for effectiveness. Happily,
this is being acquired without losing the gem-like sparkle of her verse.
Perhaps the most attractive thing of all is her puckish fighting spirit.[49]

"The poems are lean and quick as a snake," Garreta Busey added.[50]

The book was originally called *Songs for the Nearest Harmonica* but upon publication it appeared with another funereal title. *Sunset Gun*[51] was dedicated simply "To John," a current admirer (perhaps John Farrar) who, noted one friend, was replaced by another "John" while the book was in press. It, too, sold for two dollars.

Sunset Gun shows Dorothy Parker's attempt to expand the brief epigrammatic form by cycles of poems ("A Pig's-Eye View of Literature [pp. 30–32], "Verses in the Night"[pp. 57–59]), but except for these, often forced, there is only one poor poem ("For R. C. B.," p. 23), for Benchley, which she later omitted from her collected poems. Occasionally, poems here seem easy or imitative ("There Was One" [p. 24], "Frustration" [p. 53]) but there is also the stronger, more successful influence of Housman.

> New love, new love, where are you to lead me?
> *All along a narrow way that marks a crooked line.*
> How are you to slake me, and how are you to feed me?
> *With bitter yellow berries, and a sharp new wine.*
> New love, new love, shall I be forsaken?
> *One shall go a-wandering, and one of us must sigh.*
> Sweet it is to slumber, but how shall we awaken—
> Whose will be the broken heart, when dawn comes by?
>
> ("The Last Question," p. 66)

Other Roman echoes can be found in "The Trusting Heart" (p. 37), "The Gentlest Lady" (p. 39), "Afternoon" (p. 46), "The Whistling Girl" (p. 51), "Landscape" (p. 55), and the impressive "Liebestod" (p. 60). Still other poems look back to Millay and capture, better than elsewhere in Dorothy's poetry, the gaiety of the Twenties ("On Cheating the Fiddler" [p. 26], "Pour Prendre Congé" [p. 71]).

But the best poems in the book still mine the epigrammatic tradition of Martial, still locate tonal purity and economic wit. Here she shows considerable advance in her ability to energize a tired proverb and to pack into a quatrain level upon level of potential meanings all available to any careful reader. One such example is "Thought for a Sunshiny Morning" (p. 38); a similar poem, "Daylight Savings," conflates Roman form with the Elizabethan theme of the union of poetry and immortality, itself an allusion to the classical concept of art, in which small social acts become metaphorical indicators without surrendering their initial concrete signification (p. 42). Poems such as "Post-Graduate," for all their simplicity, still have this impacted quality:

> Hope it was that tutored me,
>   And Love that taught me more;
> And now I learn at Sorrow's knee
>   The self-same lore. (p. 56)

"Superfluous Advice" (p. 67) and "But Not Forgotten" (p. 69) are similar achievements: "penning a tract against self-pity, cant, and affectation, and at the same time taking a kind of Pharisaical delight in putting herself on the perverse side of the text" as Henry Morton Robinson has it in *The Bookman*.[52]

Moreover, Dorothy Parker varies the basis of her irony. She still relies on reversal ("Surprise" [p. 43]), but more and more she employs irony of situation ("Penelope" [p. 34]) and irony of condition ("Wisdom" [p. 74]). In poems of dazzling simplicity, she manages to imply allusions ("Two-Volume Novel" [p. 70]); even the eternal battle of the sexes is rendered as openly metaphorical ("The Second Oldest Story" [p. 29], "Mortal Enemy" [p. 33], "Dilemma" [p. 63]). Her new ability to jam philosophy, attitude, and judgment into foreshortened space, the maturing wit that enables her to condense coordinates of time into reckless and yet provocative juxtapositions may be seen here in one of the best poems she ever wrote, "Partial Comfort":

> Whose love is given over-well
> Shall look on Helen's face in hell,
> Whilst they whose love is thin and wise
> May view John Knox in paradise, (p. 14)

where a review of the lines shows how evenly balanced the choice is between "Helen" and "Knox," "over-well" and "wise." Read sardonically, the poem supports paganism; read meditatively, it supports individual conscience (Methodism). When we admit the variety of tonalities that the simple quatrain permits, it becomes almost impossibly equivocal in its twin condemnations.

Such expanding linguistic powers she appears to examine in "For a Lady Who Must Write Verse," perhaps her own credo.

> . . . Show your quick, alarming skill in
> Tidy mockeries of art;
> Never, never dip your quill in
> Ink that rushes from your heart. . . .
> Never print, poor child, a lay on
> Love and years and anguishing,
> Lest a cooled, benignant Phaon
> Murmur, "Silly little thing! " (p. 72)

Such deliberate caution, such quickening critical intelligence is especially necessary in a book that attempts, for the first time in any significant way, autobiographical poetry. "Bohemia" works because of the wise-cracking bravado of the earlier "Resumé":

> Authors and actors and artists and such
> Never know nothing, and never know much.
> Sculptors and singers and those of their kidney
> Tell their affairs from Seattle to Sydney.
> Playwrights and poets and such horses' necks
> Start off from anywhere, end up at sex.
> Diarists, critics, and similar roe
> Never say nothing, and never say no.
> People Who Do Things exceed my endurance;
> God, for a man that solicits insurance! (p. 35)

The governing pun on "insurance"—that which provides stability and hedges against future uncertainties, opposed to that which locks one into business so that life goes out of "soliciting" in its original sense—has a kind of quick sing-song rhythm that parcels out lines like a businessman, even as it frolics more for amusement than instruction. Whichever way we take the poem, we cannot be so simple about it as the persona who speaks the final line.

This kind of autobiography-as-metaphor always works for Dorothy Parker. Riskier, and less often successful, is the "serious" Dorothy Parker who ventures the sonnet form in "A Dream Lies Dead."

> A dream lies dead here. May you softly go
> Before this place, and turn away your eyes,
> Nor seek to know the look of that which dies
> Importuning Life for life. Walk not in woe,
> But, for a little, let your step be slow.
> And, of your mercy, be not sweetly wise

> With words of hope and Spring and tenderer skies.
> A dream lies dead; and this all mourners know. (p. 47)

The new, quietly lyrical, even mournful tone is still the product of a rueful surrender to the transient, even the unreachable, quality of happiness. There remains a fundamental skepticism of love's permanence, and so a residual resistance against idealistic notions of endurance. *Sunset Gun* begins to reveal in Dorothy Parker's poetry an unstated conflict in loyalty between the disappointing truths of love's experience and an apprehension of, for all time, man's inherent folly.

d. Death and Taxes: *"Where I may look, the frosted peaks are spun"*

Death and Taxes, Dorothy Parker's third volume of poetry, was named for our only certainties. Published in 1931 by a new publisher (Viking), the book is dedicated, at last, "To Mr. Benchley."

Reviewing *Death and Taxes* in the *Saturday Review of Literature*, Henry Seidel Canby remarked that

one should quote Latin rather than English to parallel the edged fineness of Dorothy Parker's verse. This belle dame sans merci has the ruthlessness of the great tragic lyricists whose work was allegorized in the fable of the nightingale singing with her breast against a thorn. It is disillusion recollected in tranquillity where the imagination has at last controlled the emotions. It comes out clear, and with the authentic sparkle of a great vintage . . . there is no frailty in her poetry, and its brevity is in space not in time. [53]

Raymond Kresensky noted in the *Christian Century* that "it is a well known fact that often the court jester is a serious philosopher beneath his cap and bells"[54]; seeing the same dominance of seriousness, F. P. A. commented in *Books* that "In this new collection the painful hunger for beauty and the heartbreak of its impermanence, the uncompromising idealism, are even acuter than in her previous volumes. It is her saddest and her best book."[55] Elsewhere, comments were generally favorable.[56]

Once again, Dorothy Parker revised a number of poems that reappear here.[57] But she did not eliminate "wisecrack verses" that hearken back to her earlier contributions to *Life* and to the *Saturday Evening Post*, such as "Prologue to a Saga" (p. 61). This poem opens with a series of classical allusions that, in the forward march of chronology, are displaced in the second quatrain by medieval references. None of them, however, prepares us especially well for the last line: here the twist is fun for its slang and abruptness, but it is only a surprise; it does not reverberate, as good poetry always does. Other examples that seem a residue of her earlier moods and practices are "The Evening Primrose" (p. 17), "Salome's Dancing-Lesson" (p. 20), "Little Words" (p. 24), "Purposely Ungrammatical Love Song" (p. 49), and "The Danger of Writing Defiant Verse" (p. 14). She also enjoys an easy joke on Catullus ("From a Letter from Lesbia" [p. 48]) and still experiments with French verse forms ("Ballade of Unfortunate Mammals" [p. 46], "Ballade of a Talked-off Ear" [p. 56]).

But she has not in the process lost her ability to write fine epigrams. "The Flaw in Paganism," resembling Martial in form, borrows its theme from Horace and Juvenal:

> Drink and dance and laugh and lie,
> Love, the reeling midnight through,
> For tomorrow we shall die!
> (But, alas, we never do.) (p. 13)

"Distance" (p. 16) is something new—Housman's lexicon and spirit converted to the leanness characteristic of Martial—while "Sanctuary" returns again to an Horatian use of popular phrase.

> My land is bare of chattering folk;
> The clouds are low along the ridges,
> And sweet's the air with curly smoke
> From all my burning bridges. (p. 18)

Here our sense of plague or damnation in line 1 (a barren landscape) seems transformed by pleasant clouds (l. 2) when we learn that the clouds are not nature's doing, but the persona's; it is not really cloud but clouds of smoke which, in turn, cause a geographical barrenness that resembles the barren love affair, the persona now left behind. When Dorothy Parker so intertwines lines and vocabulary, her work is far superior to "Prologue to a Saga." "Cherry White" is also lapidary, adding the familiar Dorothy Parker corrosiveness.

> I never see that prettiest thing—
> A cherry bough gone white with Spring—

> But what I think, "How gay 'twould be
> To hang me from a flowering tree." (p. 19)

The macabre humor of the final line both lifts and depresses our spirits as we read it. "In the Meadow" (p. 37) is unusual for Dorothy Parker since it works almost exclusively through natural symbol; idea and mood are equally well compacted in "The Apple Tree" (p. 38). "Iseult of Brittany" realizes a deep psychological awareness of the fated medieval heroine: unlike Horace and Juvenal, who tend to portray types, Dorothy Parker's poem frees the tragedy and the individuality of Iseult from the books of courtly romance. Again in *Death and Taxes*, she displays her powers by writing a cycle of epigrams, "Tombstones in the Starlight" (pp. 26–31).

What is fundamentally new in *Death and Taxes*, however, is a note of lyricism. There are faint anticipations of it in the lively and witty "The Little Old Lady in Lavender Silk" (pp. 32–33) if we notice how the choric line informs the spirit of the poem throughout, but it takes its newer and more characteristically solemn tones in "Midnight" (p. 51) and in the satiric portrait of "Ninon de l'Enclos, on Her Last Birthday":

> So let me have the rouge again,
>   And comb my hair the curly way.
> The poor young men, the dear young men—
>   They'll all be here by noon today. . . .
> So bring my scarlet slippers, then,
>   And fetch the powder-puff to me.
> The dear young men, the poor young men—
>   They think I'm only seventy! (p. 52)

Quiet tone is married to classical simplicity in "Of a Woman, Dead Young: (J. H., 1905–1930)" (p. 54). Here the sentiment is so honest and moving that Dorothy Parker returns to *vers libre*, relying on assonance to do the work of her normally end-stopped lines and masculine rhymes; the whole effect is one of subdued but persistent bewilderment and admiration. This hushed tone, toward which the whole volume works, is heard also in "Prayer for a New Mother" (the Virgin Mary [p. 50]) and "Sonnet on an Alpine Night" (p. 58) which the *China Weekly Review* of Shanghai compared to a poem of Yang I (about 1000 A. D.): "Upon this tall pagoda's peak/My hand can nigh the stars enclose."[58]

But the consummate poem, as poem, opens the book. "Prayer for a Prayer" uses the quiet tone to introduce a meditative moment that merges life and death, time and eternity, memory and forgetfulness, purpose and purposelessness.

> Dearest one, when I am dead
>   Never seek to follow me.
>   Never mount the quiet hill
>   Where the copper leaves are still,
>   As my heart is, on the tree
> Standing at my narrow bed.
>
> Only, of your tenderness,
>   Pray a little prayer at night.
>   Say: "I have forgiven now—
>   I, so weak and sad; O Thou,
>   Wreathed in thunder, robed in light,
> Surely Thou wilt do no less" (p. 11).

The majesty and awe that prompt the final lines, reduced suddenly to the personal level, are neither mockery nor blasphemy, but work to bring to a still close a poem that opens with personal choice juxtaposed to the forces of nature; and "Prayer for a Prayer" becomes mercy for mercy instead of measure for measure. Here, as elsewhere in *Death and Taxes*, Dorothy Parker breaks new ground—not new to Millay and Wylie, but new to her—while maintaining the lucidity, simplicity, and economy that distinguish her epigrammatic wit. Anguish is more openly displayed here, death closer to the surfaces of life, the laughter more hidden and more brittle. The increased seriousness really signals the end of her poetry—for her concerns will be turned over now, and more directly, to prose essay and fiction; it is as if with *Death and Taxes* she is already anticipating her famous statement in the years ahead of her: "There is nothing funny in the world any more." ("Investigations: Where'd the Money Go?" *Newsweek*, March 7, 1955, p. 26.)

e. Not So Deep as a Well: *"a terrible sorrow along with the sight"*

By 1936, when Dorothy Parker's collected poetry was published under the title *Not So Deep as a Well*, she had married, moved to Hollywood, and given up most writing for political activities. *Not So Deep as a Well*—the title is from Mercutio's sardonic death speech in *Romeo and Juliet* (III, i, 97)[59]—reprints her three volumes of poetry, omitting only the least of her poems,[60] and adds five new ones: "Sight," "The Lady's Reward," "Prisoner," "Temps Perdu," and "Autumn Valentine." Although critics received the work well, they did so in terms of Dorothy Parker, Algonquin wit, as Louis Kronenberger remarked:

> One comes back to Mrs. Parker's light verse with the greatest pleasure; with its sharp wit, its clean bite, the perfectly conscious—and hence delightful—archness, it stands re-reading amply. Here her high technical polish has great virtue, sometimes cracking out a surprise effect with an absolute minimum of wind-up, sometimes achieving a foreseen effect by means so dexterous it is exhilarating to watch them. Mrs. Parker can extend anticlimax to irresistible bathos by altering the pitch of her language (from the high-flown to the highly colloquial) at the exact moment she alters her meaning. But what, of course, is more important is the sense of personality that converts what might otherwise be merely a witty idea into a dramatic, however cockeyed, situation; a sense of personality that gives us not cynicism in the abstract but laughter applied to an objective. There is no one else in Mrs. Parker's special field who can do half as much. I suspect that she will survive not only as the author of some first-rate light verse but also as a valuable footnote to the Twenties, out of whose slant on existence that light verse sprang.[61]

But the new poems are a product not so much of the Twenties as of Dorothy Parker's late serious poetry, of the early Thirties. Rather like "Prayer for a New Mother," grounded in a dramatic tension between the stated beliefs of natural motherhood and the implied countercurrent of Christianity founded in love that shocks us to new and deeper truths about humility and sacrifice, so these new works too start simply, traditionally, only to lead in new directions. Consider "Sight":

> Unseemly are the open eyes
>   That watch the midnight sheep,
> That look upon the secret skies
>   Nor close, abashed, in sleep;
> That see the dawn drag in, unbidden,
>   To birth another day—
> Oh, better far their gaze were hidden
>   Below the decent clay. (p. 198)

Here the ideas of Housman take on a more subdued tone, a more regretful attitude: Housman stoicism is displaced by Parker sympathy. "Autumn Valentine" (p. 202) sounds more like earlier poems, but it too ends with a sad (and unanswered) refrain. "Prisoner" demonstrates Dorothy Parker's continuing skill as epigrammatist.

> Long I fought the driving lists,
> Plume a-stream and armor clanging;
> Link on link, between my wrists,
> Now my heavy freedom's hanging. (p. 200)

Earlier end-stopped lines and full rhymes are reinforced by her later interests in assonance and consonance. Grief and death are given lingering and beguiling memorial in the appropriately titled "Temps Perdu" (p. 201) where the verse is harder than Millay's, more clipped than Wylie's, yet holds the same sad lyricism that characterizes their work.

"The wittiest woman of our time suddenly took on stature," William Rose Benêt said in response to *Not So Deep as a Well*;[62] although she remained, as always, neither too obscure nor too erudite, Dorothy Parker moves in her poetry from surprise and slapstick to memorable solemnity and memorably subdued tones. In the nexus of love and death that moved from the cocky response to the unrequited role women play in society to the deeper and richer awareness of death as impersonal, blind to distinctions of sex and customs of romance, she admits another kind of worldliness, reaches new audiences. We are reminded of Auden's lines—"Rummaging into his living, the poet fetches / The images out that hurt and connect." She finally sensed that, too, behind her Iseults and her Martials, behind Horace's satires and Catullus' love for Lesbia.

III Fiction: "Nothing comes easily"

In her profile of Hemingway for *The New Yorker* (November 30, 1929), Dorothy Parker observed that:

With the possible exception of Ring Lardner, he is less the literary character-part than any other author I have ever seen. Nothing is done about the thrill of creating, nor the need for expression, nor even the jolly good fun of spinning a yarn. He works like hell, and through it. Nothing comes easily to him; he struggles, sets down a word, scratches it out, and begins all over. He regards his art as hard and dirty work, with no hope of better conditions. ("The Artist's Reward," p. 29)

She was then writing her stories by hand before retyping them, two fingers at a time; "It takes me six months to do a story. I think it out and then write it sentence by sentence," she told Marion Capron; "I can't write five words but that I change seven."[63] So she may have seen herself in Hemingway and seen affinities in their work. "Seventy times he rewrote the concluding pages of A Farewell to Arms. He had no idea of ever being completely satisfied with them; he merely hoped that the words would eventually come nearer to his meaning" ("The Artist's Reward," p. 29). Accustomed as she was to the simplicity, purity, and economy of language from writing poetry, she transferred those values to her fiction. Since even her lyrical poetry was essentially dramatic, she made her fiction equally so, like Hemingway deleting background material so as to focus on voices that would reveal situations even as they exposed shallowness and hypocrisy. In foreshortening time and space, Dorothy Parker's stories have surface similarities to "slice-of-life" fiction, but the real emphasis more nearly resembles Joyce. Whether acts and the people who perceive them are substantial or trivial, her fiction deals with epiphanic moments of self-awareness or self-exposure (hence our awareness) so that her fiction takes on a modern cast.

a. Early Experiments: "Mrs. Parker—she talks enough for two"

Dorothy Parker's early stories reveal, as do her early verses, an evolving mastery of technique. "A Certain Lady" (NY, February 28, 1925), shows a middle class woman with upper class pretensions: "Although she lives as far from Park Avenue as it is possible to do and still keep out of Jersey, Mrs. Legion is cozily conversant of all the comings and goings, or what have you, of Avenue dwellers" (p. 15). The story seems indistinguishable from such essays as "Professional Youth" (SEP, April 28, 1923), but it is unique; other early work is almost exclusively in dialogue. "Oh, He's Charming!" (NY, February 16, 1925) dramatizes a woman anxious to meet the famous author Freeman Pawling, but when she does, she monopolizes the conversation, her gaucheries betraying her stupidity, the author's indulgences revealing his. The sketch is the prototype for "Travelogue" (NY, October 30, 1926), where the characters are a matronly clubwoman and a young traveler, and later, for "An Arrangement in Black and White." *(Laments for the Living*, p. 221–30.) "A Terrible Day Tomorrow" *(NY*, February 11, 1928) is considerably more subtle; in this story, a young man and woman visiting a speakeasy affect Bohemian conversation and attitudes. Although the girl is anxious to leave, her boyfriend plies her with drinks until alcohol undoes them both.

Attending the theater regularly, writing theater criticism, and lunching at the Algonquin with actors, producers, and playwrights, Dorothy was heavily influenced from the first by writing for the stage. Nowhere is this clearer than in her monologues. Based on stock situations in which the monologuist is somehow victimized—as the girl in "The Waltz" *(After Such Pleasures*, pp. 97–106) is forced to dance with a poor dancer or not dance at all—these stories use interior consciousnesses, occasionally interrupting into speech, to imply a completed story. Dialogue is often alluded to, although the story itself is done in a single voice, the satire stemming in part from the monotonous quality of the isolated and deceived perception of the narrator. "The Garter" *(NY*, September 8, 1928) uses as the stock situation a woman whose garter snaps at a party; the gimmick is that the protagonist is named Dorothy Parker. As these situations are formulaic, so her language and sentiments in such stories are trite; much of the satire is grounded in a character thinking how unique—and how alone—she is, while the author Dorothy Parker embalms her in clichés. "But the One on the Right—" *(NY*, October 19, 1929) follows the same format, using as the stock situation a woman seated between a poor conversationalist and one who pays no attention to her at a dinner party, Enacted, such a story could be a script for a revue like *No, Sirree!*

The same germ for a story—that irony is present when one shallow person condemns another—also lies behind later, more sophisticated stories. In "Advice to the Little Peyton Girl" *(HB*, February 1933), Sylvie seeks Miss Marion's advice about a boyfriend who has left her because she is too spoiled, ignorant, and demanding. She accepts Miss Marion's insults; after Sylvie leaves, Miss Marion calls *her* lover, revealing herself as Sylvie's double. Duplication through parallel situations amused Dorothy; "Mrs. Carrington and Mrs. Crane" *(NY*, July 15, 1933) is a dialogue of two women who criticize their friends while inwardly imitating them; as the story unfolds, they also begin imitating each other. At first surprising is "The Road

Home" (NY, September 16, 1933) in which the young lovers driving home after a party quarrel and then make up. We do not expect reconciliation in Dorothy's stories until we realize that their temporary pact of peace is precisely analogous to the conclusions of other stories—to the woman who agrees to have a man fix her garter, to the clubwoman's plan to visit the world traveler, to the affected Bohemians drinking. Ironically, the coming together is only temporary.

All these stories, then, chart the same course; by such a formula we are to know them. On the one hand, they affect sophistication, while nevertheless displaying the manners of the "booboisie." We may think them silly now; but we must realize they were prevalent then. The bohemian style following World War I fit awkwardly on a Puritan society such as ours, but many who would be smart or fashionable failed to witness in others their own affectations. Dorothy Parker had a superb eye and ear: she saw in the sweep of their gestures and the vacuity of their conversations apt significations of the hollowness of their values and the emptiness of their spirits. Drawing on the colloquial speech she had used in light verse and prose for *Life*, she writes similar fiction, repeatedly showing us, by the disjunction of intention and performance, numerous acts of self-exposure. Such use of the ignorant narrator was not then new, but embodying in that ignorance the values and practices of her own readers, Dorothy Parker's broader and more acid criticism was. That kind of barbed satire is both incisive and subtle.

In the same period she was writing to so predictable a pattern, however, Dorothy Parker also wrote one of her half-dozen best stories. "Such a Pretty Little Picture" (*The Smart Set*, December 1922), tells the story of a dead marriage, the truth of which unwinds first through a distant objective narration, then the wife's blind conversation and habit, and finally by the inner thoughts of the husband. His daydream shows (well before Walter Mitty) how frustrated and lonely he is, routinely clipping his hedge each week.

> It was about a man who lived in a suburb. Every morning he had gone to the city on the 8:12, sitting in the same seat in the same car, and every evening he had gone home to his wife on the 5:17, sitting in the same seat in the same car. He had done this for twenty years of his life. And then one night he didn't come home. He never went back to his office any more. He just never turned up again. (pp. 75–76)

This fond and foolish fable emphasizes the depressed, hopeless condition of Mr. Wheelock's life. Its drab and static quality, signified in his name, is the subject of his realization; his final decision to resign himself is the subject of the story. It is sympathetically told; Dorothy Parker saves her irony for Mr. Wheelock's wife, child, and neighbors, who think of the Wheelock marriage as conventional and hence ideal. No story of its day surpasses this in recounting the common tragedy of the common man.

b. *Fictive Considerations: "a window and a record"*

"I am an intemperate admirer of short stories," Dorothy Parker wrote in the June 1962 issue of *Esquire*.[64] She reserves her highest praise for this form in her literary criticism; it is defined in the anthology *Short Story*, which she edited with Frederick B. Shroyer:

A short story . . . is always about something: usually about people or objects (which ultimately say something about people); it always entails conflict of one sort or another (and some of the greatest conflicts are decided by mute artillery within the skull, and not with guns and knives); and it invariably says something about universal problems as well as about its characters.[65]

Short fiction is accomplished by restricting either the compass of the subject or the manner of presentation, or both. Dorothy Parker usually limits her focus by a single scene, the single perspective of an unreliable, innocent, or ignorant narrator, and the insinuation of background detail. As with her poetry, she uses dramatic narration to economize space and maximize effect; she does not identify herself with the narration, however, since she means to tell her stories ironically: her own perception is thus deeper and clearer than the narrator's. Her stories are occasionally dramatic in their unfolding ("Big Blonde" [*Laments for the Living*, pp. 169–217], "Here We Are" [*After Such Pleasures*, pp. 37–55]) but, more often, they are static—the change occurs not in character or circumstance but in the reader's awareness of what the author is really signifying. Whether she is writing soliloquy, monologue (this implies a second voice), or narration, she resorts, as in her poetry, to hyperbolic action or remark, repetition, parallelsm, clichéd diction, and extravagant tone in order to convey to the reader a meaning somewhat different from that understood by her characters. Her scenes may be scenes

of action, but they are more likely to be chains of dialogue that
center around a trivial detail. Little elements—a snapped garter,
clipping the hedge, false consent—dovetail into mockery of the
mediocre, allowing us to understand and analyze both the subtlety
and the acerbity of Dorothy Parker's fictional satires. We must learn
to distrust the proud or spiteful misjudgments of her characters.
Because Dorothy Parker carefully observes accuracy of nuance and
precision of detail, her contracted space is, therefore, perhaps the
most misleading thing about her fiction.

Dorothy Parker's practices are similar to Hemingway's, whose
early short fiction she read with great admiration, and her practices
anticipate his remarks in *Green Hills of Africa* (1935) as well as
Shroyer's and her own in *Short Story*:

> A good short story . . . is the product of craft and intelligence. . . .[A]
> good story is much "longer" than its wordage. . . . A short story is some-
> what like an iceberg; the mass of ice seen above the water is much smaller
> than that which is submerged and which supports it. The author before and
> in process of writing his story has ranged much further across the lives of his
> characters than his story permits him to cover explicitly. The finished story
> is supported by this unseen but massive intellectual and emotional in-
> volvement on the part of the author. This is the relationship that the reader
> feels when he reads a short story and senses that he knows more about its
> people and their world than the author has told him directly. (p. vii)

The "iceberg theory" is Hemingway's, and it is instructive to compare his early fiction with Dorothy Parker's.

Take Hemingway's first collection, *In Our Time* (1925). The fight
over who owns certain logs in "The Doctor and the Doctor's Wife"
stands, as cleaning the rifle does, as a synecdoche for the doctor's
character and for the strain on his marriage. The catalogue of details
in the final two paragraphs of "A Very Short Story" shows (but does
not tell) the ending of a love affair, conveys all its pathos. Central to
the meaning of "Big Two–Hearted River: Part I" is the analogy
between the loss of Hopkins and the death of the mosquito; the
ritual of cooking in "Part II" is an act of willful blindness, to put out
of mind other things. These last two stories use analogy and ritual as
Dorothy Parker uses them in "The Banquet of Crow" (*NY*, December 14, 1957) and "Song of the Shirt, 1941" (*The Viking Portable
Dorothy Parker*, pp. 99–109), while Mr. Wheelock is as successful in

clipping his hedge as the doctor is in cleaning his rifle as a means to submerge present realities.

In a review of *Men Without Women* (1927) called "A Book of Great Short Stories" (*NY*, October 29, 1927), Dorothy Parker commended Hemingway's "clean, exciting prose" and noted "this prose, stripped to its firm young bones, is far more moving, in the short story than in the novel" (p. 92). She called his story of a couple nervously discussing a coming abortion ("Hills Like White Elephants") "delicate and tragic"; later she would write one similar in its nervousness but gayer in tone ("Here We Are"). In "Ten Indians," Nick's unusual interest in Prudie leads to our growing awareness of his romance with a young Indian girl, just as the accretion of various viewpoints in Dorothy Parker's "The Banquet of Crow" leads to our knowledge of the impossibility for a separated couple of achieving any reconciliation.

Dorothy Parker doubtless owes something, too, to her friend Scott Fitzgerald's use of setting and to his ability to choose details that will at once reveal and satirize his characters. In "A Woman with a Past" (1930), from *Taps at Reveille* (1935), we find an opening that resembles Dorothy Parker especially well.

This was New Haven—city of her adolescent dreams, of glittering proms where she would move on air among men as intangible as the tunes they danced to. City sacred as Mecca, shining as Paris, hidden as Timbuktu. Twice a year the life-blood of Chicago, her home, flowed into it, and twice a year flowed back, bringing Christmas or bringing summer. Bingo, bingo, bingo, that's the lingo; love of mine, I pine for one of your glances; the darling boy on the left there; underneath the stars I wait.[66]

The beginning of "The Ice Palace", from *Flappers and Philosophers* (1920), is also similar, as is the description of the library in Part III. Other analogous passages, where Fitzgerald's minute cataloguing of setting and manners turns them into metaphor, may be found in the opening of Parts I and II of "Bernice Bobs Her Hair" (1920) and in the opening of Part II of "May Day" (1922) which has strong resemblances to Dorothy Parker's "The Standard of Living" (*The Portable Dorothy Parker*, pp. 29–34). In both Hemingway and Fitzgerald, Dorothy Parker found what she later praised in Thurber: "Superbly he slaps aside preliminaries. He gives you a glimpse of the startling present and lets you go constuct the astounding past."[67]

Dorothy Parker also drew on the Ring Lardner of *Round-Up*.[68] She wrote of Lardner's book, in the review "Hero-Worship":

It is difficult to review these spare and beautiful stories; it would be difficult to review the Gettysburg address. What more are you going to say of a great thing than that it is great? You could, I suppose, speak of Ring Lardner's unparalleled ear and eye, his strange, bitter pity, his utter sureness of characterization, his unceasing investigation, his beautiful economy. (*NY*, April 27, 1929, p. 106)

From Lardner, Dorothy Parker learned more about using cliché and slang, the unreliable narrator, and the naive point of view (as in "Haircut"[1929]). Lardner too works with character sketches, monologues, and bits of dialogue; "Women" (1929), in which Healy complains women have ruined his career until he has his next chance to fall for one, could have been written by Dorothy Parker, and Lardner's "Zone of Quiet" has great likenesses to her "Lady with a Lamp."

"Isn't it a scream?" said Miss Lyons. "But it's true; that is, it's been true lately. The last five cases I've been on has all died. Of course it's just luck, but the girls have been kidding me about it and calling me a jinx, and when Miss Halsey saw me here the evening of the day you was operated, she said, 'God help him!' That's the night floor nurse's name. But you're going to be mean and live through it and spoil my record, aren't you? I'm just kidding. Of course I want you to get all right."[69]

Gilbert Seldes has praised Lardner for "the swift, destructive, and tremendously funny turn of phrase, the hard and resistant mind, the gaiety of spirit which have made him a humorist";[70] his special combination of sympathy and irony allows him to embody virtue and burlesque at the same time in the middle class characters he describes and ridicules. The quarrel and its resolution in "The Golden Honeymoon," one of Lardner's best-known stories, uses the same pattern and presentation as much of Dorothy Parker's work; for like her, he is highly conscious of personality types. "A Day with Conrad Green" is fundamentally analogous to Dorothy's "Little Curtis" (*Laments for the Living*, pp. 125–53) and the themes of "The Love Nest" to "Such a Pretty Little Picture." A common concern, the pathetic lack of communication between people, is the subject of

Lardner's "Anniversary" and Dorothy's "Mr. Durant" (*Laments for the Living*, pp. 15–39). For both writers, communication is frustrated because, although their characters talk excessively, they are always too preoccupied with themselves. Even their best stories are analogous. Midge Kelly, the "Champion" who ruthlessly uses everyone in his anxious climb to the top in prizefighting is the inverse of Hazel Morse, the "Big Blonde," who exists only to be used by everyone she meets: as Lardner uses the sports world as a microcosm of the larger society, so Dorothy concentrates on the relations between the sexes for figuring human relationships generally. His later stories, like hers, turn much darker.[71]

"First there must be talent, much talent," Hemingway proposes in *Green Hills of Africa*.

Then there must be discipline. The discipline of Flaubert. Then there must be the conception of what it can be and an absolute conscience as unchanging as the standard meter in Paris, to prevent faking. Then the writer must be intelligent and disinterested and above all he must survive. Try to get all these in one person and have him come through all the influences that press on a writer. The hardest thing, because time is so short, is for him to survive and get his work done. But I would like us to have such a writer and to read what he would write.[72]

Dorothy was not totally disinterested, but surviving for her, and for Frederick Shroyer, too, meant living; and living was the other necessary coordinate. "We believe that a good short story is both a window into a segment of the human experience and an interpretive record of it by one who has either lived it himself or who has somehow understood and experienced it vicariously" (*Short Story*, pp. vii–viii).

Frederick J. Hoffman has argued that the 1920s were a period when ideas and abstractions not tested and verified by personal experience were dismissed as a basis for art,[73] and surely Hemingway made every effort to live a full life and to record his past—in Michigan, Paris, Africa, Spain, and Cuba. In these terms, Lardner's problems with alcoholism and his story "Cured!" might be placed alongside Dorothy Parker's alcoholism and "Big Blonde." Like both men, Dorothy Parker persistently turned to anecdotes she observed or lived for much of the material of her mature fiction.[74]

c. Laments for the Living: *"They hate you whenever you say anything like that"*

In his review of *Laments for the Living* (New York, 1930),
Dorothy Parker's first collection of sketches and stories, T. S. Matthews observed in the *New Republic* for September 17, 1930, that
she was motivated to making an indictment of the human race.

> Dorothy Parker is an able prosecutor, and one who knows the limitations
> of her case. No one could write with such unhappy wit, no one could
> manage such a savage humor, who did not feel herself a blood sister to her
> victims, who did not also regard them as a pernicious race of odious little
> vermin. Dorothy Parker is very much of our day: the thrust of her wit is apt
> to tickle as it wounds; her most sympathetic gesture always has some horror
> in it.[75]

This collection of thirteen pieces, published by Viking and dedicated to Adele Quartley Lovett, wife of the banker Robert Lovett
and a close friend at the time, is uneven, containing some of
Dorothy Parker's more popular but lesser stories as well as some of
her best. Some remind us of her early, experimental fiction.
"Dialogue at Three in the Morning" (pp. 233–37), between "the
woman in the petunia-colored hat" (p. 233) and "the man with the
ice-blue hair" (p. 233), is the angry, trivial monologue of a woman
who feels she is being jilted and a man who wishes to apologize but
gets no opportunity: its chief technique is repetition; its end, our
boredom, paralleling the boredom of the characters. "The Mantle of
Whistler" (pp. 93–98) is representative flapper dialogue between a
couple who have just met at a party. "You Were Perfectly Fine" (pp.
115–22) unravels the night before as a woman helps her companion
recall some of the stunts he performed when drunk; the irony of the
title builds as referents to it multiply. "Just a Little One" (pp. 43–51)
is another study in jealousy—as the couple converse in a speakeasy
dark as Mammoth Cave, the woman gets more and more drunk; on
the way home she asks for a little horse as she had spent the evening
asking for little drinks. "New York to Detroit" (pp. 55–62), in which
an estranged couple discuss their separation, uses a bad telephone
connection to insinuate their own faltering relationship. And "Arrangement in Black and White" (pp. 221–30), although quite daring
for its time, follows the familiar Parker outlines, the woman anxious
to display her tolerance by talking to the colored Walter Williams
and finally overcome by her ability to shock her husband Burton in

reporting what she has done. In all of these, the situation is clear nearly at once, and thus the irony is heavy and the satire blunt.

"Mr. Durant" parallels a man's cruelty to his secretary, Rose, whose affair with him ends in an abortion he will only partly pay for, and to his children, whose dog he intends to be rid of as soon as they are in bed. Yet his coldness is not the subject so much as the cause of his coldness: his need for order and discipline. His inability to live naturally—to enjoy his family and their pet—is thus symbolized in his willingness to kill the foetus he has helped to produce. Dorothy Parker shows no shred of sympathy in this story—she achieves the distancing Hemingway asked for—but she has a fine sensitivity in "The Sexes" (pp. 3–12) and "The Last Tea" (pp. 157–65). In the former, a young man is puzzled and spiritually defeated by the unreasonable jealousy of his date; in the course of his manly attempt at reconciliation, he finds himself falling to her standards. "The Last Tea," narrating the breakup of a romance at which both parties interrupt each other to express the demands on them by other dates, works surprisingly well because their clichés cover up not so much their shallowness as the impasse between them; what each fights to maintain is not so much reputation as self-respect. "A Telephone Call" (pp. 101–12), one of Dorothy Parker's most anthologized works, is an overextended analysis of despair in which repetition throws our attention, along with the character's, to a temporary dodging of the self where frequent references to God display the hollowness of the secular catechism for not receiving a call.

Three stories in *Laments for the Living* are full and, in distinct ways, moving. "The Wonderful Old Gentleman" (pp. 65–90) shows the parasitic nature of humanity; two daughters and a son-in-law share differing responses to an old man's imminent death. He is staying with the Bains, whom he has milked without cause throughout his life; the barrenness of their existence is revealed in the description of their dark, uncomfortable furnishings. The analogy to the meanness and squalor of the Bains' lives is obvious and offset only by the refined dress of Mrs. Whittaker, whose sorrow is mere ritual. The Bains come to realize that they have been used and so temper their grieving. The story thus studies the variations of funereal sorrow, the irony inherent in the slow revelation of the Bains' exploitation succeeded, in the final lines, by the blatant unconcern of Mrs. Whittaker.

We can see Dorothy Parker's use of social detail—reminiscent of

Fitzgerald—in the opening of "Little Curtis," but what seems at first too elaborate, with its shaggy-dog ending, is only the story's premise, for Mrs. Matson continues to apply the same polished surface to her treatment of people, her staff, and her friends (where, at a party, she presents cheap favors), as to her adopted son Little Curtis. As the story proceeds, our own indignation mounts: Mrs. Matson's activities change from the trivial to the significant, but her manner is immobile, impervious to change. Yet it is Little Curtis himself, deprived of her love and his playmates, who saves himself: by laughing at one of Mrs. Matson's friends with a speaking-horn, he exposes the Matsons' total reliance on ritual. Only Mrs. Kerley's clichés—the verbal equivalent of Mrs. Matson's behavior—restores an artificial equilibrium to the Matsons' hollow household.

All of these stories gain strength through their concentration. Yet Dorothy Parker's best story, "Big Blonde," is astonishingly panoramic. In its portrait of the birth and growth of alcoholism and suicidal despair and in its clinical analysis, painfully detailed and piercingly accurate, we have an unrelenting study of the possible brutality of life. Despite the breadth of time, the sharp focus on Hazel Morse is close and steady.

From the start, Hazel Morse finds no advantage in living. She never knew the pleasure of family; her later popularity is artificial. But she has no distorted sense of herself; she is willing to settle for Herbie Morse to gain some security and stability. Herbie leads Hazel to alcohol, which in turn produces tenderness, self-pity, "misty melancholies" (p. 175). Herbie finally leaves her, despising himself, despising him in her, and she becomes a partygirl.

Hazel Morse is mirrored in her husband, the speakeasies, her lovers, and finally, the maid, yet all these painful doublings are not nearly so pathetic as the comparison Dorothy Parker makes between Hazel and a wretched horse nor as tragic as Hazel Morse looking at herself in an actual mirror when taking veronal. Here, at the moment of suicide, the best she can manage is a bad joke: " 'Gee, I'm nearly dead, . . . That's a hot one!' " (p. 207).

But that is not the end of Hazel Morse. As she survived desertion by her husband and subsequent lovers, so she survives the deadly poison: her punishment is to remain alive amidst the squalor of the poor and unfortunate yearning to breathe free. Yet what survives is at best what we see when Hazel Morse, drugged, is at greatest peace with herself.

Mrs. Morse lay on her back, one flabby, white arm flung up, the wrist against her forehead. Her stiff hair hung untenderly along her face. The bed covers were pushed down, exposing a deep square of soft neck and a pink nightgown, its fabric worn uneven by many launderings; her great breasts, freed from their tight confiner, sagged beneath her arm-pits. Now and then she made knotted, snorting sounds, and from the corner of her opened mouth to the blurred turn of her jaw ran a lane of crusted spittle. (p. 208)

The spittle doubtless descends from her prototype, the suicidal Emma Bovary, from whose mouth at death trickles black bile; but Emma leaves a respectable husband, a doctor, and their daughter. Hazel lives, and has no one. She remains, at story's close, symbolically in a bed, a bottle close at hand—and no more pills. In the depth of its felt understandings, the severity of its detail, and the economy of its presentation, "Big Blonde," O. Henry Prizewinner as the Best American Short Story of 1929, has the beauty of bones stripped bare of artifice and detail, clean with truth.

d.   After Such Pleasures: *"the product of craft and intelligence"*

Dorothy Parker's second volume of fiction (New York, 1933) *After Such Pleasures,* was dedicated to Ellen and Philip Barry; its title is from John Donne's "Farewell to Love": "Ah cannot wee, / As well as cocks and lyons jocund be,/ After such pleasures?" (title page). Edmund Wilson was excited by it. "Dorothy Parker's new book has seemed to me amazingly good," he wrote Louise Bogan on December 12, 1933, "particularly the last story ["Glory in the Daytime"]. You should read it, if you haven't—I'll send you my borrowed copy, if you'll promise to send it back."[76]

The anonymous reviewer for *The Nation* had a more measured tone; he liked the book, but sensed that Dorothy Parker's pathos might be the consequence of romanticism and result in sentimentality.

She is the disillusioned romantic who can turn her disillusionment into biting understatement, into a damning likeness of what is boring and trivial. . . . But she is an authentic wit and an excellent satirist and she is just enough surprised to find that love descends to boredom to make her description of it passionate as well as pointed.[77]

Dorothy Parker's authentic wit is found in her soliloquies, five of which are included here. Her most widely performed piece, "The

Waltz" (pp. 97–106) is so sharply caustic that we forget the stereotyped situation it elaborates (and forget having ourselves been in it). What holds our attention is the everfertile imagination of the speaker in thinking of ways to be ironic about herself, so as not to rec· ꞵ nize her own joy in the dance. Equally well done, with its precisely chiseled tone and its rhythmic choric phrases, is "From the Diary of a New York Lady" (pp. 85–93).

> *Monday.* Breakfast tray about eleven; didn't want it. The champagne at the Amorys' last night was *too* revolting, but what *can* you do? You can't stay until five o'clock on just *nothing.* They had those *divine* Hungarian musicians in the green coats, and Stewie Hunter took off one of his shoes and led them with it, and it *couldn't* have been funnier. (p. 85)

It couldn't have been funnier partly because Stewie Hunter was her date and, as the week is reviewed, we learn her only date although always her last resort. She is, then, cheering herself up. But the way she usually cheers herself up is to consider how common others are in a trite language that ironically reveals her own commonness. Her week unwinds in a kind of wild dervish, its frenzy mounting because she cannot break loose from what is, in the end, conventional, dreary, and imprisoning. Her language reveals manners that redefine "lady," and while the narrator commiserates with herself, her narration shows us why her husband ignores her: as usual with Dorothy Parker, two stories unfold simultaneously, establishing distance and irony. This story may have a particular source in "Extracts From a Secretary's Diary" by L. L. Jones, published in *Vanity Fair* for October 1918 (or that may be her pseudonym): the format and even occasional prose rhythms are precisely analogous. Other sketches in *After Such Pleasures* are "The Little Hours," the complaint of an insomniac that is somewhat less amusing, where again the protagonist is named Dorothy; "Sentiment" (pp. 157–67), the memories of a girl who takes a taxi past haunts she had once shared with a past love and that ends, suddenly, with a gimmick, a misplaced memory; and "Lady with a Lamp" (pp. 185–200), a monologue by a rival to the sick Mona who delights in telling Mona indirectly that her boyfriend has left her. In all five of these works, Dorothy Parker reapplies her successful formula of exposing shallowness and hypocrisy by carefully selected detail, but her patterns of development are now so well established that we delight in these stories only because of the vitality and humor of her style.

Yet fuller stories that evolve out of dialogue can also become painfully obvious. "Dusk before Fireworks" (pp. 109–40) is at first amusing, because the girl who pretends she will never be jealous again is so foolishly certain of herself. Her accusations against such other women as Evie Maynard redound on her, but she is as oblivious to this as she is to her own weakness (her possessiveness) and her own stupidity (in misunderstanding the function of the phone calls). "A Young Woman in Green Lace" (pp. 171–81) just back from France and trying to impress a man at a customary party of a friend, has an even more fragile base—the woman does not know that the color green suggests not only fertility but (as with the green sleeves of the Middle Ages) prostitution.

More effort is expended in the writing, and more is gained, in "Glory in the Daytime" (pp. 203–32) "Horsie" (pp. 3–34), and "Too Bad" (pp. 59–81). The drama in the first of these inheres in the juxtaposed varieties of love: Mrs. Murdock's girlish adoration of a great actress; Mrs. Noyes' lesbian relationship with the actress; and Miss Wynton herself, filled only with self-love. Ironic distance is maintained, since the story is related through the myopic vision of little Mrs. Murdock, the fan, yet we share her joy if not her naiveté. Caught in the mood of celebration, she does not recognize that Mr. Murdock's derisive name for Mrs. Noyes—he calls her "Hank," not "Hallie"—shows that he knows her for what she truly is. "Horsie" is likewise the story of an average woman, who as a home nurse for a well-to-do family enters into a magical time and into a fairyland of her own. She is called "Horsie" by the husband because of her facial features and his final gifts to her—some flowers and a taxi ride home ending the good meals, the recognition, and the escape from her usual dull life—are his cruel joke. But Miss Wilmarth rises above this because she takes a genuine pleasure in his gifts, and her joy highlights the callousness of the Crugers for trying to make a joke of her. Even through her sentiment, Dorothy Parker could wage satiric battle.

"Too Bad" details the death of yet another marriage, seen from several perspectives as a basis for our own all-embracing view. The routines of Mr. and Mrs. Weldon are disagreeable to each other, but they do not even tell each other this: they no longer share anything. They are puzzled at what has happened to their marriage, but genuine caring left it long ago. Dorothy Parker achieves a superbly realized analysis of what can go wrong in such marriages with the kind of detail Fitzgerald might employ, the diction of Lardner, the selectivity and understatement of Hemingway. But there is, in addition, her own special irony. It is obtained here by framing the exposure of the Weldons—again an ironic name—with the vacuous analysis of two neighbors. Mrs. Ames and Mrs. Marshall try to understand the separation of their "friends," but in doing so only reveal their own superficial standards. They lack any deep understanding of the Weldons, as the Weldons did, finally, of each other.

The only story in this volume superior to "Too Bad" is "Here We Are"—superior because of the lightness of touch by which it reveals the longings, fears, and hesitations, the desires, joys, and expectations that together describe the wedding night. If the bride pays more attention to herself than her husband does to himself here— for he has the greater passion—they both quarrel out of shared nervousness. They mean to be truly wed before the night is out, to make the night memorable despite their fears.

> "Look at us—we're on our honeymoon. Pretty soon we'll be regular old married people. I mean. I mean, in a few minutes we'll be getting in to New York, and then we'll be going to the hotel, and then everything will be all right. I mean—well, look at us! Here we are, married! Here we are!"
> "Yes, here we are," she said. "Aren't we?" (p. 55)

There is significance in ending the story with a question. For beneath the youth in this fiction is the coming maturity when such quarrels and misunderstandings, such delays despite the best of intentions, may transform this couple into the Weldons. The fiber of this story depends on our double perspective. In its presentation of both possibilities, its modulation of tone beneath the apparent casualness, the story has a kind of toughness that makes this, too, one of Dorothy Parker's half-dozen best short stories.

e.   Here Lies: *"She liked to picture herself in the gracious act"*

Dorothy Parker published her collected stories under the title *Here Lies* (New York, 1939) and dedicated them to Lillian Hellman. She preserved only twenty-four,[78] including three new ones: "The Custard Heart," "Clothe the Dead," and "Soldiers of the Republic." In reviewing the book for the *Spectator*, William Plomer observed,

> The urbanity of these stories is that of a worldly, witty person with a place in a complex and highly-developed society, their ruthlessness that of an

expert critical intelligence, about which there is something clinical, something of the probing adroitness of a dentist: the fine-pointed instrument unerringly discovers the carious cavity behind the smile. . . . Mrs. Parker may appear amused, but it is plain that she is really horrified. Her bantering revelations are inspired by a respect for decency, and her pity and sympathy are ready when needed.[79]

Ann Springer, however, alluded to Dorothy Parker's sentimentality in the *Boston Evening Transcript*,[80] and it is a proper charge against "The Custard Heart," a story reminiscent of "A Certain Lady." "The Custard Heart" (pp. 349–62) is a portrait of a woman whose carefully controlled life suggests the totality of her pride; she is blind to beggars with pencils on the street, the view of garbage from her window, the reason the chauffeur Kane left after getting her maid Gwennie with child. The satire here is obvious, the conclusion of the story in its first lines.

"Clothe the Naked" (pp. 155–70), on the other hand, illustrates Dorothy's new social conscience; it uses a blind black boy adopted by the washerwoman Big Lannie to illustrate the virtues of communism over a capitalism that puts Lannie out of work and deprives them both of necessities and luxuries without giving them recourse. The story is not so much sentimental as it is angry and, with Big Lannie, the allegorical nature of the characters is more successful than with the boy Raymond.

Then he came out into the yard, and turned his face in the gentle air. It was all good again; it was all given back again. As quickly as he could, he gained the walk and set forth, guiding himself by the fence. He could not wait; he called out, so that he would hear gay calls in return, he laughed so that laughter would answer him.

He heard it. He was so glad that he took his hand from the fence and turned and stretched out his arms and held up his smiling face to welcome it. He stood there, and his smile died on his face, and his welcoming arms stiffened and shook.

It was not the laughter he had known; it was not the laughter he had lived on. It was like great flails beating him flat, great prongs tearing his flesh from his bones. It was coming at him, to kill him. It drew slyly back, and then it smashed against him. It swirled around and over him, and he could not breathe. He screamed and tried to run out through it, and fell, and it licked over him, howling higher. His clothes unrolled, and his shoes flapped on his feet. Each time he could rise, he fell again. It was as if the street were perpendicular before him, and the laughter leaping at his back.

He could not find the fence, he did not know which way he was turned. He lay screaming, in blood and dust and darkness. (pp. 168–69)

The laughter that grinds Raymond beneath it is the laughter of the exploitative construction workers; the use of race is unnecessary. This is unlike Dorothy Parker's certain economy elsewhere; it is a consequence of her own passionate hatred of the dismissal of humanity that for her had become the way of life outside communism. Raymond is dressed in hand-me-down shoes and Mr. Ewing's old full-dress coat, yet these sorry tokens are not meant to parody communistic sharing so much as to exalt it. The unsuitable clothes reflect the blindness of the giver rather than the need of the receiver, lending a power to the integrity that prompted this hybrid between allegory and social documentary.

The best story of this collection, "Soldiers of the Republic" (pp. 259–66) is an autobiographical slice-of-life that captures the tension and horror of war. The setting is a "big café in Valencia" where a Swedish girl and the narrator, an American, try to bring a moment's relief to soldiers only temporarily off duty. Life here is urgent, and refined social custom has no place.

They like Americans in Valencia, where they have seen good ones—the doctors who left their practices and came to help, the calm young nurses, the men of the International Brigade. But when I walked forth, men and women courteously laid their hands across their splitting faces and little children, too innocent for dissembling, doubled with glee and pointed and cried. "*Olé!*" Then, pretty late, I made my discovery, and left my hat off; and there was laughter no longer. It was not one of those comic hats, either; it was just a hat. (p. 262)

The soldiers talk of their families back home but, not hearing from them, do not dare to write inquiring letters. To do so might endanger their families, since they fight for the Spanish Loyalist cause. Nor do they dare leave the front now to look for them; they must be content to know that, as one was told, they "were all alive . . . and had a bowl of beans a day" (p. 265). Only after they leave do the Swedish girl and American narrator learn that the men have paid for their drinks. It is a small thing, but in this context it is both moving and significant. The men have found a token by which to signify their loneliness and their relief and pleasure in this accidental meeting in a big café in their tiny, yet major, war. *In Our Time* and

Men Without Women are just behind the documentary quality of this story.

f. *Later Stories: "a product of creative arrangement"*

Dorothy Parker's chief concern in her fiction is the failure of human sympathy, of human communication. This emerges through repeated motifs: the battle of the sexes, the anxieties of love, the hypocrisy of society; repeatedly her settings are a dance, a dinner, a party, a restaurant. But in the midst of such social scenes, the subjects are alienation and loneliness as much as pride; her women are often self-absorbed snobs, her men philanderers, scoundrels, or subservient husbands, dishonest or weak. Neither men nor women are able to attain their inflated self-images.

Dorothy Parker works with a reductive realism, as F. P. A. notes. "Dorothy Parker's stories are as tightly and compactly written as her verse. . . . Short stories they are, but only technically. Each is a novel, and in the unbridled hands of some of the wordier novelists—and I could name you plenty—would have become a novel of at least 500,000 words."[81] Radically condensed, her stories and sketches are tips of icebergs.

Yet her resources remain everywhere in the customs of society. "She is one of those rare storytellers," Vernon Loggins has said, "who can create a memorable fiction out of an apparent nothing—a casual conversation."[82] Whatever the generative impulse, her stories are, like Swift's, implicit in their satire: the terms for judgment remain outside the works. By asking us to supply the proper terms, she makes collaborators of us, enforces our involvement. By the same token, her satire is so broadened (because of a potentially wide readership) that she often is forced to distort her setting and to make people into caricatures to insure her meaning. Consequently, much of her fiction—despite its realistic base—seems to us more fable than story.

These generalizations apply to all her fiction, but her later stories take on new density, grow increasingly autobiographical. Five new stories were added to those of *Here Lies* for *The Viking Portable Dorothy Parker* (1944), dedicated to Lieutenant Alan Campbell. "Cousin Larry" (pp. 488–95; also *NY*, June 30, 1934) is an early monologue in which a woman recalls her affair with another woman's husband and is puzzled when the wife is upset: the speaker, wearing an ugly dress and holding a dead cigarette, her mouth resembling that of a fish, is one of Dorothy Parker's least subtle portraits. "Mrs. Hofstadter on Josephine Street" (pp. 236–47; *NY*, August 4, 1934) is loosely autobiographical; it recounts a Hollywood couple, unable to shift for themselves, who hire a black manservant who slowly and subtly comes to tyrannize them. There is a bitter comparison of the intolerance shown blacks and Jews, and Dorothy carefully pruned the story for its republication.[83] "Song of the Shirt, 1941" resembles "The Custard Heart"—Mrs. Martindale, superfluously wealthy as her day seems "extraordinarily bright" (p. 99), is so caught up in her own charity that she is blind to the real need of others. But the story is subsequent to Dorothy Parker's political activity and so has grimmer overtones: here the organization of headquarters and the production line making hospital gowns signify a misguided capitalism, preventing Mrs. Martindale from expressing herself naturally and so precluding the sharing that a higher form of patriotism might inspire.

"The Standard of Living" (pp. 53–60) and "The Lovely Leave" (pp. 21–40) are the best of these added stories. In the former, two secretaries amuse themselves by pretending what each would buy for herself if given a million dollars. The story celebrates their game (though it equates success with money), approving their meager fabrications to make a mundane life bearable in a way the post-Marxist Dorothy would not approve. Here, Annabel and Mimi ask less of life than they deserve, and so she spares them any cynicism or excessive sympathy. "The Lovely Leave," based on Dorothy's own separation from Alan, depicts with obvious feeling a young married couple about to be separated by war. Steve's weekend leave has been reduced to a few hours, and Mimi's surprise and disappointment causes them to expose their anxieties. Under the strain of perfecting an impossibly short time together, they quarrel. " 'You see,' she said with care, 'you have a whole new life—I have half an old one. Your life is so far away from mine, I don't see how they're ever going to come back together' " (p. 31). She openly fears estrangement; he wants to savor, for a few moments, the creature comforts of a home bath. They feel and talk at cross-purposes; their language and behavior, acts and intentions are at odds. When Steve leaves, Mimi is asked by a friend if the leave were lovely and she says it was—the first lie the war will cost her. Living with fictions was Dorothy's chief realization and both these stories—one comic, one pathetic—deal directly with that theme, advancing stoic (but not detached) irony.

Her last five stories are among her better works of fiction. "The Game" (*Cosmopolitan*, December 1948, pp. 58;90–102), putatively written with Ross Evans, is openly savage. In the apartment of newlyweds Bob and Emily Lineham where "Each room . . . already had museum qualities" (p. 90) and decorators' chalk marks help place the furniture, an older woman, jealous at the happiness the Linehams exhibit, plots a game of charades so as to expose the first Mrs. Lineham's suicide to the new bride. The horror is suggested at the story's opening but it moves inexorably and painfully in a style that is recognizably Dorothy Parker's.

"I Live on Your Visits" (*NY*, January 15, 1955, pp. 24–27) is an acidic portrait of a divorced woman who lives vicariously on the appearances of her son, when she can attack her former husband and his new wife. Her drunkenness is an outer sign of her self-indulgence; her friendship with a vulgar woman astrologer betrays her coarseness of spirit. The boy, who alternates between protecting his mother and being embarrassed for her, is Dorothy Parker's occasion for displaying the cruelty and pain that may lie in marriage; "I Live on Your Visits" is a study of love as power. The story suffers not so much from being obvious as from its obsessive theme: it is presented without sympathy, without relief.

"Lolita" (*NY*, August 27, 1955, pp. 32–35) is a plain girl whose mother, long separated from her husband, keeps as unbecoming as possible. Still the girl marries handsome John Marble, and, slowly, all Mrs. Ewing's defenses against her old age and unhappiness unwind. The story is a subtle portrait of the cost of solitude and old age, of the essential loneliness of life; Mrs. Ewing is at last reduced to hoping her daughter will be abandoned as she was, "For Mrs. Ewing was not a woman who easily abandoned hope" (p. 35).

The ritual meeting—this time between economic and social classes rather than generations—is the focus of Dorothy Parker's ironic scrutiny in "The Bolt behind the Blue" (*The Portable Dorothy Parker* [New York, 1977 ed.], pp. 394–415). The story opens with the consummately crafted sentences that distinguish her late fiction, combining colloquialism with formality of tone.

Miss Mary Nicholl was poor and plain, which afflictions compelled her, when she was in the presence of a more blessed lady, to vacillate between squirming humility and spitting envy. The more blessed lady, her friend Mrs. Hazelton, enjoyed Miss Nicholl's visits occasionally; humility is a seemly tribute to a favorite of fate, and to be the cause of envy is cozy to the ego. The visits had to be kept only occasional, though. With the years, Miss Nicholl grew no less flat in the purse and no more delightful to the eye, and it is a boresome business to go on and on feeling tenderness for one whose luck never changes.

Miss Nicholl worked as secretary to a stern and sterling woman. For seven hours a day she sat in a small room lined with filing cabinets where at half-past twelve precisely was put upon her desk, next to her typewriter, a tray set forth with the produce of the stern and sterling one's favorite health-food shop. The job was permanent and the lunches insured Miss Nicholl against constipation, yet it is to be admitted that her daily round lacked color and height. Those were fine occasions for her when, her work done, she might cover her typewriter and go to call on Mrs. Hazelton, to tread the gleaming halls, to sit in the long blue drawing room, to stroke the delicate cocktail glass and warm her spirit in its icy contents.

The duplicity of both women, only insinuated here, is fervently staged throughout their meeting, Mrs. Hazelton showing off her dog, her daughter, and her wardrobe, Miss Nicholl pretending gratitude for the gift of an old sequinned purse for which she has no possible use. But unlike her other mature fiction, "The Bolt behind the Blue"—the title disappointingly obvious and weak—fractures openly at the close into divergent perspectives that remind us of Dorothy Parker's earlier fiction and poetry. Once alone, Miss Nicholl's thoughts are full of hatred and scorn while Mrs. Hazelton, conversely, scolds her daughter for disparaging Miss Nicholl while ruefully considering the secretary's professions of contentment. No bolt crosses the blue mood of either woman since such disparate reactions are likewise only pretense: Dorothy Parker exposes the condition of both women as twinned through their boredom with life, their consequent loss of self-respect, and their desperate pettiness at attempting to deceive themselves by deceiving each other.

Like all her late stories, "The Banquet of Crow" (NY, December 14, 1957, pp. 39–43) is also a study in estrangement. Written shortly after Dorothy Parker's reconciliation with Alan Campbell, it is highly disciplined—her best story. It opens metaphorically:

It was a crazy year, a year when things that should have run on schedule went all which ways. It was a year when snow fell thick and lasting in April, and young ladies clad in shorts were photographed for the tabloids sunbathing in Central Park in January. It was a year when, in the greatest prosperity of the richest nation, you could not walk five city blocks without being besought by beggars; when expensively dressed women loud and lurching in public places were no uncommon sight; when drugstore counters were stacked with tablets to make you tranquil and tablets to set you leaping. (p. 39)

This is the year Guy Allen left his wife Maida. Mrs. Allen, puzzled and upset, responded in several ways: by complaining to her friends until they will have no more to do with her; by asking her husband's friends how he is; by seeking other women who were friends in the long past; by going to a psychiatrist. Only Dr. Langham helps, by telling Maida her husband is going through male menopause. His sudden return to fetch a suitcase seems to support this, but by extraordinarily subtle hints Dorothy Parker has already told us that nothing will save the marriage. Maida Allen does not know her husband and she does not know herself.

"Why were you unhappy? " she said.
"Because two people can't go on and on and on, doing the same things year after year, when only one of them likes doing them," he said, "and still be happy."
"Do you think *I* can be happy, like this? " she said.
"I do," he said. "I think you will. I wish there were some prettier way of doing it, but I think that after a while—and not a long while, either—you will be better than you've ever been." (p. 43)

Guy Allen's revelation thus demonstrates his own ignorance to us. But he leaves no doubt about the fate of the two of them: the crow Maida Allen would have her husband eat is a meal they both share; Dorothy Parker points to the cause in her final line: "She went to the telephone and called Dr. Langham." In Dorothy Parker's world even psychiatrists do not communicate, and men and women both, like doctor and patient, are born to be estranged.

IV   Criticism: *"superlatives make tiresome reading"*

Alexander Woollcott began it in New York City: capsule drama criticism punctuated by quip and insult was characteristic of his reviews in the *New York Times* as early as 1914.

To send what he has across the footlights, Mr. Klein takes the ordinary human motives and their consequences and multiplies them by ten.

Their play is a melodrama and a peculiarly livid one, with violence as one of its properties and an unusually prominent part in the cast assigned to Chance.[84]

He was not the first to develop the mode; in *Shouts and Murmurs* (1922) he fondly recalls two by Eugene Field: " 'So-and-so played Hamlet last night at the Tabor Grand. He played it till one o'clock'. . . . 'Mr. Clarke played [King Lear] all evening as though under constant fear that some one else was about to play the Ace.' "[85] Lists of Woollcott's own quips are now living legends.[86] He provided a theoretical basis for them in his essay "Capsule Criticism."

What we are looking for, of course, is the happy sentence that speaks volumes. As an example, consider the familiar problem presented by the players who can do everything on the stage except act. I have in mind a still celebrated beauty to whom that beauty opened wide the stage-door full thirty years ago. Since then she has devoted herself most painstakingly to justifying her admission. She has keen intelligence and great industry. She has learned every trick of voice and gesture that can be taught. She has acquired everything except some substitute for the inborn gift. Something to that effect, expressed, of course, as considerately as possible, ought, it seems to me, to be a part of any report on her spasmodic reappearances.[87]

Woollcott's daily reviews and Sunday column for the *Times*, "Second Thoughts on First Nights," were regarded as the best drama criticism being written when Dorothy Parker worked at *Vogue* and *Vanity Fair;* and when she met Woollcott at the Algonquin shortly before undertaking her monthly drama reviews for *Vanity Fair*, she must have heard the barbs her own work would in time emulate.

Criticism in the days when Dorothy Parker began writing was focused on the art of performance, whether theatrical or literary. Convention, critics believed, corrupts taste; and absolute adherence to convention corrupts absolutely: her chief standard was the convincing reality of the art, the honesty of presentation. She developed, as she wrote reviews for *Vanity Fair*, [88] *Ainslee's, The New Yorker*, and *Esquire*, firm if implicit standards. She hated improbabilities, stereotypes, excesses, meaninglessness, and overt sweetness. For her the theater involved the art of scenic management: gesture, costume, and set all played an integral part in the performance of a play, while in literature she sought individuality and integrity in vision and in style.

Yet if her standards were strict and substantial, her tone was light, bright, personal, her criticism conversational and hyperbolic by turn; her favorite practice was to damn by irrelevancy or incongruity, thinking of an actress' sable wrap, for example, rather than her acting (*VF*, March 1919, p. 36).[89] She quickly adopted the persona of the disillusioned idealist but, in avoiding praise, she was often bored, and her distractions led to digressions in both her drama and book reviews. A frequent ploy in the former was to discuss the audience rather than the play.[90] With Woollcott, she set a style still famous and still imitated in the personal reviewing of plays, records, and books and films today.

a. *Drama Criticism: "No woman could look on the things I have seen and keep her girlish character"*

i. Vanity Fair

Dorothy Parker wrote monthly drama reviews for *Vanity Fair* from April 1918 through March 1920. The job was difficult for, as she would later admit, she might review a play that had disappeared long before the magazine reached newsstands. Moreover, monthly summaries meant she could give very little space to any single play and, to give her columns coherence, she had to relate a number of different plays each month.

She began reviewing cautiously; she often awarded compliments and—at the start—even superlatives.

Of John Barrymore's performance . . . I can only say that, to me, it was flawless. ("The New Plays," December 1918, p. 89)

"Dear Brutus" is to me the event of the season. ("The Midwinter Plays," February 1919, p. 39)

There is no greater tribute to her acting than that her audiences never consider the play—it's all Mrs. Fiske. ("The New Plays," April 1919, p. 41)

She was careful to praise the friends of the Round Table, too: Lynn Fontanne and Constance Collier ("The New Plays," November 1918, p. 53), Helen Hayes (February 1919, p. 39), Peggy Wood ("The Oriental Drama," January 1920, p. 94). For style, she rested almost entirely on her wit.

Not even the presence in the first-night audience of Mr. William Randolph Hearst, wearing an American flag on his conventional black lapel, could spoil my evening. "A Succession of Musical Comedies," (April 1918, p. 69)

The cast contains two of the most virulent young lovers ever beheld—they bubbled, and chased each other around tables, and were so exuberant that I prayed—in vain—for the scenery to fall on them, and quiet them down. (December 1918, p. 84)

If you would get the best out of the evening, by all means leave after the first act, take a brisk walk around the Reservoir, and get back just as the curtain rises on the last act. You won't miss a thing. ("The First Hundred Plays Are the Hardest," December 1919, p. 39)

The only unacknowledged contribution to the performance is *Aphrodite's* costume which was evidently furnished by the Atlas Paint Company. (January 1920, p. 39)

As time passed, however, she grew increasingly disappointed, increasingly negative. She turned to "capsule criticism."

I have heard it said that it took Messrs. Shipman and Hymer just three and a half days to write their drama. I should like to know what they were doing during the three days. (February 1919, p. 39)

I should have heard a good deal more of the proceedings if I had left the Vanderbilt Theatre and gone and stood out in the middle of Forty-seventh Street, in which direction [the actors] were all facing. (February 1919, p. 74)

The second act numbers are all by Irving Berlin; whose music sounds like a medley of all his past hits. ("The First Shows of Summer," August 1919, p. 23)

Such quips were worthy of Woollcott's praise.

To study Dorothy Parker's twenty-three essays for *Vanity Fair* is to observe a slowly evolving critical consciousness. Her taste grew; her insights improved. She noted of one production what could be a theatrical maxim: "In their care to hold themselves aloof from commercialism, they seem to veer dangerously close to amateurishness" (March 1919, p. 92). And of the Amercian temper: "Gloom may be all very well for a lot of unshaven Russians, but for a good hustling American, there's nothing like chasing sunbeams. Say what you will, the pen with the smile wins" ("Optimism in the Drama," VF, March 1920, p. 41). She came too to test classifications of plays, finding that in revues cleverness comes in not doing the expected ("The New Order of Musical Comedies," *VF*, May 1918, p. 49), noting that "one successful play" results in "a long succession of others," ("The New Play," *VF*, April 1919, p. 41) and observing that Irish plays rely on patriotic sentiment, ("The Close of a Perfect Season," *VF*, July 1919, p. 33)

While thus generalizing, she also learned that personal commentary added focus and wit to her column.

In fact, so thoroughly was I baffled as to the real identity of the thief that, at the end of the first act, I regarded all the members of the cast, the leader of the orchestra, the hat-room boy, and the ordnance officer in the right-hand stage-box, with equal suspicion. (Of *The Blue Pearl*, "The Fall Crop of War Plays," October 1918, p. 106)

And, after seeing war plays,

From my couch in the sanatorium, I pen these few poor lines. I am a little better now. In fact, they say that, with careful nursing, I may pull through. If no one ever mentions the words "Over Here," or "One of Us,"or "Crops and Croppers" in my hearing, I still have a fighting chance. (November 1918, p. 53)

Still, as she continued her monthly grind of reviewing, it is clear she found the experience wearing. Her patience grows thinner; she is quicker to spot (and report) the commercial and the meretricious; she becomes bored. As counterforce, her remarks become considerably more barbed.

This play holds the season's record, thus far, with a run of four evening performances and one matinee. By an odd coincidence, it ran just five performances too many. ("The Anglo-American Drama," February 1920, p. 41).

Pictorially, the production rates about A plus; vocally, at a generous estimate, D; and, humorously, somewhere along about V minus. (February 1920, p. 102)

But by then, she had already compared Billie Burke to Eva Tanguay (January 1920, p. 94). She was learning that while her wit might save her spirits, it would not save her job. With her next assignment, she would strive to achieve better balance in her reviewing.

ii. Ainslee's.

Dorothy Parker's monthly column for *Ainslee's,* "In Broadway Playhouses," succeeded Alan Dale's column "Plays and Players" in May 1920 and ran every month through July 1923. The audience of *Anslee's* was far less sophisticated than that of *Vanity Fair*, but she seems to have had more editorial freedom even as she adopts a kind of cloying persona of the put-upon "little woman" to make the column enjoyable for those who could not get to New York to see Broadway theater. She still attacks pretension, conventionality, "stickiness," and overly elaborate productions, but the plays become vehicles for her wit or her persona of the tired reviewer more intelligent than the material she is forced to appraise.

Over the course of three years, she began to develop clear prejudices. She liked Shaw and O'Neill and Cohan (though she chided him on his perpetual announcements to retire); she lavished praise on Mrs. Fiske, Roland Young, James Barton, Margaret Lawrence, Leslie Howard, Laurette Taylor, Ethel Barrymore, Glen Hunter (in a variety of roles), Jeanne Eagels ("great" in Maugham's *Rain*, ("Three Rousing Cheers," February 1923, p. 157), Jane Cowl, Estelle Winwood, and the Theater Guild. But she was equally quick to scorn Milne, Billie Burke, Eddie Cantor, Marie Dressler ("If this lady is the world's most side-splitting comedienne, then I am Laddie Boy," "Nothing from Nothing," April 1923, p. 155), Shakespeare on stage, and David Belasco "the famed Wizard of the Drama," ("Let 'er go," November 1922, p. 157). She was off-again, on-again regarding Zeigfeld, always wondering where he got whole cadres of gorgeous girls the likes of which she never saw in real life.

Frequently for *Ainslee's* readers she continued her wisecracks.

[On Fannie Hurst's wordiness in *Back Pay*]: The stage hands had to keep sweeping up periodic sentences, so that they wouldn't clutter up the wings and the actors climbed laboriously over stacks of similes every time they made an entrance or an exit. ("Plays and Plays and Plays," December 1921, p. 156)

Miss [Dorothy] Mackaye's best moments [in *Getting Gertie's Garter*] were those when she was off stage. ("Comedy Relief," November 1921, p. 155).

Undeniably, Miss [Dorothy] Ward is more at home on the Winter Garden stage than she was on that of the Shubert Theater. There is more room for her vivacity. And perhaps some day, if she is allowed to play where she has enough space—in the Yale Bowl, say, or the Grand Central Terminal—she may be perfectly great. ("Fair to Middling," September 1921, pp. 157–58).

The trouble with [*Nice People* by Rachel] Crothers . . . is, that when they are bad, they are very, very good, and when they are good, they are awful. . . . the conclusion of her plays being always a pollyanticlimax. ("Nights Off," June 1921, p. 158)

Here as at *Vanity Fair*, the need to "wrap up" a month's plays led to digressive and personal introductions that were space fillers then and are tiresome now. But it is on *Ainslee's* that her keen and reliable taste was formed, and in covering major plays—which she sometimes recognized when others did not—she helped to make New York City theater, until then somewhat provincial, nationally significant. She found *The Bat* excessive in its crimes and melodrama ("Words and Music," October 1920), but raved about Maugham's *The Circle*—"You owe it to yourself and your family to see 'The Circle,' if you never see anything else" ("Take Them or Leave Them," January 1922, p. 156)—and was the only reviewer to analyze responsibly Andreyev's *He Who Gets Slapped:* "It is a curious blending of strangely interesting scenes, and uniquely uninteresting ones, never wholly clear, and never hopelessly baffling" ("And Still They Come," April 1922, p. 158). She generally admired Shaw, but thought *Back to Methuselah* should have remained on the library shelf.

In the middle of the [first] evening, the thoughtful management served coffee to those who were sitting up with the actors. How one envied those fortunate souls whom coffee keeps awake! If the management really wanted to do the thing up right, they would serve hair shirts. . . . [The end of the cycle] was crammed to suffocation with words. . . . Better fifty lines of "Candida" than a cycle of "Back to Methuselah." ("Back to Methuselah, or Thereabouts," June 1922, p. 157)

And despite the frivolous chatter that often crowded her columns, she was the only major reviewer who understood and so praised George M. Cohan's *The Tavern;* she alone caught the parodies, the twists on convention in the repeated bits, and the weird collocation of costumes. Only on the digressive surfaces does the theater criticism of *Ainslee's* resemble that of *Vanity Fair*, for this was her critical turning point, where her taste came of age.

iii.   The New Yorker

Dorothy Parker thus displays assured competence when, from February 21 to April 11, 1931, she substituted for Robert Benchley, reviewing plays for *The New Yorker* in what she called her "Reign of Terror" ("Valedictory," *NY*, April 11, 1931, p. 30). She often began with a mock sense of humility and closed with a public plea to Benchley to hurry his return, but the criticism is some of her best on the theater.

Here Dorothy Parker shows respectful praise for Elinor Wylie ("Willow, Willow, Waley," March 7, 1931, p. 34), and she is one of the first to discover the talents of Jo Mielziner ("Kindly Accept Substitutes," February 21, 1931, p. 25). But as in her earliest drama criticism, she seems happiest at criticizing the stars and the successes: she complains of Katherine Cornell's delivery; the dullness of *The Admirable Crichton;* Estelle Winwood's unearned facility; and two "extraordinarily over-rated young men," Rodgers and Hart. Her criticism remains the assertion of a singular taste, neither argument nor demonstration.[91] Her most famous quip is here—"I may mutter only that 'The House Beautiful' is, for me, the play lousy" ("No More Fun" March 21, 1931, pp. 28, 36)—but "Mother," as she terms herself infrequently, saves her best remarks for her old irritant A. A. Milne. Her column for March 14, titled "Just Around Pooh Corner," deals mostly with Milne's *Give Me Yesterday.* "Its hero is caused, by a novel device, to fall asleep and adream; and thus he is given yesterday. Me, I should have given him twenty years to life" (p. 31). Dorothy Parker never had a tolerance for Milne's whimsey.

The cabinet minister stretches himself out on his old bed, and slips picturesquely to slumber. Darkness spreads softly over the stage, save for a gentle blue beam on Mr. Calhern. Music quivers; then come lights. Then there appear two—not one, but two—Christopher Robins, each about eleven years of age, both forced, poor kids, to go quaintsy-waintsy in doings about knights and squires and beauteous maidens. (I should have known when the program listed their roles as "Nite" and "Squier" that the Charles Hopkins Theatre was no place for me, nor ever would be.) These are part of the cabinet minister's dream, and into it comes a Buteus (sic) Maiden in the person of a lady, say, of ten years, with all the poise of the Sphinx though but little of her mystery. For a few minutes, everything is so cute that the mind reels. Then the cabinet minister himself gets into the dream—I do not pretend to follow the argument—and meets up with his boyhood sweetheart, who wears, and becomingly, the dress of her day. And then, believe it or not, things get worse. (pp. 30, 32)

The column concludes: *"Personal: Robert Benchley, please come home. Whimso is back again"* (p. 38).

Yet there are, in *The New Yorker* reviews, the kind of authority she learned while writing for *Ainslee's*. Convictions are quick, clean, and, if not explained, generally brief. She remains attracted to the glittering possibilities of the theater and disappointed in its vain, indulgent, or meretricious realities. The attraction never really wanes—only the pose seems to make it so. Benchley was, before and after her, on *Life* and for *The New Yorker,* always more concise, always less self-conscious. It is as if Dorothy Parker wished to write satire, to write her own fine pieces, and was instead forced to cavil about someone else's: as if at heart she knew that she was at least as commercial from time to time as were the targets of her wisecracks.

b. *Literary Criticism: "the hard, bright purity"*

Dorothy Parker's literary criticism is another matter: concentrating here on modes of writing she herself tried to perfect, she writes astringently, authoritatively, perceptively. She may have thought of herself in terms she applied to Katherine Mansfield.

She was not of the little breed of the discontented; she was of the high few fated to be ever unsatisfied. Writing was the precious thing in life to her, but she was never truly pleased with anything she had written. With a sort of fierce austerity, she strove for the crystal clearness, the hard, bright purity from which streams perfect truth. She never felt that she had attained them.[92]

In her book reviews for *The New Yorker* and *Esquire*, she could choose her texts (as she was unable to choose the plays under review) and so she was able to pursue certain repeated concerns. She admired genuine talent and decried its waste; she despised the commercial, the pompous, the prejudicial, the second rate. Occasionally, she made her anger obvious by choosing a novel by Mussolini or the biography of Aimee Semple McPherson, for she felt they not only exposed bad writing but the faults of a culture that could encourage them. Her work was "a combination of acumen and nonsense," John Farrar has remarked, her "delicate claws of . . . superb viciousness" making scratches "subtle in phrasing but by no means subtle in the sentiments they [convey]."[93]

From her first book review, of Kathleen Norris' *Norma Sheridan* for *Life* ("The Latest Books," November 17, 1921, p. 22) to the writing of her last years for *Esquire*, she concentrated primarily on fiction, championing the short story over the long novel, looking for new talent, partial to first works. Her early praise for Hemingway and Lardner may now seem extravagant to us, but the terms in which she presented it were shrewd; and they were precisely the terms that would cause her to praise, in our own time, Updike's *The Poorhouse Fair* and James Purdy's *Malcolm*, Nabokov and Malamud. Her literary criticism is directed by the art itself, not at her sophisticated audiences; and it is a criticism of a high order still.

i. The New Yorker

Dorothy Parker first alluded to herself as "Constant Reader" in a drama review for *Vanity Fair* ("Signs of Spring in the Theatre," May 1919, p. 41); she used the pseudonym for all forty-six book reviews she published in *The New Yorker* between October 1, 1927, and March 18, 1933. The mannerisms of her drama reviews appear only in her persistent self-portrait as a feckless, lazy reader whose self-doubts concerning popular taste lead her to nausea (as in her nearly irrelevant discussion of "the case of the rams" in a review of Fannie Hurst and Booth Tarkington, "Re-enter Miss Hurst, Followed by Mr. Tarkington," *CR*, pp. 49–50), but her criticism generally is prompter, more efficient, and more particular in its standards. Talent and taste remain the fundamental prerequisites for good writers; "It is the first job of a writer who demands rating among the great, or even among the good, to write well," she remarks in a review on Dreiser ("Words, Words, Words," p. 140). This credo is further defined in her reviews of Hemingway and Lardner. She found Hemingway's style "exciting" because it was "clean" ("A Book of Great Short Stories," p. 16)—"Hemingway has an unerring sense of selection. He discards details with a magnificent lavishness; he keeps his words to their short path. His is, as any reader knows, a dangerous influence. The simple thing he does looks so easy to do" (p. 17)—itself a sign of "writing well," and she went out of her way in 1929 to acknowledge *Round-Up* and praise Lardner for the same virtues. He is "a great writer" ("Hero Worship," p. 113), she vows, because of his "spare and beautiful" writing (p. 114). Good and tasteful work for Dorothy Parker, then, results from a severely disciplined talent.

Her column, which was called "Recent Books" until October 29, 1927, when its permanent title, "Reading and Writing," was assigned it, has often been cited for her famous quips. This is where she reviewed the autobiography of Margot Asquith, Countess of Oxford ("Re-enter Margot Asquith—A Masterpiece from the French," *CR*, pp. 10–11), Elinor Glyn's *It* ("Madame Glyn Lectures on 'It,' with Illustrations," p. 23), and Milne's *The House at Pooh Corner* ("Far from Well," p. 101). And there are others.

[Of W. G. Harding and Nan Britton]: they seem to have been, at best, but a road-company Paolo and Francesca. ("An American DuBarry," *CR*, p. 6)

"Crude" is the name of Robert Hyde's first novel. It is also a criticism of it. ("Re-enter Margot Asquith," *NY* October 22, 1927, p. 100)

[Of Aimee Semple McPherson]: It may be that this autobiography is set down in sincerity, frankness, and simple effort. It may be, too, that the Statue of Liberty is situated in Lake Ontario. ("Our Lady of the Loudspeaker," *CR*, p. 69)

[Of Mussolini's novel]: If *The Cardinal's Mistress* is a *grande romanzo*, I am Alexandre Dumas, *père et fils*. ("Duces Wild," *CR*, p. 96)

Attending to such *bon mots*, Harold Clurman observes: "Her manner was more suited to the trivial stuff which she too frequently chose to discuss."[94]

But in studying these reviews, we find that serious commentary outweighs such cracks, outweighs even the coy, self-conscious affectations by which Dorothy Parker tries to identify a credible person named "Constant Reader." Here her taste, unlike that displayed in her drama criticism, was idiosyncratic for her time, but not for our own. She finds the unrealistic work of James Branch Cabell "a transcendent imagery, a lacy slyness, a frosty irony" ("A Book of Great Short Stories," *NY*, October 29, 1927, p. 94). She admired Upton Sinclair's "courage, his passion, his integrity," thought him "a fine novelist" but "as a literary critic he is simply god-awful" ("The Socialist Looks at Literature," *CR*, p. 29). She also saw two opposing forces in Fannie Hurst's work.

There have been times when her sedulously torturous style, her one-word sentences and her curiously compounded adjectives, drive me into an irritation that is only to be relieved by kicking and screaming. But she sees and she feels, and she makes you see and feel; and those are not small powers. ("Re-enter Miss Hurst," *CR*, p. 52)

In the same review, she says of Booth Tarkington: "he has no equal at setting down in exquisite words the comic manifestations of youthful love-agony, though never does he dare let his pen touch the agony itself. He is, I am afraid, too merciful a man for greatness" (p. 53). Comparing Ford Madox Ford's *The Last Post* ("not a good book," ["A Good Novel, and a Great Story," *CR*] p. 54) to the history on which it was based, she observed "that there are certain things set down in black on white beside which even distinguished, searching, passionate novels pale to mediocrity" (p. 55). She also distrusted the talent and taste of Sinclair Lewis.

The Man Who Knew Coolidge is Babbitt broadened by a mile, and Babbitt, Lord knows, was never instanced as an exercise in the subtle. ("Mr. Lewis Lays It On with a Trowel," *CR*, p. 87)

I think Mr. Lewis's latest work is as heavy-handed, clumsy, and dishonest a burlesque as it has been my misfortune to see in years. (p. 86)

A strong advocate of realism, she was equally critical of Dreiser: "to me Dreiser is a dull, pompous, dated, and darned near ridiculous writer" ("Words, Words, Words," *CR*, p. 140).

But she also praises and here—unlike the reviews of drama—she says specifically why. She noted of Dashiell Hammett:

Brutal he is, but his brutality, for what he must write, is clean and necessary, and there is in his work none of the smirking and swaggering savageries of a Hecht or a Bodenheim. He does his readers the infinite courtesy of allowing them to supply descriptions and analyses for themselves. ("Oh, Look—A Good Book!" *CR*, p. 135)

She sees in G. B. Stern's *Debonair* a weakness she might have seen in her own work: "Miss Stern has had that thing happen to her which befalls most fine satirists. By the nature of her gift, she writes superbly of the people she hates; but when she tries to do a character whom she likes and wishes her reader to like, the result is appalling" ("These Much Too Charming People," *CR*, p. 92). She thought Anne Parrish's *All Kneeling* "a quick and deft and constantly amusing satire, the portrait of a lady who so sharply suggests almost all other ladies that you get a little bit frightened" ("Duces Wild," p. 99).

Yet there are marked and obvious lapses. Dorothy Parker can still judge authors and intentions rather than works. She notes of Isadora

Duncan: "She was no writer, God knows. . . . But, somehow, the style of the book makes no matter. . . . She was a brave woman. We shall not look upon her like again" ("Poor, Immortal Isadora," *CR*, pp. 44, 47). Before works of huge dimension, such as Gide's *Counterfeiters*, she can do embarrassingly little: "*The Counterfeiters* is too tremendous a thing for praises" ("Re-enter Margot Asquith," *CR*, p. 13). She chooses some easy targets (Britton, McPherson) and some easy works (Mussolini's novel, Milne's whimsey). She is better at general than specific analysis. She is more fascinated by craft than substance. She is impatient with posturing and self-parody (as in Lewis); she enjoys too quickly what is, like her own writing, "economical." Her criticism is often sidetracked by the personal commentary that was general to the literary criticism of the 1920s.

Yet more because of these than in spite of them, her sensibility grows with this reviewing, and what is first grounded exclusively in taste comes to be bolstered by certain principles. If her critical eye is predictable, it is also keen and widely sympathetic (from Duncan to Mansfield). Her comments, despite the dated flavorings, stand time's test remarkably well, as often instructive now as entertaining. It is a body of criticism that, straining to develop its own self-image, lays down standards that reveal a deep and necessary respect and awareness of the art of prose and prose fiction.

ii. Esquire

Dorothy Parker's last major accomplishment was for *Esquire* magazine where, between December 1957 and December 1962, she wrote forty-six columns and reviewed two hundred eight books—more works with less froth than she had published, in about the same period, for *The New Yorker*. She began with a year's wrap-up—"Best Fiction of 1957" in her mid-sixties—and briefly conducted the column "Esquire on Books." But within a month this became "Dorothy Parker on Books," and her name from then on took equal prominence.

Her standards, three decades later, are unchanged. In April 1960 she attacks Alan Kapelner's *All the Naked Heroes* because

The book is written in a manner less breathless than panting, so that punc-tuation and paragraphing are swept away in the onrush, and interminable descriptive stretches are composed of words loosely strung together by more "and's" than you ever saw before in your life. Too, though this is a minor matter, Mr. Kapelner has taken to himself a trick of diction that causes me to summon the men in the white coats to carry me away from it all. That's the transforming of nouns into verbs—thus, if you go to a lunch counter to buy a cup of coffee, you are not served with a cup of coffee; you are coffeed; and when you have drunk the brew, you dime the counter. This goes on over and over, but the book and I parted company when the traveling brother saw a child who lilac'd a grave. ("Excursions and side trips: Seven selected adventures," pp. 41, 42)

By the same token, she confesses admiration for Beckett but could neither understand nor appreciate *Murphy* ("Best Fiction of 1957," December 1957, p. 64).

There is much of the old acidity of Dorothy Parker throughout this late work. She titled her review of Errol Flynn's autobiography "Flynn-flam" and remarks, "I do not quite believe that anybody has to be that rugged, nor do I at all believe most of the book" (March 1960, p. 59). Of *The Memoirs of Casanova* she finds "a certain lack of variety" ("The way to exercise is not always through sitting down and reading," March 1961, p. 50). The most she can say of Irving Stone's *The Agony and Ecstasy* is that it has "perhaps the most embracing title since *War and Peace*" ("From tabloids to Colette to Yates and on to a bum voyage," June 1961, p. 38) and she complains of Graham Greene (in reviewing *A Burnt-Out Case*), "I sometimes wish that Mr. Greene had not joined the church quite so vehemently" *(Ibid.)*. Once more she has fun with personalities whose biographies or commercialism anger her—Zsa Zsa Gabor ("To me, the lady is a figment of mythology," ["Lovely Lady and Lively Ghost," December 1960, p. 90], George Sanders, and Gerold Frank—but the subject that angers her the most is the meretricious treatment and dispassionate exploitation of sex.

Poor dear sex is crammed into spaces where there is scarcely room for it by itself, and its joy must be left outside. The nowadays ruling that no word is unprintable has, I think, done nothing whatever for beautiful letters. The boys have gone hogwild with liberty, yet the short flat terms used over and over, both in dialogue and narrative, add neither vigor nor clarity; the effect is not of shock but of something far more dangerous—tedium. (December 1957, p. 60)

What Milne was to her reviews in *The New Yorker*—the running metaphor for all that was bad—Jack Kerouac becomes in *Esquire*.

It says, on the dust-cover of *The Subterraneans,* that the Beat Youth believe that how to live seems much more crucial to them than why. (I don't know why they need give themselves such airs about it; if memory serves me, that is the way most generations believed.) But the "how" of the Beat Boys and Girls is of an appalling monotony. . . . He narrates these episodes [of physical love] play-by-play—what do these new writers do, anyway? Keep score-cards? ("Second thoughts on some major themes," May 1958, p. 42)

Much more devastating, she quotes in its entirety Kerouac's affected and silly preface to Jack Micheline's *River of Red Wine and Other Poems;* it reads like the worst kind of parody:

I like the free rhyme, and these sweet lines revive the poetry of open hope in America, by Micheline, though Whitman and Ginsberg know all that jive, and me, too, and there are so many other great poets swinging nowadays (Burroughs, Corso, Steve Tropp I hear, McClure, Duncan, Creeley, Whalen, especially Whalen & Snyder, and Anton Rosenberg, I don't know where to turn and I never pretended to be a critic till now) so I quit and abdicate. When you sit on a curbstone at dawn on Times Square at age 171, what's the difference, or 17? Right, man? Just look at the sky and say, "As though I didn't know already" ("This September's song: too much is too much," September 1958, p. 12).

Not one to miss an opportunity, Dorothy Parker concludes her own column with two of these same sentences.

Her insights, read now, are for the most part unerring. She was the first to acknowledge Tillie Olson (June 1962) and Richard Yates (*Revolutionary Road* in 1961; *Eleven Kinds of Loneliness* a year later), and she praised Auberon Waugh (who she thought surpassed the contemporary work of his father, in October 1961) and Updike's *The Poorhouse Fair* (February 1959). She examined John Hersey and Horace Gregory, William Golding and Niccolo Tucci ("enormous and enormously brilliant" she says of *Before My Time* ["A magnificent book on a less-than-magnificent time and its people," September 1962] p. 62). Her comments on Weidman, Robert Penn Warren, Isherwood, Shirley Ann Grau, and Henry Roth have not been appreciably bettered. Her acuity can be epigrammatic: she thought Nabokov's *Lolita* "An anguished book, but sometimes wildly funny" ("Sex—without the asterisks," October 1958, p. 103); Donleavy's *The Ginger Man* "a rigadoon of rascality, a bawled-out

comic song of sex" more of Dublin than Brooklyn; and James
Purdy's *Color of Darkness*, which most others had not discovered,
the work of "a striking new American talent, sure and sharp and
painful" (both "Four rousing cheers," July 1958, p. 20). She was
much taken with Katherine Anne Porter's *Ship of Fools*. "There is
never a slackening of its pace, never a lazily written passage, never a
portrait roughed in" ("The Pyramid, other monuments, and needles
in haystacks," July 1962, p. 129). But she could as quickly dispute
other critics, and fearlessly. She was annoyed by the extravagant
reviews of James Gould Cozzens' *By Love Possessed*—"It seems to
me that we might all admire Mr. Cozzens' people and their world
more, if Mr. Cozzens himself did not admire them so much"; "*By
Love Possessed* seemed to me cold, distant, and exasperatingly pa-
tronizing"—and goes on to praise instead John Cheever's *The Wap-
shot Chronicle* (both December 1957, p. 62). Nearly always, she was
more a barometer for our time than hers.

If we cannot fault her judgments, we can complain that she still
employs summary impressions rather than detailed analyses. She
still refers us to implied standards of taste; what she loses in convincing argument she gains in the ease with which her columns
could be appreciated by persons who themselves rarely read books.
Her convictions could train even them.

She knew, too, the weakness of her own work.

There are so many ways to damn a book, and so few by which to extol it.
How scant are the words of praise! "Delightful," "engrossing," "fascinating," "fine," "distinguished," and sometimes (though this is the one that
leads to trouble) "great." And the reciting of them acts on a reader as does a
big bowl of sodium amytal, with sugar and cream. ("Acclaim for four finds:
glittering, charming, fascinating, fine," April 1959, p. 31)

Yet there is a marked change here from her earlier criticism—where
in *The New Yorker* she had come with bright and brittle wit to scorn
and amuse, in *Esquire* she clearly wishes to discover, to admire, and
to argue high standards as much positively as negatively. These
reviews are, in a way, a summing of what she meant to stand for;
indirectly, they point to what she had always meant, in her own
poetry and fiction, to do. It is tempting, therefore, to find in her
review of Anthony Powell's *At Lady Molly's* respect for what she
knew was her own fundamental technique in fiction.

Mr. Powell writes of highborn English society—writes with so straight a face and so meticulously guided a pen that at first you think, "Good Lord, the man admires these creatures!" And then it comes upon you, as refreshingly as if you came suddenly upon a garden of spices, that Mr. Powell, never once widening his face or slipping his tongue into his cheek, is telling of these people with a cool, clean perception, is dissecting their lives and their fairly stately homes, and their preoccupations and their idiocies and their musical chairs of loves and marriages, with the delicate scalpel of high comedy. It is not a book at which you roar with laughter—except when a bit comes back to you and you find yourself taken with bellowing in embarrassing places—but it is, I think, as funny a work as you can find, and surgically exquisite a one. . . . *At Lady Molly's* is English humor at its civilized best. ("A curtsey or two, and a bow with a lunar arrow," December 1958, p. 48)

It is valuable, in those waning days of her life when she grew to despise the albatross of necessarily living a life of repartee, when she came often to public recollections of self-hatred, that she still had a window on her own record, however meager she felt it to be in retrospect. Wilfrid Sheed commented in the *New York Times Book Review* some years back that "She spat venomously on the old Algonquin legend. Having to be Dorothy Parker had damn-near ruined her."[95] He was only half-right. She rose, like a phoenix, transplated in time and place, from the Roaring Twenties to the Rebellious Sixties, from women's magazines to a man's magazine, and she returned with acerbic wit and standard of purity intact. Reading Dorothy Parker's last criticism, despite its occasional mannerisms, helps us to the most reliable means of our own judgment of what she was, and is, and remains.

CHAPTER 4

Conclusions

A S Dorothy Parker's life seems so paradigmatic of the "smart" period from 1915–1929; the Marxist period, 1933–1941; the war period, 1941–1945; and the rebellious aftermath when she wrote stories and plays defending women, defending the mad and the lonely, her work too was clearly a product of its times even as it on occasion transcends them. The novelist Allan Seager once told me that he taught creative writing by asking his students to imitate the short fiction of DeMaupassant until they had a clear sense of mastering form and technique. Then, he said, they could break loose and find their own voices. Whether Seager had formulated this method during his early days on *Vanity Fair* with Dorothy Parker or whether *Vanity Fair* itself suggested this practice, I do not know, but it is clear that Dorothy Parker herself followed it.

In retrospect, her work still invites our attention because she chose excellent models and lent to them her own identifiable voice, a voice both of a time and place (the "smart" age) and beyond it (the rueful, sardonic, and despairing feminine voice). She knew great poetry arises from intense experience such as Catullus' love for Lesbia or Horace's disappointment in Rome, and she brought her own life to her work; from their use of precision of detail, purity of language, and economy of expression, her own poetry took at its maturity their clarity of tone and compactness of form. "The tragic poet," Schiller remarked in 1795, "is supported by the theme, while the comic poet, on the contrary, has to keep up the aesthetic character of his theme by his own individual influence. The former may soar, which is not a very difficult matter, but the latter has to remain one and the same in tone; he has to be in the elevated region of art, where he must be at home."[1] Even while the Algonquin wits restrained Dorothy Parker's humor to spoken bon mots and sarcastic repartee, she herself searched other modes—Horace's satire,

164

Catullus' lyrics, Millay's sonnets. She saw the range of humor, stretching from open sarcasm to a tired and mordant stoicism, and her poetry reflects this wider perspective. "Her poems," Corey Ford has observed, "were exquisite cameos, poignant and haunting" as well as sudden comic reversals.[2]

She looked for the same characteristics in fiction and found them nearer home, in Hemingway and Lardner and the best of Fitzgerald. These became her models for fiction—for she felt, while proudly proclaiming her hardwon feminism,[3] that thinking of herself only as a woman would ruin her.[4] Although such sketches as "The Waltz" now seen thin and attenuated beneath the robust surfaces of situation and self-mocking characterization, these monologues and soliloquies like her stories are chiseled down to their elements, their bones wiped clean (as she remarked of Hemingway's style). She combined the impeccable grammar of "The Conning Tower" and *The New Yorker* with the casual attitude advocated by both, yet she brought to her colder, even reticent fiction a woman's eye for detail of place and costume, habitual gesture and social manner, observations so accurate and dialogue so reliable that they enrich and extend rather than dilute the acerbic satire that, from a sharply disappointed sentimentality, is the chief impulse of all her prose fiction. Her fiction is no more polished than some early essays and the middle and late criticism, but it is, in its way, less self-conscious and so less mannered. The fiction is all of a piece—the sketches, portraits, satires, and stories—but except in rare instances, such as "Dialogue at Three in the Morning," it never seems to reach toward self-parody.

The wonder of it is that, knowing her life, she could manage to write so well and for so long a time. If Charles Brackett's portrait of her in *Entirely Surrounded* is as accurate as Woollcott claimed, then she was always unhappy, self-pitying, embarrassing, sentimental. She had highs that only temporarily broke the lows; she seems, on the whole, to have been deeply perceptive, but also deeply lonely and despairing. She was a member of her own "lost generation," James R. Gaines contends, too young for World War I, too old to be a Fitzgerald "flapper."[5] In the riot of her own time and place— among the other giants and humorists—she saw only absurdity, duplicity, and heartbreak. Her most helpful response, despite her hatred of hard work and her awkward lack of self-respect, was to write. "She has had successes of many kinds, some of which have

seemed to her exacting and fastidious intelligence grotesquely un-
worthy of enjoyment, and others of which must greatly have eased
the burden of living," as James Gray puts it,[6] yet she asked of
herself, as she asks of her readers, anger at injustice, unfailing res-
ervoirs of mercy, and a piercing insight that dismisses pretensions,
with a cruel exposure. If this helped her come to terms with the
melancholy and terror of her own life and the extravagances and
silliness of her major creative periods, it still lends a unique and
difficult complexity of tones within and sometimes beneath the
many layers of which her satires are so carefully constructed. "She is
obviously," Robert Spiller once remarked, "a good deal more than a
pert humorist"[7]—there are reasons why everyone still knows
Dorothy Parker. She herself recognized what she meant to do, and
did, in remarks she made for *The New Yorker* on Samuel Hoffenstein in which we can sense both anger and disgust. "Probably his
book will be listed under the head of light verse. I don't know who
weigh verse, or what their measure is, but the fact that these true
and bitter stanzas are dazzlingly witty seems to me to make them in
no way less profound than far more cumbersome poetry" ("A Very
Dull Article, Indeed," *NY*, March 31, 1928, p. 99).

She was forever attracted to the melancholic or tragic; with Wyatt
Cooper she once raced to see a destructive forest fire ("Whatever
you think Dorothy Parker was like, she wasn't," *Esquire,* July 1968,
p. 61). "What upsets you?" David Susskind asked her in 1959 on his
television talk show "Open End." She replied, "Many things. Injustice, Intolerance, Smugness, Stupidity. . . . Segregation. I'm *very*
disturbed about that."[8] But if she despised the rich and educated
because they cared too little, she trusted and loved the little man
and woman because they asked so little.

> There is about all these characters, even the angry ones, a touching quality.
> They expect so little of life; they remember the old discouragements and
> await the new. They are not shrewd people, not even bright, and we must
> all be very patient with them. Lambs in a world of wolves, they are, and
> there is on them a protracted innocence.[9]

We think of Big Lannie or Hazel Morse. Although the words are
Dorothy Parker's speaking of Thurber, her price in her own work
was to move toward sentimentality ("Horsie") or, forcing her reserve, toward a kind of dazzling and painful coldness ("I Live on

Your Visits"). Sometimes—as with "Big Blonde," *The Coast of Ilyria, The Ladies of the Corridor,* "Portrait of the Artist"—she struck the right balance, and these victories outweigh the false starts. "Only the emotion of love takes higher rank than the emotion of laughter."[10]

"Mrs. Parker's published work does not bulk large," Woollcott wrote. "But most of it has been pure gold and the five winnowed volumes on her shelf—three of poetry, two of prose—are so potent a distillation of nectar and wormwood, of ambrosia and deadly nightshade, as might suggest to the rest of us that we all write far too much."[11] Even so, he—and we—have misjudged her. We are still amused at the surfaces of her work but neglect to consider their sardonic depths. We have praised her fiction beyond her poetry and her criticism beyond either, yet her earlier criticism can be cloying, her fiction until the mid-1930s repetitive, formulaic, mannered, emphazing her "obsession [with the rich]—all of those mousy ladies who live in drab two-room apartments and visit their 'betters' for a charitable cocktail, all of those black or Irish servants who suffer in silence and *endure.*"[12] Still she had, in the end, unerring taste and leaves in the pages of *Esquire* some of the very best personal literary criticism of the modern and postmodern periods. But her greatest success remains the epigram, a form always more European than American. Here is her chief triumph: she is the best epigrammatic poet in our country, in this century. It is not much; it is a great deal; had she been willing to believe it, she might have stopped her searching. Fortunately, she did not, and so no matter where we come upon her, she leads us back to the best of her poetry, fiction, and criticism and outward to the rest. Each still has its proportionate rewards.

Notes and References

Preface

1. Mrs. Roger Barbee in Donald Ogden Stewart's *The Crazy Fool* (1925) and Daisy Lester in Charles Brackett's *Entirely Surrounded* (1934); and Mary Hilliard in George Oppenheimer's *Here Today* (1932), Julia Glenn in George S. Kaufman and Moss Hart's *Merrily We Roll Along* (1934), and Paula Wharton in Ruth Gordon's *Over Twenty-One* (1944). The characters of Daisy and Julia are embarrassingly honest; the other three portrayals are genial and adoring, Mrs. Barbee being especially unpredictable and whimsical.

2. The challenge followed F. P. A.'s equally witty use of *meretricious:* "I wish you a meritricious and a Happy New Year."

3. Nora Ephron, *Crazy Salad* (New York, 1976 ed.), p. 139.

4. Dale Kramer, *Ross and 'The New Yorker'* (Garden City, N.Y., 1951), p. 116.

5. Margaret Case Harriman, *The Vicious Circle* (New York, 1951), p. 52.

6. Sheilah Graham, *The Garden of Allah* (New York, 1970), p. 141.

7. John Mason Brown, *The Worlds of Robert E. Sherwood* (New York, 1965), p. 132.

8. Margaret Lawrence, *The School of Femininity* (New York, 1936), p. 174

9. W. Somerset Maugham, "Variations on a Theme," in *The Viking Portable Dorothy Parker* (New York, 1944), pp. 14–15.

10. Corey Ford, *The Time of Laughter* (Boston, 1967), p. 54.

11. Lillian Hellman, *An Unfinished Woman—A Memoir* (Boston, 1969), p. 219.

12. "Books of the Times: A Magnificent Surprise From Russia," *New York Times*, July 1, 1964, p. 36.

13. Graham, p. 138.

14. Hellman, p. 226. Other Jews who were associated at one time or another with the Round Table were Groucho, Chico, Zeppo, and Gummo Marx; Dorothy Schiff; Howard Dietz; Jascha Heifitz; S. N. Behrman; Art

169

Samuels; Herman Mankiewicz; Al Getman; Raoul Fleischmann; George and Ira Gershwin; Oscar Levant; and Ben Hecht.

15. Irving Howe, *World of Our Fathers* (New York, 1976), pp. 606, 618, 564, 599, 557, 595; but see Part 4 generally.

16. "Excuse It, Please—Americans at Play; This Sentimental Grand Vizier," *New Yorker*, February 18, 1928, p. 79.

17. Jane Grant, *Ross, 'The New Yorker,' and Me* (New York, 1968), p. 120.

18. Morton Cooper, " 'Men seldom make passes/ At girls who wear glasses,' " *Diner's Club Magazine*, October 1964, p. 46; John Keats, *You Might As Well Live* (New York, 1970), p. 296.

19. "Not Enough," *New Masses*, March 14, 1939, p. 3.

20. James Gray, *On Second Thought* (Minneapolis, 1946), p. 197.

21. Oliver Goldsmith, "A Comparison between Laughing and Sentimental Comedy," in *The Comic in Theory and Practice*, ed. John J. Enck et al. (New York, 1960), p. 12.

22. Henry Fielding, "Author's Preface" to *Joseph Andrews*, Modern Library ed. (New York, 1939), p. xxx.

Chapter One

1. W. Cooper, "Whatever you think Dorothy Parker was like, she wasn't," *Esquire*, July 1968, p. 57; Harriman, p. 169.

2. Keats, p. 17.

3. W. Cooper, p. 27. Her mixed parentage "means she has the cast-iron effrontery of the Jew when put up against the world, and the cast-iron sense of superiority which is the temperamental inheritance of the Scot," Margaret Lawrence, *The School of Femininity* (New York, 1936), p. 173. "It also means that she has the knife-blade bitterness of the Jewish tongue put together with the emotional economy of the Scot. This leads her to set her remarks within the smallest containing phrase and to aim them at the bull's eye."

4. Keats, pp. 18–19.

5. "Miss Parker Never Poses," *New York Times*, January 8, 1939, IX, 4:2.

6. Marion Capron, "Dorothy Parker," in *Writers at Work*, ed. Malcolm Cowley (New York, 1959), p. 76.

7. Keats, p. 22.

8. "The New Plays," *Vanity Fair*, June 1919, p. 100.

9. Keats, p. 24.

10. Capron, p. 72.

11. Frank Crowninshield, "Crowninshield in the cub's den," *Vogue*, September 15, 1944, pp. 163, 197.

12. Capron, p. 73.

13. Frederick J. Hoffman, *The Twenties* (New York, 1962), p. 110.

14. *The Portable Ring Lardner* (New York, 1944), p. 735.

15. Robert C. Benchley, "Mr. Vanity Fair," *The Bookman,* January 1920, pp. 429–33.

16. *Vanity Fair,* ed. Cleveland Amory and Frederic Bradlee (New York, 1960), p. 11.

17. Amory and Bradlee, p. 7.

18. Crowninshield, pp. 197–98.

19. Hoffman, p. 71; cf. Charles A. Fenton, "Ambulance Drivers in France and Italy, 1914–1918," *American Quarterly,* Winter 1951.

20. "Plays of War and Peace," *Vanity Fair,* January 1919, p. 72.

21. Capron, p. 73.

22. Robert Benchley, "The Art of Being Bohemian," *Vanity Fair,* March 1916, p. 43.

23. Keats, p. 47.

24. Frank Case, *Tales of a Wayside Inn* (New York, 1938), pp. 60, 62; see also pp. 299, 349, for comments by Gertrude Atherton and Heywood Broun. Additional comments are in Harriman, pp. 7, 11, 29–31 and passim. Others joined later; see George Oppenheimer, *The Passionate Playgoer* (New York, 1958), p. 5. The best bon mots are collected in Robert E. Drennan, *The Algonquin Wits* (Secaucus, N.J., 1968).

25. Gertrude Atherton, *Black Oxen* (New York, 1923). The Sophisticates are described as "workers, engaged in doing the things they think most worth while—which are worth while because they furnish what the intelligent public is demanding just now, and upon which the current market places a high value" (p. 151). They are contrasted with the character Anne (p. 150), and one of their innumerable night parties, with word games, is dramatized in chap. XXVIII (pp. 153–61).

26. Edna Ferber, *A Peculiar Treasure* (New York, 1939), pp. 292–93. Harriman agrees, p. 229. In *George S. Kaufman and His Friends* (Garden City, N.Y., 1974), Scott Meredith (p. 223) reports Ferber's annoyance with Tess Slesinger, an imitator of Dorothy; when Slesinger asked a clerk for one of her own books, Ferber gave her one by Parker. For other accounts of the Round Table, see Meredith, chap. 10.

27. Case, p. 66.

28. Dave Smith, "Dorothy Parker and Friends: Reminiscences of the Algonquin," *Los Angeles Times,* May 4, 1976, 4:1; the occasion—where Heywood Hale Broun added she was the only one who noticed children like himself—was a meeting of the Friends of the USC Libraries. Case also recalled (p. 63): "A young girl named Dorothy Parker was frequently at the Round Table, where she would simply sit, now and then saying something at which the others would laugh." Loos (*A Girl Like I* [New York, 1966], pp. 148–49) remembers "she seldom spoke, and when she did her remarks, although bitter, were not snide and they were cleansed of offense by their wit."

29. "The Curtain Rises at 8:30, Sharp," *McCall's*, March 1928, p. 4.

30. "The Oriental Drama," *Vanity Fair*, January 1920, pp. 94, 39. Ironically, these remarks were kinder than others in the same article: she says of the actor Wallace Eddinger, "He has almost entirely lost his trick of hurrying through his speeches and ending them with a prolonged whine"; that Lillian Lorraine "has said something" when she calls herself a bad actress; and that for *The Little Blue Devil*, "Harold Atteridge has badly mangled the book and lyrics and with Harry Carroll has slightly rewritten most of the musical successes of the last few seasons." Apparently all these producers, who did not advertise in *Vanity Fair*, could be attacked with impunity.

31. "Vanity Fair Editors Out," *New York Times*, January 13, 1920, p. 10:3. The two offended who wrote him were Ziegfeld and Billie Burke, in separate letters which arrived the same day.

32. See also Keats, pp. 55–56.

33. Capron, p. 74. She should not have been startled; in 1917 Benchley had resigned from his job on the *New York Tribune Graphic* because his friend Ernest Gruening had been fired for allegedly pro-German sentiments.

34. "Life's Valentines: Florenz Ziegfeld," *Life*, February 16, 1922, p. 17.

35. Quoted by Nathaniel Benchley in *Robert Benchley* (New York, 1955), pp. 144–45.

36. Nathaniel Benchley, p. 145.

37. Keats, p. 59.

38. "Song of the Open Road," *Life*, April 7 and May 5, 1921. This note accompanied the republication: (p. 660): "Mr. Henry C. Sheridan of New York, . . . was so greatly entertained by it that he promptly forwarded a five pound box of candy to the author, a box of Corona-Corona cigars to the editorial board, and a check for $100 to LIFE's Fresh Air Farm. We reproduce the poem herewith, in the hope that it will inspire other readers to similar outbursts of generous enthusiasm."

39. "Paging Saint Patrick," *Life*, March 16, 1922, p. 3.

40. "Life's Valentines: Mr. Avery Hopwood," *Life*, February 16, 1922, p. 17.

41. "The Far-Sighted Muse," *Life*, March 9, 1922, p. 3.

42. "Fragment," *Life*, January 5, 1922, p. 1.

43. "The New Books," *Life*, November 17, 1921, p. 22.

44. Another spoof by Marc Connelly, "I Approve of Reading," tells of a business that encourages reading good books on the job and a photograph shows Dorothy visiting one of the factories to observe the plan. The issue is described and the picture reprinted in Ford, pp. 43–47. Another account is in T. L. Masson, *Our American Humorists* (New York, 1922), pp. 388–91.

45. They included several types: parodies of popular figures of folklore or pot-boiler fiction, playlets about middle-class manners, rhymed and unrhymed lyrics on the follies of love.

46. *Vanity Fair,* October 1923, p. 15.

47. Hellman, p. 35.

48. George S. Kaufman and Moss Hart, *Merrily We Roll Along* (New York, 1934), Act I, Scene iii, p. 83.

49. Edmund Wilson, in a letter to F. Scott Fitzgerald May 26, 1922. See Wilson, *Letters on Literature and Politics 1912–1972,* ed. Elena Wilson (New York, 1977), p. 85.

50. Herman Liebert in conversation with AFK at Beinecke Library, Yale Universtiy, June 28, 1964.

51. The Puncheon Club later became Jack and Charlie's; see Keats, p. 70.

52. Polly Adler describes her place as a "combination club and speakeasy." See *A House Is Not a Home* (New York, 1953), p. 96.

53. See James Thurber, *The Years with Ross* (Boston, 1958), p. 6 and passim.

54. Nancy Milford, *Zelda: A Biography* (New York, 1970), pp. 66–69.

55. Ring Lardner, Jr., *The Lardners* (New York, 1976), p. 136 and passim.

56. Howard Teichmann, *Smart Aleck: The Wit, World and Life of Alexander Woollcott* (New York, 1976), p. 169. Cf. all of Chapter 13, and see also Samuel Hopkins Adams, *A. Woollcott* (New York, 1945), pp. 184–86. Charles Brackett's novel (*Entirely Surrounded,* 1934) is about the island; Woollcott (*Letters* [New York, 1944], p. 135) wrote Noel Coward August 11, 1934, "The portrait of Dorothy Parker is the most astonishingly skillful."

57. Babette Rosmond, *Robert Benchley* (New York, 1970), p. 65.

58. Quoted in Keats, pp. 60–62.

59. Capron, p. 79.

60. Quoted in Keats, pp. 82, 74.

61. Loos, *A Girl Like I,* p. 150.

62. Ben Hecht, *Letters from Bohemia* (Garden City, N. Y., 1964), pp. 193, 187.

63. *Enough Rope* (New York, 1926), p. 51.

64. Quoted in Graham, p. 144.

65. *Sunset Gun* (New York, 1928), p. 75.

66. Quoted in Keats, p. 100.

67. Harriman, p. 159.

68. Nancy Hoyt, *Elinor Wylie* (Indianapolis, 1935), p. 94.

69. *Sunset Gun,* p. 21.

70. The complete program is in Harriman, pp. 89–97; lyrics are in Brown, p. 171; Dale Kramer, *Heywood Broun* (New York, 1949), p. 137.

71. Meredith, pp. 104–106, assigns the failure to high costs, few seats, and the aging May Irwin as interlocutor.

72. "Optimism and the Drama," *Vanity Fair*, March 1920, p. 41.

73. For statistics on the expanding Broadway theater of 1924, see Abel Green and Joe Laurie, Jr., *Show Biz* (New York, 1951), p. 207.

74. Quoted in Keats, p. 102.

75. Earlier that year she urged people to support a show put together by McMein, Woollcott, and Connelly for the Ellin Speyer Hospital for Animals and the American Humane Association. See "What Is a Benefit?" in *New York Times*, February 24, 1924, VII, 2:4.

76. Stage directions, Kaufman and Hart, Act II, Scene i, p. 95.

77. Stage direction, Kaufman and Hart, Act I, Scene ii, p. 41.

78. Quoted by James R. Gaines, *Wit's End* (New York, 1977), p. 156.

79. For a fuller discussion, see Calvin Tomkins, *Living Well is the Best Revenge* (New York, 1971); also, Carlos Baker, *Ernest Hemingway* (New York, 1969), pp. 158 and passim.; Andrew Turnbull, *Scott Fitzgerald* (New York, 1962), pp. 154 and passim.

80. Quoted in Gaines, p. 113.

81. F. Scott Fitzgerald, *Letters*, ed. Andrew Turnbull (New York, 1963), p. 305.

82. Thurber, *The Years with Ross*, p. 6.

83. Ferber, p. 320.

84. Lardner, p. 171.

85. Bennet Cerf, *Try and Stop Me* (New York 1945), p. 112; this may be apocryphal since it is also a scene in Charles Brackett, *Entirely Surrounded* (New York, 1934), p. 22–23. She was a guest of Swope at the opening of *Mourning Becomes Electra* in 1931. See Arthur and Barbara Gelb, *O'Neill* (New York, 1962), p. 751; Gaines, *Wit's End*, p. 72.

86. *Enough Rope*, p. 74.

87. *New York Times*, April 9, 1928, 44:6–7. Eddie Parker later remarried, but died childless of an overdose of sleeping powders (*Hartford Courant*, January 8, 1933, I, 6).

88. Keats, pp. 156–57.

89. Quoted in Keats, p. 161.

90. Quoted in Keats, pp. 124–25.

91. *Enough Rope*, p. 61.

92. Genevieve Taggard, "You Might As Well Live," *New York Herald Tribune*, March 27, 1927, VII, 7:3.

93. *Enough Rope*, p. 59.

94. The entry for November 17, 1926: "To the office, and so home and at my scrivening, and then Dorothy Parker come to see me, and I overjoyed to see her, and she told me about her peregrinations abroad, and I asked her about Ernest Hemingway, and how old he was, and she said, 'Well, I don't know. You know all writers are either twenty-nine or Thomas Hardy.'

And we talked of this and that, and I told her unless somebody should be John Milton in a few days I should have to award her a watch for the best piece wrote in my column this year. Which would be good news to those that have appointments with her, I think."

For other poems, parodies, and her influence, see as examples the columns for November 16, 23, and 24, 1926; February 22, March 10, 16, August 31, 1927; February 3, March 6, May 25, December 12, 1928; March 15, April 8, 1929.

95. Edmund Wilson, "The Muses Out of Work," *New Republic,* May 11, 1927, p. 321.

96. John Farrar, "Anonymously—John Farrar," *The Bookman,* March 1928, p. 70.

97. Quoted in Morris W. Yates, *The American Humorist* (Ames, Iowa, 1964), p. 227. Other accounts are in Grant, Kramer, Thurber, and Brendan Gill, *Here at "The New Yorker"* (New York, 1975).

98. Thurber, *The Years with Ross,* pp. 20–21.

99. "Re-enter Margot Asquith—A Masterpiece from the French," *New Yorker,* October 22, 1927, p. 98; "The Professor Goes in for Sweetness and Light," *New Yorker,* November 5, 1927, p. 90; "Far from Well," *New Yorker,* October 20, 1928, p. 98; rep. *Constant Reader* (New York, 1970), pp. 10–11, 19, 101. Later references are included within the text. Grant (p. 9) calls the remark on Milne "the most hypersensitive literary criticism the magazine ever published, and the best." Meredith notes (p. 319) that Dorothy once told Kaufman "she sometimes reviewed a book without reading it, simply looking at the jacket blurb and forming her opinion that way." She might have been joking with Kaufman, whom she did not especially like, but her reviews—carefully phrased as they are—do not often go into detail on the contents of the books.

100. " 'You've got to watch Woollcott and Long and Parker,' " Ross told Thurber, " 'they keep trying to get double meanings into their stuff to embarrass me.' " Quoted in Thurber, p. 12.

101. Leon Whipple, "Letters and Life," *The Survey,* November 1, 1928, 170:2.

102. The story is recounted in Keats, p. 151.

103. T. S. Matthews, "Curses Not Loud But Deep," *The New Republic,* September 17, 1930, p. 133.

104. Henry Seidel Canby, "Belle Dame sans Merci," *Saturday Review,* June 13, 1931, p. 891.

105. Capron, p. 75.

106. Ogden Nash, "The Pleasure Is Ours," *Saturday Review,* November 4, 1933, p. 231.

107. Mark Van Doren in Keats, p. 181.

108. Quoted in Keats, p.132.

109. *New York Times,* August 11, 1927, 1:5; 2:3, 4.

110. G. Louis Joughin and Edmund M. Morgan, *The Legacy of Sacco and Vanzetti* (New York, 1948), p. 282.

111. Keats (p. 146) finds twenty-eight shared similarities and notes the resemblance to "Such a Pretty Little Picture." "Big Blonde" is Dorothy Parker's most frequently reprinted story.

112. Fitzgerald, p. 215.

113. John Emerson and Anita Loos, "Movies—The Eighth Art," *Vanity Fair*, March 1920, p. 104.

114. But the boom that peaked in 1924 began to slide into serious depression by 1929. The decline was steady, except for 1935–36, when the situation improved slightly, until it bottomed out in 1941. A chart and authoritative discussion are in Jack Poggi, *Theater in America* (Ithaca, N. Y., 1968), chapters 3, 4.

115. In an advertisement for *Hard Lines* in *Saturday Review* for June 17, 1931 (p. 544); the lines are from Montana-Vermala, and Nash's reply accompanies them. Warner Brothers also made a short, "At the Round Table," in the early 1930s in which she may have appeared.

116. Dorothy Emerson, "Poetry Corner," *Scholastic*, March 13, 1936, p. 11.

117. It has since been popular in summer stock. Oppenheimer's witty comments on it are in *The Passionate Playgoer: A Personal Scrapbook* (New York, 1958), pp. 5–6.

118. Details are in Keats, pp. 187–89.

119. International News Service reported on June 15, 1934, that she and Alan were married in October 1933 at her sister's home on Long Island; her divorce papers submitted in 1947 assign the marriage to 1934 in Raton, New Mexico. International News Service also reported on July 12, 1934, a prank whereby Denver's socially prominent people were invited to a party at the Campbells' that Alan and Dorothy knew nothing about. The *Los Angeles Times'* first reference is headed "Dorothy Parker's Secret Marriage to Actor Bared." The report was handled variously in various papers.

120. Undated letter from 3783 Meade St., Denver, now bMS Am 1449 (1280) (4) in Houghton Library, Harvard University.

121. Graham, p. 11. alan Campbell once told Charles Champlin: " 'The rooms were dark, the tapestries dingy, the furniture ugly and the beds were hard,' " but the only choice was the Beverly Hills Hotel where Dorothy claimed "the elephants go to die." *Los Angeles Times*, June 18, 1967, Calendar, p. 6.

122. Graham, p. 140.

123. *New York Times*, "Miss Parker Never Poses," January 8, 1939, IX, 4:2.

124. Keats, p. 182.

125. Undated ts letter to Woollcott, bMS Am 1449 (1280) (5), Houghton Library, Harvard.

126. Teichmann, p. 252; Richard Corliss, *Talking Pictures* (Baltimore, 1975), p. 257; Graham, p. 108. See also Corliss, p. 5.

127. Graham, p. 146; LH to AFK, August 11, 1964.

128. Keats, pp. 179, 184; Graham p. 141.

129. Milford, p. 290.

130. Quoted by Gilmore Millen, "Dorothy Parker, Noted N. Y. Wit, Yearns for Farm Life," *Los Angeles Times,* September 24, 1936.

131. Unsigned, "Dorothy Parker, Farmer: Gets 111 Acres near Doylestown, Pa.; Restoring Homestead," *New York Times,* August 24, 1936, p. 13:5.

132. Anita Loos, *Kiss Hollywood Good-by* (New York, 1974), p. 119. Other names on the impressive list were Zoë Atkins, Maxwell Anderson, Michael Arlen, Vicki Baum, Benchley, Stephen Vincent Benet, Fitzgerald, Hart, Hecht, Samuel Hoffenstein, Sidney Howard, Aldous Huxley, Christopher Isherwood, Kaufman, MacArthur, S. J. Perelman. All were short-term contracts that were not usually renewed.

133. SELZNICK INTERNATIONAL PICTURES, INC.
                9336 Washington Boulevard, Culver City, Cal.
Dear Gerald [she often joked with pseudonyms],
    So last week, the board of directors of Selznick Pictures, Inc., had a conference. The four members of the board sat around a costly table in an enormously furnished room, and each was supplied with a pad of scratch paper and a pencil. After the conference was over, a healthily curious young employe[*sic*]of the company went in to look at those scratch pads. He found:
    Mr. David Selznick had drawn a seven-pointed star; below that, a six-pointed star; and below that again, a row of short vertical lines, like a little picket fence.
    Mr. John Hay Whitney's pad had nothing whatever on it.
    Dr. A. H. Giannini, the noted California banker, had written over and over, in a long, neat column, the word "tokas," which is Yiddish for "arse."
    And Mr. Meryan Cooper, the American authority on technicolor, had printed, in the middle of his page, "RIN-TIN-TIN."
    The result of the conference was the announcement that hereafter the company would produce twelve pictures a year, instead of six.
    I don't know. I just thought you might like to be reassured that Hollywood does not change.
Undated letter to Woollcott, bMS Am 1449 (1279) (3), Houghton Library, Harvard.

134. Donald Ogden Stewart, "Writing for the Movies," *Focus on Film* 5, November-December 1970, p. 52.

135. "Hollywood, The Land I Won't Return To," *Seven Arts* 7, pp. 133, 135.

136. CB to AFK, August 1964.

137. Bob Thomas, *Selznick* (Garden City, N. Y., 1970), p. 118. This film "gave the industry's big-city screenwriters a chance to vent their cynicism about the prevailing rural-American dream" (Corliss, p. 15).

138. Graham, pp. 144, 145.

139. Quoted in Rudy Behlmer and Tony Thomas, *Hollywood's Hollywood* (Secaucus, N. J., 1975), p. 190.

140. *New York Times* film review rep. *New York Times Film Reviews 1913–1968*, 6 vols. (New York, 1970), II, 1284. Hereafter cited as *NYTFR*.

141. *NYTFR*, II, 1326.

142. Anonymous, "So They Say," *The Golden Book Magazine*, July 1932, p. 13.

143. Rudy Behlmer, ed., *Memo from David O. Selznick* (New York, 1972), p. 98; Behlmer and Thomas, p. 81; Thomas p. 113; Lardner, p. 190.

144. *NYTFR*, II, 1384–85.

145. It was likely at this time and likely about Miriam Hopkins, mistress of William Randolph Hearst, that Dorothy spontaneously composed a jingle recalled by Anita Loos in *A Girl Like I* (p. 149). It had to do with Hopkins' special dressing room with a statue of the Madonna at the entrance: "Upon my honor/ I saw a Madonna/ Standing in a niche/ Above the door/ Of a prominent whore/ Of a prominent son of a bitch."

146. The film was produced by Hunt Stromberg for MGM; it featured Frank Morgan, Ray Bolger, and Mischa Auer—a varied cast to write for.

147. *NYTFR*, III, 1569.

148. "The Time and the Place," Amory and Bradlee, p. 300.

149. Edmund Wilson, "It's Terrible! It's Ghastly! It Stinks!, " *New Republic*, July 21, 1937, p. 312.

150. Quoted by Donald Ogden Stewart in *Fighting Words* (New York, 1940), p. 37.

151. Harold Clurman, "Dorothy Parker—A Wit at Whatever Cost," *Los Angeles Times*, November 29, 1970, Book Review, p. 24.

152. "The Fall Crop of War Plays," *Vanity Fair*, October 1918, p. 56; November 1919, p. 37; "Duces Wild," *The New Yorker*, September 15, 1928, p. 95.

153. Walter B. Rideout, *The Radical Novel in the United States, 1900–1954* (Cambridge, Massachusetts, 1956), pp. 138–39.

154. Keats, p. 192.

155. Clurman, p. 24.

156. See Jay Martin, *Nathanael West, The Art of His Life* (New York, 1970), p. 345; Hoffman, p. 421; Malcolm Cowley, *Exile's Return* (New York, 1956), pp. 294–96. Lincoln Steffens wrote his wife Ella Winter when she was in Russia, "Get it all; all but the details. Get it as a whole. . . . Russia is just what Dorothy Parker, Hemingway, Dos Passos and all the Youth school

of writers lack and need." Quoted in Alfred Kazin, *On Native Grounds* (New York, 1942), p. 377.

157. "Not Enough," *New Masses*, March 14, 1939, p. 3. The Anti-Nazi League did a reading of Irwin Shaw's "Bury the Dead" with Frederic March and Florence Eldredge, Stewart recalls, and they were accused of being communists. Thalberg closed his doors to all of them and investigations into their loyalties increased. They refused to "clear" themselves. Three important primary accounts are Stewart, pp. 53–54; Arnaud D'Usseau, "A Screenwriter Speaks," *New Masses*, September 12, 1939, pp. 29–31; and Dalton Trumbo, *The Time of the Toad* (privately printed, 1947; New York, 1972). Dorothy read and approved Trumbo's book; see Trumbo, *Additional Dialogue: Letters of Dalton Trumbo*, ed. Helen Manfull (New York, 1970), Mrs. Trumbo to Mrs. Williams, February 23, 1956.

158. Stewart, *Fighting Words*, p. 119.

159. Quoted in Martin, p. 347. His discussion of leftist Hollywood movements is perceptive and succinct.

160. "Not Enough," *New Masses*, March 14, 1939, p. 3.

161. "Authors Aid Roosevelt," *New York Times*, October 19, 1936, p. 2:6; Graham, p. 160.

162. Lardner, p. 258.

163. Much of the photography was in Morales, outside Madrid, where the cameramen saw a Republican attack and were sniped at themselves. Leicester Hemingway, *My Brother, Ernest Hemingway* (Cleveland, 1962), pp. 197–98.

164. Lillian Hellman, *Pentimento* (Boston, 1973), p. 103.

165. Quoted in Burton Bernstein, *Thurber* (New York, 1975), p. 279.

166. "Incredible, Fantastic. . . and True," *New Masses*, November 23, 1937, p. 16.

167. Samuel Hopkins Adams, *A. Woollcott: His Life and His World* (New York, 1945), p. 296; the second remark was in a letter to Rebecca West, February 21, 1938. See Woollcott's *Letters*, ed. Beatrice Kaufman and Joseph Hennessey (New York, 1944), p. 203.

168. Leon W. Schloss, "Dorothy Parker Quits Her Role as Humorist," *Los Angeles Times*, January 7, 1939.

169. "Review and Comment," *New Masses*, June 27, 1939, p. 21.

170. Fitzgerald, *Letters*, p. 430. Earlier that year, the *New York Times* reported that Frank Case of the Algonquin was suing Dorothy and Alan Campbell for failure to pay for a party they claimed they had not requested, on December 2, 1938, honoring Philip Barry on the opening of his play *Here Come the Clowns* ("488 Party No Joke to Dorothy Parker," *New York Times*, March 16, 1939, 25:2; March 19, IV, 2:6).

171. Hellman, *Pentimento*, pp. 176–78; LH to AFK August 11, 1964.

172. *NYTFR*, III, 1818.

173. Letter to Woollcott dated September 2 (1942?) from Fox Farm, Pipersville, Pa.; b MS Am 1449 (1278) (2), Houghton Library, Harvard.

174. Ruth Gordon's play *Over Twenty-One* (New York, 1944) is about "Soldiers coming alone, girls tracking right along with them" (p. 31); it is fairly factual about the Campbells at Miami Beach. The play was later a film starring Irene Dunne and Alexander Knox.

175. "Destructive Decoration," *House and Graden*, February 1942, p. 34.

176. Introduction, *Watch on the Rhine*, quoted in Richard Moody, *Lillian Hellman, Playwright* (New York, 1972), p. 134.

177. "Miss Brass Tacks of 1943," *Mademoiselle*, May 1943, pp. 85, 144, 146; rep. as "Are We Women or Are We Mice?" in *Reader's Digest*, July 1943, pp. 71–72.

178. "War Fund Women to Seek $1,000,000," *New York Times*, September 27, 1944, p. 24:5; "War Fund Women Raise $1,337,335," November 17, 1944, p. 23:8.

179. Maugham, "Introduction," *The Viking Portable Dorothy Parker* (New York, 1944), pp. 17, 18.

180. John O'Hara, untitled, *New York Times*, May 28, 1944, VII, 5:1–5; 28:1–3; J. Donald Adams, "Speaking of Books," *New York Times*, June 11, 1944, VII, 2:2–5.

181. *The Viking Portable Dorothy Parker*, p. 534.

182. Matthew J. Bruccoli, *The O'Hara Concern* (New York, 1975), p. 180; Dorothy selected *The Great Gatsby, Tender Is the Night,* "Absolution," "The Baby Party," "The Rich Boy," "May Day," "The Cut-Glass Bowl," "The Offshore Pirate," "The Freshest Boy," "Crazy Sunday," and "Babylon Revisited."

183. Keats reports (p. 252) later productions of the play in London and Edinburgh, but they failed to materialize. Minutes of the Edinburgh Festival Society approved a production of "The Incomparable Sister" on February 8, 1949; in March 1949, the Society approved Dorothy's change of title to "Coast of Illyria," while on March 29 they declined still another title change by Dorothy to "Mary is from Home" [sic]. Clearly Dorothy had much at stake with this work and she continued fussing—she revised so heavily that Flora Robson declined the role of Mary Lamb and on June 21 it was announced by the Artistic Director of the Edinburg Festival that performances of the play were suspended and the production was replaced by Peter Ustinov's *The Man in the Raincoat* (Edinburgh Festival Society minutes; 1949 Edinburgh Festival Program; letter to AFK from G. W. Bain, September 1, 1977). Peter Ustinov has no further recollection of what happened (Ustinov to AFK, June 28, 1977).

184. She admitted nothing, but Frederic March was more open; he admitted giving an ambulance to the Loyalists and one to Finland and France during the Russo-German pact in 1940, although he did not implicate Dorothy.

185. Trumbo, *Additional Dialogue*, p. 133.

186. Lillian Hellman, whom Berkeley cited as being with Dorothy at a communist organizational meeting, was asked about them both in a hearing before the House Un-American Activities Committee on May 21, 1952; the transcript is in Eric Bentley, *Thirty Years of Treason* (New York, 1971), pp. 535 ff. Hellman denies the charges in *Scoundrel Time* (Boston, 1976), p. 81. Ironically, Reuters announced on April 18, 1959, that a Moscow publishing house had just released a volume of Dorothy Parker's stories, but the fact came too late for the McCarthy hearings.

187. Charles Grutzner, "Red Fronts Face Fund Appeal Ban," *New York Times*, February 26, 1955, 1:7; 5:2—4; "Investigations: Where'd the Money Go? " *Newsweek*, March 7, 1955, pp. 25–26.

188. Capron, p. 79.

189. Keats, p. 263; Brooks Atkinson, "At the Theater" *New York Times*, October 22, 1953.33: 5—6; Woolcott Gibbs, "The Lost Lady" *New Yorker*, October 31, 1953, pp. 58–60; *Newsweek* (review) November 2, 1953, p. 65. Atkinson's reviews were negative, as was an unsigned review in *Time* for November 2, 1953 which read in part, "despite its virtues, the play comes, somehow, to make too much of a bad thing," p. 82.

190. Hellman, *Pentimento*, p. 161.

191. AG to AFK, May 10, 1963.

192. Janet Winn, "Capote, Mailer, and Miss Parker," *New Republic*, February 9, 1959, pp. 27–28.

193. Murray Schumach, "Dorothy Parker Discusses TV," *New York Times*, May 6, 1962, II, 17:6–8.

194. Mary Ann Callan, "Students Appalling to Dorothy Parker," *Los Angeles Times*, April 28, 1963, 1:30.

195. CB to AFK, September 23, 1964.

196. Mrs. Barbara Holdridge to AFK, August 12, 1964; Howard Sackler, who directed the production, wrote: "Miss Booth seemed to me the ideal reader of Parker: her whole style is flavored with the 'sophistication' of the period, she *illuminates* it through those women. And I feel that it *is* dated—as Wilde is, or Sir Thomas Overbury—and that one should perform a dated piece—when it's worth doing—in its own terms, i. e. to set it squarely in its time and atmosphere, and not 'bring it up to date': it becomes untrue. Coriolanus, after all, is not Mussolini." HS to AFK, September 12, 1964. But Shirley Booth had also performed Dorothy Parker in the 1930s (see above, p. 52).

197. "My Home Town," *McCall's*, January 1928, p. 4.

198. "New York at Six-thirty P.M.," *Esquire*, November 1964, p. 100.

199. Brendan Gill, "Introduction," *The Portable Dorothy Parker* (New York, 1977 ed.) p. xvi.

200. Teichmann, p. 317. She later attacked Adams' biography of Woollcott *(New York Times*, June 24, 1945, VII, 21:2–3), noting: "I am bitterly angry that I must write 'the late' before his name."

201. Capron, p. 82.

202. Wyatt Cooper, *Esquire*, July 1968, pp. 111–12.

203. FS to AFK, August 20, 1976.

204. "The Middle or Blue Period," *The Portable Dorothy Parker*, p. 596.

205. Donald Ogden Stewart, *Fighting Words*, pp. 38, 39.

206. "Dorothy Parker, Venerable Critic at 70, Explodes Several Legends about Herself," *The New Haven Register*, October 13, 1963, p. 12.

207. Lardner, p. 190.

208. Keats, p. 296.

209. Quoted in Moody, p. 340.

210. Alexander Woollcott, *While Rome Burns* (New York, 1934), p. 149.

211. N. Benchley, p. 249.

212. Woollcott, *While Rome Burns*, p. 148.

Chapter Two

1. Grant Showerman, *Horace and His Influence* (Boston, 1922), p. 43.

2. Aldous Huxley, "The Importance of the Comic Genius," in *Vanity Fair*, ed. Amory and Bradlee, p. 83.

3. Gilbert Seldes, *The Seven Lively Arts* (New York, 1924; rep. 1962), p. 121.

4. *Enough Rope*, p. 109.

5. *Enough Rope*, p. 34.

6. Max Eastman, *Vanity Fair*, June 1916, p. 63.

7. Eastman, pp. 63, 124.

8. The portrait of Herford is a good example of the Round Table members supporting each other; Beatrice Herford as "The Algonquin Girl" would close the Round Table's show *No, Sirree!* a year later (April 30, 1922) with a monologue. The program is reprinted in James R. Gaines, *Wit's End* (New York, 1977), p. 63.

References to magazine pieces will be given in the text whenever possible. The following abbreviations will be used: *VF (Vanity Fair), LHJ (Ladies' Home Journal), SEP (Saturday Evening Post), NY (New Yorker), NYT (New York Times), RD (Reader's Digest), HB (Harper's Bazaar)*.

9. "On the Trail of a Wife," *VF*, December 1919, pp. 60, 61; "Our Great American Sport," *VF*, January 1920, pp. 62–63; "The Throes of First Love," *VF*, March 1920, pp. 68, 69. "Fish" is profiled in *VF*, December 1919, p. 59.

10. "Why I Haven't Married," *VF*, October 1916, pp. 51, 122.

11. "Why I Haven't Married"; "Our Tuesday Club," *LHJ*, July 1920, pp. 4, 83; "A Dinner Party Anthology," *LHJ*, August 1920, pp. 4, 121; "A Summer Hotel Anthology," *LHJ*, September 1920, pp. 32, 194; "An Apartment House Anthology," *SEP*, August 20, 1921, pp. 10, 11, 66, 71; "Men I'm Not Married To," *SEP*, June 17, 1922, pp. 13, 42. Shorter portraits appear in *Life* in 1921–1923.

12. "As the Spirit Moves," *SEP*, May 22, 1920, pp. 8, 9, 108, 111; "Welcome Home," *SEP*, July 22, 1922, pp. 9, 60, 62, 64; "Our Own Crowd," *SEP*, October 21, 1922, pp. 10, 125, 126; "You Must Come See Us Sometime," *SEP*, September 1, 1923, pp. 10, 11, 38, 41.

13. "My Home Town," *McCall's*, January 1928, p. 4; "The New York Type," *McCall's*, February 1928, p. 8; "The Curtain Rises at 8:30, Sharp," *McCall's*, March 1928, p. 4; "Spring Song," *McCall's*, April 1928, p. 8; "Toward the Dog Days," *McCall's*, May 1928, p. 8. Cf. "At the Dog Show," *Cosmopolitan*, May 1934, pp. 62, 63, 114.

14. Ernest Hemimgway, "On the American Dead in Spain," *New Masses*, February 14, 1939, p. 3.

15. John Bright, "Orchids for Dorothy Parker," *New Masses*, December 7, 1937, p. 17.

16. Other of her essays, discussed in Chapter 1, are: "Out of the Silence," *NY*, September 1, 1928, pp. 28, 30, 32; "Hollywood, the Land I Won't Return To," *Seven Arts* 5, pp. 130–40; "Destructive Decoration," *House and Garden*, February 1942, pp. 33–35, 88; "What Is a Benefit?" *NYT*, February 24, 1924, VII, 2:4; "Miss Brass Tacks of 1943," *Mlle*, May 1943, pp. 85, 144, 146, rep. *RD*, July 1943, pp. 71–72; "Who Is That Man?" *Vogue*, July 1944, pp. 67, 138, 139, rep. *RD*, September 1944, pp. 79–81, with letters of reply.

17. Louis Kronenberger, "Introduction," *An Anthology of Light Verse* (New York, 1935), pp. v–vi.

18. See, for example, *The World*, March 19, 1922, 11:1; January 2, 1925, 9:1. The first series here lists Dorothy's "hate songs" in *VF*, the second her "hymns of hate" in *Life*.

19. Quoted by F. P. A. in *Innocent Merriment* (New York, 1942), pp. 159–60. For F. P. A.'s parodied response see his column in *The World* for September 23, 1924, 13:1. F. P. A. credits Villon with teaching him the form. An early example of Dorothy Parker's rondeaus, uncollected, is in *SEP*, November 11, 1922, p. 84.

20. For an example, see *The World*, August 16, 1929, 11:1; for an unsuccessful poem that draws largely on Wylie, see "How Bold It Is," *The World*, February 22, 1923, 13:1.

21. Cf., for example, "Ich trat in jene Hallen" or "Es liegt der heisse Sommer," which Joseph Auslander translates:

> The fervent flame of Summer
> Lies in your lovely cheek;
> But in your heart the Winter
> Lies old and cold and bleak.
> All this will change, my precious,
> And sooner than you seek:
> The Summer in your heart, dear,
> The Winter in your cheek.

(Heinrich Heine, *Bittersweet Poems* [Mount Vernon, N.Y., 1956], p. 19.)

22. The best-known imitator of Dorothy Parker is Fanny Heaslip Lea. See as an example her "Obituary" in *Harper's Bazaar*, March 1931, p. 156. Thus far, my research has uncovered sixty-eight poems in *Life* between 1920–1926 that Dorothy omitted from her volumes of published poetry, as well as fifteen from *Vanity Fair* (1915–1920), six from *The World* (1923–1929), five from *New Yorker* (1925–1938), and eight from *Saturday Evening Post* (1922–1923).

23. Elmer Rice, *The Living Theatre* (New York, 1959), p. 15. *Close Harmony* was first copywritten as *Soft Music* in 1924, taking its present title in 1929.

24. Robert Benchley, *Life*, December 18, 1924, p. 18. Cf. Heywood Broun, "Seeing Things at Night," *The World*, December 1, 1924, 9:6; Alexander Woollcott, *The Sun*, December 1, 1924, 20:4–5; John Anderson, *Post*, December 1, 1924, 14:1; Robert Littell, "Main Street in the Theatre," *New Republic*, December 24, 1924, p. 20.

25. Broun, *Sunday World*, December 7, 1924, Metropolitan Section, 3:1–2.

26. *Close Harmony* (New York, [1929]), p. 85. Further references are given in the text.

27. Louis Bromfield, "The New Yorker," *The Bookman*, February 1925, p. 742.

28. Keats, p. 102.

29. See details above, p. 180, n. 183.

30. Keats, p. 252.

31. Eric Bentley, *The Dramatic Event* (New York, 1954), p. 154.

32. Milton Bracker, "Lonely 'Ladies of the Corridor,' " *New York Times*, October 18, 1953, II, 1:4–6, 3:4–7.

33. Bentley, *Dramatic Event*, p. 154.

34. Brooks Atkinson, "At the Theatre: Edna Best and Betty Field Are Starred in 'The Ladies of the Corridor,' " *New York Times*, October 22, 1953, 33:5–6; subsequently, he reported that five of eight critics approved the play, two "with fervor," but while admitting that it "is beautifully played in every part by the most notable cast of the season," he insisted that the play "is hardly more than a literal report of the obvious" ("Hotel Widows: 'The Ladies of the Corridor' Who Have Money, But No Personal Resources," *New York Times*, November 1, 1953, II, 1:1–2). One of the five was Woolcott Gibbs, who reported in the *New Yorker* that this "monumental enterprise" was partly the work of Dorothy Parker, "who is in the habit these days of irritably deprecating her reputation as a wit, is responsible not only for the precise and deadly wit that frequently punctuates the script but also for the acute understanding of human loneliness, cruelty, stupidity, and occasional glowing, unpredictable fortitude that gives the characters their intermittent flashes of absolute fidelity to life" ("The Lost Ladies," October 13, 1953, p. 58).

35. *The Ladies of the Corridor* (New York, 1954), p. 3. Further references are given in the text.

36. "What is more morbid than meaninglessness? Or bad art?" Bentley, *Dramatic Event*, p. 155.

Chapter Three

1. *Enough Rope*, p. 31. Further references will be given in the text.

2. John Jay Chapman, "The Poets of the Future," *Vanity Fair*, July 1919, p. 45.

3. Kenneth Quinn, *The Catullan Revolution* (Melbourne, 1959), p.26.

4. Karl Pomeroy Harrington, *Catullus and His Influence* (Boston, 1923), pp. 46, 51–53.

5. Harrington, pp. 62, 219.

6. Harrington, p. 218.

7. E. A. Havelock, *The Lyric Genius of Catullus* (Oxford, 1939), pp. 98–100.

8. Harrington, p. 220.

9. *The Poems of Catullus* (New York, 1931); the poems were being circulated earlier than that. Cf. Catullus, numbers 57, 69, 72.

10. Compare "One Perfent Rose" (p. 73) and "The Choice" (p.96) in *Enough Rope*.

11. George L. Watson, *A. E. Housman: A Divided Life* (London, 1957), pp. 138, 203, 219. Reviews of *A Shropshire Lad* (p. 161) point to qualities common to Dorothy Parker's poetry; Housman too collected and published with his brother parodies and light verse. See Laurence Housman, *A. E. H.: Some Poems, Some Letters and a Personal Memoir by his Brother* (London, 1937), pp.229–47.

12. Cyril Connelly in *The New Statesman* for May 23, 1936, quoted in Grant Richards, *Housman: 1897–1936* (New York, 1942), p. 365.

13. Letter to Sydney Cockrell January 15, 1932, quoted in Richards, p. 387; Watson, pp. 213–14.

14. Miriam Gurko, *Restless Spirit* (New York, 1962), pp. 13, 240; Anne Cheney, *Millay in Greenwich Village* (University, Ala., 1975), p. 114; Watson, pp. 213–14.

15. Cf. James Gray, *Edna St. Vincent Millay*, University of Minnesota Pamphlets on American Writers 64 (Minneapolis, 1967), p.45.

16. Gurko, pp. 124–25.

17. Edna St. Vincent Millay, *A Few Figs from Thistles* (New York, 1922), p.9.

18. Millay, *A Few Figs*, p. 12. Other appropriate poems in *Figs* are on pp. 13–15, 19–21, 23–26, 33, 34, 36, 37. Her attitude toward woman's independence as well as her tight form and classical allusions are common to Dorothy's work; Louise Bogan has spoken of it as Millay's influence (LB to AFK, August 4, 1964). *Figs* was Millay's third book; but see also "Sonnet II" in *Renascence* (1919) and, in *Second April* (1921), pp.27, 37–39, 47–48,

56–57. "Vincent's first appearance on the Vassar dramatic scene was when she recited, in Latin and nestling in her hands a dead song-sparrow borrowed from the Museum of Natural History, Catullus' 'Passer Mortuus Est' " (Gurko, pp. 62–63); the poem is in *Second April*, p. 29. See also Millay's fourth book,, *The Harp-Weaver and Other Poems* (1923), pp. 10, 11, 17, 19, 22, 23, 26, 27, 56.

19. Cf. Gurko, p. 130. There are, in fact, too many connections to be studied here. Cf. Gray, p. 16: "Despite the many sidelong references to the physical relationship, the enclosing interest is that of human love as a total experience of the psyche involving, on the positive side, the endless warfare of two egos that cannot effect a complete surrender into oneness."

20. A good discussion of Wylie is in Thomas A. Gray, *Elinor Wylie* (New York, 1969), chap. 2; for their friendship, see p. 40 above. Wylie's *Collected Poems* (1932) and *Last Poems* (1943) show more interest in the soft line and enjambment and a considerably more romantic cast. A comparison can be made with "Valentine" (*Collected Poems*, p. 41) and the contrast seen with "Restoration Love Song" (*Last Poems*, p. 90).

21. Warren H. Cudworth, Preface, *Odes of Horace* (Norwood, Mass., 1917), p. xi.

22. Louis Untermeyer, *Including Horace* (New York, 1919), pp. xiii–xiv.

23. These characteristics were associated then with Horace; see Grant Showerman, *Horace and His Influence* (Boston, 1922) and Tenney Frank, *Catullus and Horace* (New York, 1928). Like Dorothy, Horace read widely but not deeply; he was especially concerned with society and manners and found it difficult, therefore, not to write satire. Housman published a number of papers on Horace and felt his *Ode IV. vii* "the most beautiful poem in ancient literature" (Tom Burns Haber, *A. E. Housman* [New York, 1967] p. 96); Housman's own brief corpus of one hundred and three odes in four books may be a direct imitation of Horace. See Norman Marlow, *A. E. Housman: Scholar and Poet* (London, 1958), p. 60. Horace was popular with the Round Table, and Broun even named his Connecticut home Sabine Farm.

24. Quoted in Charles H. Dennis, *Eugene Field's Creative Years* (Garden City, N. Y., 1924), p. 167.

25. Eugene Field, *Echoes from the Sabine Farm* in *Works of Eugene Field* (New York, 1898), VI, 380.

26. Dennis, pp. 167–68.

27. Gilbert Seldes, *The Seven Lively Arts* (New York, 1924; rep. 1962), p. 246. Seldes recalls (p. 245) that Adams used to quarrel about the quantitative meter in Horace.

28. Quoted in Yates, *The American Humorist* (1964), p. 253.

29. Franklin P. Adams, *In Other Words* (Garden City, N. Y., 1912), p. 21.

30. Franklin P. Adams, *Tobogganing on Parnassus* (Garden City, N. Y., 1916), p. 12.

31. Besides *In Other Words* (pp. 9–43) and *Tobogganing on Parnassus* (pp. 6–29, 142), these also include *By and Large* (1914, pp. 3–23), *Weights and Measures* (1917, pp. 75–95), and *Something Else Again* (1920, pp. 3–25), all published in Garden City, N. Y.

32. Franklin P. Adams, *So There!* (New York, 1923), p. 38.

33. Franklin P. Adams, *Something Else Again* (Garden City, N. Y., 1920), p. 65.

34. Showerman, p. 135.

35. J. H. Westcott, *One Hundred and Twenty Epigrams of Martial* (Boston, 1897) , p. 164.

36. Westcott, pp. vi, x.

37. Paul Nixon, *A Roman Wit* (Boston, 1911), p. 51

38. Nixon, p. 52.

39. Walter C. A. Ker, Introduction to Martial's *Epigrams*, Loeb ed. (New York, 1930), I, xiii. Nixon's collection is stuffed with close analogies to Parker's work; in the more recent translation by James Mitchie, *The Epigrams of Martial* (New York, 1972), see pp. 25, 27, 43, 47, 121, 141, 161, 189. *Martial, the Twelve Books of Epigrams*, trans. J. A. Pott and F. A. Wright (London, 1925), is dedicated to Housman.

40. John Farrar, "This Stream of Poets," *The Bookman*, March 1927, p. 81.

41. *New York Times*, "Three Poets Who Openly Prefer Laughter to Tears," March 27, 1927, III, 6:1-3. Other comments: *The Nation*, "Books in Brief, " May 25, 1927: "a thread of traditional light verse, a wire of Edna Millay's, a hair of Elinor Wylie's. . . , and a thick strand of her own" (p. 589); Russell Crouse, *New York Evening Post* notes a "reverberating mordancy"; Herschel Brickell, also the *Post*, "Her light verse is as good as anything I know of in our time"; *Saturday Review*, "Its laughter has a biting edge, its humors are satisfyingly terse, its wistfulness begets beautiful phrases"; Herbert Gorman, *New York World*, "The book is rich with those nuggets of gold that may be removed from their setting without losing any of their sparkle": *Providence Journal*, "all the clarity of the finer sort of irony with no brutality. . . . Humor without scorn; wisdom without smugness"; *Milwaukee Leader*, "with a most every-day vocabulary, Miss Parker creates verses which are sometimes exquisite, sometimes comical; sometimes whimsical; but verses which are pointed and swift and earthy and vivid. She has, in short, done a new thing." See *Book Review Digest* 23 (1927), 571–72

42. Edmund Wilson, "Dorothy Parker's Poems," *New Republic*, January 19, 1927, p. 256.

43. Marie Luhrs, "Fashionable Poetry," *Poetry*, April 1927, p. 52–54.

44. Cf. Rabelais (*Works*, ch. 62): "You shall never want rope enough."

45. "Epitaph for a Darling Lady" (*The World*, August 3, 1925, 11:1)

originally read "shiny sands" (l. 1), "Pretty day on pretty day" (l. 5), "Gay and scented and alarming" (l. 10), and "very charming" (l. 12). The second stanza of the original version of "Story of Mrs. W—" *(The World,* June 13, 1925, 11:1) has been omitted. It read: "Here is no aching red of rose,/ Nor are there cruel fragrances,/ But each untroubling thing that blows;/ The spinster flowers, that live to please."

46. Cf. *Satires,I,x.*

47. Maugham, p. 15.

48. Genevieve Taggard, "You Might as Well Live," *New York Herald Tribune,* March 27, 1927, VII, 7:2–4.

49. *New York Times,* "Six Rhymsters in Caps and Bells," July 1, 1928, Books, 10:3–4.

50. Garreta Busey,"A Porcupine's View," *New York Herald Tribune,* July 15, 1928, XII, 7:5. She continues: "We are willing to pursue Miss Parker to her extremest thicket in spite of, or rather for the sake of, her quick and cruel barbs." F. B. B. in *The Boston Transcript* warns, "We cling to our belief that as long as she remains raucous, flippant, and ironic she is to be cherished and lauded but when she grows tender and sweetly lyrical she wanders beyond her present field," noting each new poem "had its birth in the first book" (June 30, 1928, Books, 3:8). Other reviews of interest are "New-Moon Madness," by William Rose Benet (Elinor Wylie's husband), *Saturday Review,* June 9, 1928, p. 943; "New York Wits" by Edith H. Walton in *New Republic* June 27, 1928, p. 155. F. P. A. wrote a poem in his column called "Book Review": "Oh, what a beauty! and oh, what fun/ Is Dorothy Parker's *Sunset Gun"* (May 31, 1928, 13:1).

51. The title refers to a gun fired at military bases such as those she visited when Eddie was stationed there; James R. Gaines notes on a visit to West Point this gun especially frightened Benchley. *Wit's End* (New York, 1977), p. 5.

52. Henry Morton Robinson, "Some Scrannel Pipings," *The Bookman,* September 1928, p. 96.

53. Henry Seidel Canby, "Belle Dame sans Merci," *Saturday Review,* June 13, 1931, p. 891.

54. Raymond Kresensky, "Humor and Tragedy," *Christian Century,* October 28, 1931, p. 1345.

55. Franklin P. Adams, "The Parkerian Formula, *"New York Herald Tribune,* Books, June 14, 1931, p. 7.

56. So "Books in Brief," in *The Nation* for September 23, 1931: "Such clever craftsmanship is reason enough for admiration, but there is more to be said: Mrs. Parker as a light verse writer is actually a better poet than many of our very serious composers in meter" (p. 315); *New Republic,*"Book Notes, " August 12, 1931: *"Death and Taxes.* . . incline[s] more toward sentimentality gone sour than toward the sharp mind hitting the center of an emotional situation with the sharp phrase" (pp. 348-49). In

"Nor Rosemary nor Rue" in *Poetry*, December 1931, Harold Rosenberg scored her for her sentiment, her "negligible" wit, and "the easy rhythm, the banal feelings and phrases" (pp. 159-61).

57. *Death and Taxes* (New York, 1931). References will be given in the text. Originally, the last stanza of "The Danger of Writing Defiant Verse" (p. 15) read: "He's none to come and wrench a kiss/ Nor pull me in his lap . . ./ Oh, Lord! I see, on reading this,/ He is an awful sap!" (*The World*, March 15, 1929, 15:1). Originally line 2 of "Purposely Ungrammatical Love Song" (p. 49) read, "Is willing to speed my woes away " (*The World*, December 25, 1928, 15:1); other changes were made in "Prayer for a Prayer" (p. 11), "Distance"(p. 16), "Little Words" (p.24), "The Crusader" (p. 30), "Song for the End of a Sequence" (p. 36), "From a Letter from Lesbia" (p. 48).

58. *China Weekly Review* (Shanghai), August 22, 1931, p. 479:1.

59. The reference also has the glib self-deprecation associated with Round Table wit; Mercutio's whole line (about his death wound from Tybalt) is "Tis not so deep as a well, nor so wide as a church door; but 'tis enough, 'twill serve."

60. Omitted from *Enough Rope*: "Verse Reporting Late Arrival at a Conclusion," "Day-Dreams," "Folk Tune," "Spring Song," "Finis," "Autobiography," "Biographies," and "Song in a Minor Key." Omitted from *Sunset Gun*: "For R. C. B.," "Swan Song," "Verses in the Night," and "Directions for Finding the Road"; "To Newcastle" was retitled "The Counsellor." Omitted from *Death and Taxes*: "In the Meadow."

61. Louis Kronenberger, "The Rueful, Frostbitten Laughter of Dorothy Parker," *New York Times*, December 13, 1936, VII, 28:3-4.

62. William Rose Benet, "Deep, At That," *Saturday Review*, December 12, 1936, p. 5.

63. Capron, p. 79.

64. "Six collections of short stories and a lovely novel [sic]," *Esquire*, June 1962, p. 64.

65. "Preface" to *Short Story: A Thematic Anthology* (New York, 1965), p. vii. Further references are given in the text. Shroyer actually drafted the preface after discussions with Dorothy and her approval of the contents. They were brought together by Scribner's editor Charles Pettee and they "worked on the book for over two years. We began by each of us submitting to the other a list of around 100 short stories we thought were very good. I'm proud to say that many titles appeared on both our lists! We then arrived at the stories that actually appear." FBS to AFK, August 10, 1976. Selections include stories by Hemingway, Fitzgerald, and Lardner.

66. My text is *The Stories of F. Scott Fitzgerald*, ed. Malcolm Cowley (New York, 1951), p. 364.

67. "Introduction" to *The Seal in the Bedroom* (New York, 1932), p. viii; she is talking of his drawings, however.

68. Five of the seven stories from *Round-Up* (1929) discussed here—

"Haircut," "Women," "Zone of Quiet," "A Day with Conrad Green," and "The Love Nest"—first published in magazines, were collected earlier in *The Love Nest and Other Stories* (New York, 1926).

69. Ring Lardner, *Round-Up* (New York, 1929), p. 72.

70. Seldes, *Seven Lively Arts*, p. 120.

71. See Ring Lardner, *Some Champions*, eds. Matthew J. Bruccoli and Richard Layman (New York, 1976). Like her, Lardner kept rewriting but remained unsatisfied; see Dale Kramer, *Ross and the "New Yorker,"* pp. 233–34. In 1953, John O'Hara credited Hemingway, Lardner, and Parker for his own succinct style. See Bruccoli, *The O'Hara Concern*, p. 74.

72. Ernest Hemingway, *Green Hills of Africa* (New York, 1935, 1953), p. 27.

73. Hoffman, p. 430.

74. Examples are "You Were Perfectly Fine" (see Keats, p. 137); "Just a Little One" (Keats, pp. 139, 142); "Soldiers of the Republic" (Keats, pp. 219–20); "The Lovely Leave" (Keats, pp. 238–39).

75. T. S. Matthews, "Curses Not Loud But Deep," *New Republic*, September 17, 1930, p. 133.

76. Edmund Wilson, *Letters*, p. 234.

77. "Shorter Notices," *The Nation*, December 20, 1933, p. 715.

78. She omitted "The Mantle of Whistler" and "Dialogue at Three in the Morning" from *Laments for the Living* and "A Young Woman in Green Lace" from *After Such Pleasures*.

79. William Plomer, "The Parker Probe," *Spectator*, November 17, 1939, p. 708.

80. *Boston Evening Transcript*, May 27, 1939, Books, 2 : 2–3.

81. Franklin P. Adams, "Foreword" to *Collected Stories* (New York, 1942), p. vii.

82. Vernon Loggins, *I Hear America Singing* (New York, 1937), p. 302.

83. See *The Viking Portable Dorothy Parker;* further references are given in the text. The penultimate paragraph on p. 239 originally continued: "The moment our eyes met, as they say who are literary, I knew! In all my years, I have hated no living thing as I hated Horace." A new paragraph at the top of p. 246 read as follows:

"I do not know if he did his work in the house well or ill or at all; I was impervious to all save Horace, in my hatred of him. Before Horace, I had fostered quondam hatred—fragile, fragrant, wood anemones, they seemed—for those always of my own color and mainly for those richer than I. Horace's design and status were no matter; black, white, or polka-dotted, cook or ambassador to the Court of St. James', I should have hated him. I had thought that obsessing hatred was a fine, tough emotion, conducive to sung deeds of violence. Well, it is not; hate enough, and your hate stuns you, dumbs you, renders you sick and silent. I hated Horace enough. He stood before me, all day long, dripping words bland and aqueous as ill-made custard, and I became like Harriet, the half-wit murderer. I remember once planning that at one more mention of the name of Mrs. Hofstadter on Josphine Street, I would shriek; but that was my biggest moment. Right after, I turned to the slow, soupy realms of the defeated. I knew I should never cry aloud, or even murmur."

Originally the story had one more sentence at the close: "And yet, you know, Mrs. Hofstadter on Josphine Street was not among the major reasons why I hated Horace." She made other minor changes throughout.

84. Alexander Woollcott, "New Klein Drama Is Short of Truth," *New York Times*, October 6, 1914, 11 : 3; Woollcott, "Walker Whiteside Shines in 'Mr. Wu,' " *New York Times*, October 15, 1914, 13 : 1.

85. Woollcott, "Capsule Criticism" in *Shouts and Murmurs (New* York, 1922), p. 84.

86. For examples, see S. H. Adams, pp. 98–99 (some of which are echoed by Dorothy), and Teichmann, *Smart Aleck*, pp. 84–87. His best: "The score is by Sigmund Romberg, who knows a good tune when he hears one." "Woollcott," Harriman writes (p. 161), "was a master performer in the Cult of Rudeness which had developed among the Vicious Circle, in which insult was the accepted coin of conversational exchange."

87. Woollcott, "Capsule Criticism," p. 79.

88. Some of her criticism is reprinted in Amory and Bradlee, pp. 34–35; excerpts are in Oppenheimer, pp. 42–44, 550–53.

89. "All's Quiet on the Rialto," *VF*, March 1919, p. 36; she is speaking of Gail Kane in "The Woman in Room 13."

90. P. G. Wodehouse parodies this in "Reviewing a Theatre Audience," *VF*, November 1919, p. 42.

91. *NY*, February 21, 1931, p. 26; "No More Fun," *NY*, March 21, 1931, p. 28; *NY*, March 21, 1931, p. 30; *NY*, February 21, 1931, p. 26.

92. *Constant Reader* (New York, 1970), p. 3. This recent collection includes thirty-one of her forty-six reviews for *NY*, ten of them in excerpted form. Further references are given in the text with the abbreviation *CR. CR* is reprinted in *The Portable Dorothy Parker*, rev. ed. (New York, 1973).

93. John Farrar, "Anonymously—John Farrar," *The Bookman*, January 1928, p. 555. Dorothy Parker's "A Telephone Call" appears in the same issue (pp. 500–502).

94. Clurman, "Book Review," *Los Angeles Times*, November 29, 1970, p. 24.

95. Wilfrid Sheed, "Wits' Ends and Means," *New York Times*, August 6, 1972, VII, 2. Cf. Woollcott (*While Rome Burns*, p. 150): "But it is quite true that in her writing—at least in her prose pieces—her most effective vein is the vein of dispraise. Her best word portraits are dervish dances of sheer hate, equivalent in the satisfaction they give her to the waxen images which people in olden days fashioned of their enemies in order, with ex-

quisite pleasure, to stick pins into them. Indeed, disparagement to Mrs. Parker is so habitual that she has no technique for praise, and when she feels admiration, can find no words for it. . . ."

Chapter Four

1. Friedrich Schiller, "On Simple and Sentimental Poetry," in *Essays Aesthetical and Philosophical* (London, 1884), p. 293; rep. in Enck et al, *The Comic in Theory and Practice* (New York, 1960), p. 22.

2. Ford, p. 53.

3. Capron, p. 77.

4. Drennan, p. 113.

5. Gaines, pp. 80–81.

6. James Gray, *On Second Thought*, p. 195.

7. Robert Spiller et al., *A Literary History of the United States*, rev. ed. (New York, 1953), p. 756.

8. Quoted by Janet Winn, "Capote, Mailer, and Miss Parker," *New Republic*, February 9, 1959, pp. 27–28.

9. Introduction to *The Seal in the Bedroom*, p. viii; she is speaking of Thurber's characters.

10. Max Beerbohm, "Laughter," in *And Even Now* (New York, 1925), quoted in Enck et al., p. 67.

11. Woollcott, *While Rome Burns*, p. 144.

12. Fred Lawrence Guiles, *Hanging On in Paradise* (New York, 1975), p. 83. Guiles also notes accurately the relative scarcity of male characters (p. 84).

Selected Bibliography

PRIMARY SOURCES

(For titles and sources of uncollected works, see Index under "Dorothy Parker, Works of.")

After Such Pleasures. New York: Viking, 1933. (Fiction)

The Best of Dorothy Parker. London: Methuen, 1952. (Fiction and Poetry)

Close Harmony, with Elmer L. Rice. New York: Samuel French, 1929. (Drama)

Collected Poetry of Dorothy Parker. New York: Modern Library, 1944.

Collected Stories of Dorothy Parker. New York: Modern Library, 1942.

Constant Reader. New York: Viking, 1970. (Criticism)

Death and Taxes. New York: Viking, 1931. (Poetry)

Enough Rope. New York: Boni & Liveright, 1926. (Poetry)

Here Lies. New York: Viking, 1939. (Fiction)

The Ladies of the Corridor, with Arnaud D'Usseau. New York: Viking, 1954. (Drama)

Laments for the Living. New York: Viking, 1930. (Fiction)

Not So Deep as a Well. New York: Viking, 1936. (Poetry)

The Penguin Dorothy Parker. New York, 1977. Harmondsworth, England, 1977. (Fiction, Poetry, Criticism, Journalism)

The Portable Dorothy Parker. New York: Viking, 1973. (Fiction, Poetry, Criticism, Journalism) Published in England as *The Collected Dorothy Parker.* London: Gerald Duckworth & Co., Ltd., 1973.

Short Story: A Thematic Anthology, with Frederick B. Shroyer. New York: Charles Scribner's Sons, 1965.

Sunset Gun. New York: Boni and Liveright, 1928. (Poetry)

The Viking Portable Dorothy Parker. New York: Viking, 1944. (Fiction and Poetry)

RECORDINGS BY PARKER

Dorothy Parker: Poems and "Horsie." Spoken Arts 726, n.d.

The World of Dorothy Parker. Verve V-15029, n.d.

193

SECONDARY SOURCES

CAPRON, MARION. "Dorothy Parker." In *Writers at Work*, ed. Malcolm Cowley. New York: Viking, 1957. A valuable interview, although answers occasionally resort to smart quips by Parker.

COOPER, MORTON. " 'Men seldom make passes / At girls who wear glasses'." *Diners' Club Magazine*, October 1964, pp. 46–47, 68–69. A popular article, with occasional inaccuracies.

COOPER, WYATT. "Whatever you think Dorothy Parker was like, she wasn't." *Esquire*, July 1968, pp. 56–57, 61, 110–14. A rich and reliable portrait of Dorothy Parker in her last years.

CROWNINSHIELD, FRANK. "Crowninshield in the cubs den." *Vogue*, September 15, 1944, pp. 162–63, 197–201. A valuable first-hand recollection of Parker's years on *Vogue* and *Vanity Fair* that does not always agree with Parker's account to Marion Capron.

DRENNAN, ROBERT E., ED. *The Algonquin Wits*. Secaucus, N. J.: The Citadel Press, 1975. A collection of Parker quips, pp. 110–26.

GAINES, JAMES R. *Wit's End: Days and Nights of the Algonquin Round Table*. New York: Harcourt, Brace, Jovanovich, 1977. Only apparently journalistic history, this is the best study of the Round Table and the harmful effects of its self-indulgence. The design, slightly modifying the page format of *Vanity Fair*, has some genuinely valuable photographs.

GILL, BRENDAN. Introduction to *The Portable Dorothy Parker*. New York: Viking, 1973, 1977. On balance a negative appraisal of Parker's work, seeing her as an overrated minor talent.

GRAHAM, SHEILAH. *The Garden of Allah*. New York: Crown, 1970. "The Grim Weeper," pp. 138–53, is a negative and gossipy portrait of Parker's years in Hollywood.

GRAY, JAMES. *On Second Thought*. Minneapolis: University of Minnesota Press, 1946. A brief critical summary, pp. 195–200, errs through lavish praise.

GUILES, FRED LAWRENCE. *Hanging On in Paradise*. New York: McGraw-Hill, 1975. An informed and astute study of the corruption of American writers during the heyday of Hollywood, with some special attention to Parker.

HELLMAN, LILLIAN. *An Unfinished Woman*. Boston: Little, Brown, and Company, 1969. "Dorothy Parker," pp. 212–28, is an incisive but affectionate personal memoir of Parker from 1935 until her death in 1967.

KEATS, JOHN. *You Might As Well Live: The Life and Times of Dorothy Parker*. New York: Simon and Schuster, 1970. The standard, popular biography, thin in places, but based on extensive research. Some facts and interpretations are amended or superseded by material in chap.

1 here; the literary judgments are sparse and at times surprisingly adulatory.

LAWRENCE, MARGARET. *The School of Femininity*. New York: Frederick A. Stokes Company, 1936. A slender negative account, pp. 173–76, now seems misguided and perhaps malicious.

MAUGHAM, W. SOMERSET. "Variations on a Theme." Introduction to *The Viking Portable Dorothy Parker*. New York: Viking, 1944. A sensitive and sometimes illuminating account of Dorothy Parker's craft by a fellow writer of fiction.

WOOLLCOTT, ALEXANDER. *While Rome Burns*. New York: Viking, 1934. "Our Mrs. Parker," pp. 142–52, is an early but perceptive, sensitive, and respectful account of Dorothy Parker from 1916–1934.

Index

Works are listed under the author's name. Direct quotations are indicated by *italics;* an asterisk denotes extended discussion or analysis.